"Daniel's book is essential reading – full of such wise advice, help and support. It's going to bring people together and will change lives."

– **Lorraine Kelly,** CBE, journalist and TV presenter

"Whether you're gay, not sure or know someone who's gay... read this book! Awkward conversations exist because we don't know how someone's thinking. Daniel's candid account of his experiences will help you understand, empathise, or make you realise that you're not alone. Sometimes funny, often awkward, but always honest, this is the account you need to read."

– **James Max,** presenter on TalkTV, columnist and business advisor

"A very personal, very practical guide to coming out! Be proud."

– **Laura Whitmore,** TV and radio presenter

"Hugely relatable and spoken from both the heart and the head, Gay Man Talking offers frank and funny insights into navigating the challenges around growing up, finding love and self-acceptance that many young gay men face today."

– **Professor Paul Baker,** author of *Outrageous! The Story of Section 28 and Britain's Battle for LGBT Education*

gay man talking

of related interest

In Their Shoes
Navigating Non-Binary Life
Jamie Windust
ISBN 978 1 78775 242 9
eISBN 978 1 78775 243 6

Bi the Way
The Bisexual Guide to Life
Lois Shearing
ISBN 978 1 78775 290 0
eISBN 978 1 78775 291 7

Coming Out Stories
Personal Experiences of Coming Out from Across the LGBTQ+ Spectrum
Edited by Emma Goswell and Sam Walker
ISBN 978 1 78775 495 9
eISBN 978 1 78775 496 6

How to Understand Your Sexuality
A Practical Guide for Exploring Who You Are
Meg-John Barker and Alex Iantaffi
Illustrated by Jules Scheele
ISBN 978 1 78775 618 2
eISBN 978 1 78775 619 9

gay
man
talking

all the conversations
we never had

daniel harding

Jessica Kingsley Publishers
London and Philadelphia

First published in Great Britain in 2022 by Jessica Kingsley Publishers
An imprint of Hodder & Stoughton Ltd
An Hachette Company

1

A CIP catalogue record for this title is available from the British
Library and the Library of Congress

ISBN 978 1 83997 094 8
eISBN 978 1 83997 095 5

Printed and bound in Great Britain by Clays Ltd

Jessica Kingsley Publishers' policy is to use papers that are natural,
renewable and recyclable products and made from wood grown
in sustainable forests. The logging and manufacturing processes
are expected to conform to the environmental regulations
of the country of origin.

Jessica Kingsley Publishers
Carmelite House
50 Victoria Embankment
London EC4Y 0DZ

www.jkp.com

To my Southend gays and gals.
All the beautiful colours of the rainbow and our allies, thank you.
And to Laura, for everything.

contents

introduction

Do you ever look in the mirror and think, *who the fuck are you?* Constantly? Me too.

It's incredibly hard to define who you are. When attempting to describe myself, I've always struggled. Throughout my life this has been the case in job interviews, on first dates and during awkward small talk at weddings. In fact, especially weddings. When you are wedged next to your cousin's boyfriend eating mushroom soup and you hear:

So, tell me about you.

And while mushroom soup should never be an appetiser at a wedding, as both in looks and in taste it just fails on every level, I constantly struggled with the question.

Who was I?

I could tell you without hesitation who I'd like to be. Or perhaps I could tell you about the fun, rose-tinted version of me, Daniel John Harding. The laugh (literally) and the soul of any party. All the triumphs and anecdotes of a confident man with his head screwed on (I wish). Although I actually hated the term "man." It has forever just felt like an "old" word to me. No longer a boy. Aged.

Ancient.

And I did not want to get old. At least not before I finally became comfortable with who I was, or at least until I tried a threesome. (I'm never going to try a threesome.) Because to everyone else, I was the "man" who was on camera and alive. Who had it all figured out.

Fun. Free. Sorted.

But that wasn't really who I was. That "man" was the *me* that I projected and who most likely lived on ALL my dating-app profiles. Yes, I have a few.

The filtered me.

Because in truth, I haven't always had a good relationship with myself. In fact, in high school, I despised the chubby, camp and confused fourteen-year-old who hid behind his curtain fringe. Why I ever thought that curtains on a round face were a good idea, I'll never know. But that was part of my identity, a perplexed and lost little fat boy, with his hair perfectly parted. Potentially the only thing perfect about me.

I was the boy with the over-sized bag and big dreams who was scared shitless of his reality. A reality that I hated even more than myself.

If you saw me now, five foot eleven, slim build and an air of fake confidence, you probably wouldn't have put the past me and present me together. We weren't the same.

But it was in ditching past me that I realised the relationship that we have with ourselves, be it good, bad or ugly, ripples into every other area of our lives. Unavoidably and unforgivingly.

Potentially, I had never been able to define myself because I hadn't stopped running from myself. And as RuPaul tells us twice a year during thirteen episodes, *if you can't love yourself, how in the hell you gonna love somebody else?*

Relationships, in every form, had always been a foreign concept to me. I knew the basics, and the fact that they were a requirement to live and maintain a fully functional life, but I wasn't sure that I was all that good at them. Perhaps because I was still running.

When I was nine and on holiday in Lanzarote with my family, I desperately wanted to be popular. Popularity in my mind equalled friendships, relationships and courtships, all boats that I wanted to hop on board. And none of which I was currently sailing.

Within twenty-four hours of starting the Spanish vacation, my sister had befriended a girl called Beth in the holiday club. And I, well, I pretended to be a killer whale in the pool, alone. It wasn't that I found forming friendships hard, but I was so nervous to create "actual" relationships when I didn't even understand who I was myself. I didn't. I was coasting.

How could honest bonds form when you were a fake?

So, as my sister hung out with the kid-club crew, I practised my Free Willy routine and captured the attention of a girl who was six years older than me.

Charlene was six feet tall with bouncy curls, looking like she'd just stepped off the cover of *Teen Vogue*. A glamourzon. She happened to also be Beth's sister and found me cute. Brotherly cute, not any other form. I mean, of course she did. I was a tubby kid with curtains, performing Splash! the musical. What wasn't to love?

During the course of the holiday, we exchanged lots of interesting conversations (I realise now that it was probably only two quick chats) and I convinced myself that I had a crush on this "hot girl."

At the end of the trip, Beth and my sister became pen pals, and I had an awkward photo next to Charlene to prove to the lads back home that a girl liked me. I still have that picture.

The reality was, we never spoke again and there weren't any "lads" back home. In truth, Charlene was pretty and perfect, and I had idealised her. But this wasn't a crush; this was just a confused boy, playing alone in the pool, desperately wanting to be that pretty, tall popular person with great relationships.

The girl that had it "easy."

I wanted to be her. Or anyone but me. A simpler life. And while I knew that I didn't have it easy at all, wondering who I was, I had no idea of the lions, tigers and bears waiting for me along my very own yellow brick road.

This was the start of my ripple. The journey into future relationships and understanding their impact on me. But also my impact on them. I was an awkward, confused blue-eyed boy, trying to find the right fit and his people. Idolising as I went. Placing everyone who was living a "normal" life on a pedestal, from couples who looked like they had it all to hot girls on holiday to straight boys who had it easy to celebrities who were comfortable in their own skin.

Idols.

Because I looked up to anyone who wasn't me. I was no role model. Everyone else was shiny, confident and together. Sorted.

Everyone but me.

❥

At seventeen years old, a month before my eighteenth birthday, I came out to my mum. I was scared – terrified perhaps – and it turns out she was actually the parent that I should have been most concerned about. I should have told my dad first.

"I think I'm gay, Mum."

Those were the words that fell out of my mouth. I had imagined that releasing the weight off my shoulders and slipping into my new label would confirm my identity. Define me. Finally. It didn't work. I wonder if it actually made things a little harder for me. I'd finally admitted something that I'd either denied, dodged or avoided for my whole existence. Something that surely would now place the "odd boy" in a clear box. However, instead, it set me on a path that constantly showcased that I was different. Only now I had a sticker to prove it.

Gay.

A subject I did not want to talk about. *Ever.* I'm also not sure why I said, "I think" when literally every bone in my body knew that this was my truth. I wasn't straight, I wasn't bi, I wasn't going through a stage, I was just a confused young gay boy. A twink, I guess. My new label.

"Oh no, Daniel, but you'll get AIDS!"

I winced at the words and gulped down the lump that was lodged in my throat. As if I didn't have enough to worry about; now my mum was convinced I'd die too. Because that was what happened to gay men in her eyes.

Death.

She told me that she'd pray for me every day after that. She wasn't religious at all. In fact, the last time that we were in a church was for my mum to marry her second husband...

Now that I was out, no matter how much in that moment that I wanted to, I couldn't go back. The wardrobe was wide open. I would never be able to take back those words that I'd said out loud. That confession. It was perhaps the most truthful thing that I'd ever uttered since saying, "I want to chop off my curtains!"

But in that moment I realised that it wasn't the "coming out" that would help me find myself; all that did was start me off on my brick road. Despite how hard the path ahead might be, I was about to try on lots of different people and styles to find a fit. It was going to get a lot harder before it got easy.

Maybe it never gets easy.

Now, at thirty-three, I've worn multiple labels and encountered numerous connections. But as a modern gay man, I've come to realise that it's the relationships around us, breaking us down and making us back up, that create our defining moments.

From the relationships with our parents, siblings, mobile phones, first loves, sex lives, bullies, friends, role models, to ourselves, each one has incredible significance and impact. More than we ever stop to realise.

And, although relationships had always been this alien concept my whole life and forming them started off uneasy after "coming out" to my not-so-happy mum before Sunday lunch, gradually a new world began to open up. Tired relationships got refreshed and new prospects presented themselves.

I started my own journey. And *you* will find your way. But nothing is as black and white as we may think. Sure, we come out – do the hard bit – but what next?

What happens to those relationships?

Is being the "gay best friend" really all that we have? Is it fun and inclusive or just alienating us socially?

Are we forever now just the gay uncle, brother, son, friend? Is that part of our title?

For so many of us gay men, the future relationships we will have are coloured by judgement and stereotypes. Shame and internalised beliefs that often go unchallenged. Sometimes we might be seen as just the side act, or sexually promiscuous individuals, fluid and unsettled party boys, but we are also misjudged.

Constantly.

Especially if this image runs counter to the lifestyle you seek. Because we can be "normal."

Can't we?

In this ever changing contemporary and confusing world, finding our people, acceptance and kin is the difference between surviving and thriving. I had no idea how important relationships would become to me, helping me finally answer the question, *who am I?*

Define me.

Perhaps my mum's prayers had helped me after all. Turns out I didn't need to ditch the old me from that holiday snap in Lanzarote; I needed to accept him. Stop running.

So, I finally pulled back my curtains, slipped on my size seven ruby slippers, and, for the first time, was excited to see who they'd meet. What they'd educate me on. And in turn, who would learn from me.

We sometimes just need to find good people and have the right conversations. Because when you open up dialogue, you'll be amazed by what you hear.

The conversation shouldn't stop after you've come out. It should be only just beginning.

In this book, I look into the modern gay relationships around me – from parents, siblings and friends through to lovers, enemies, technology and ourselves – unpicking stereotypes, exploring the nuances of these connections and understanding the impact they have on us.

Featuring interviews with other gay men, influential figures and Hollywood actors; relationship case studies; and insight from behavioural expert Judi James, this book delves deep into modern gay life to hopefully help readers challenge the relationships they have with others and move towards a happier, more positive relationship with themselves and those around them. Because whether you are an ally or a part of the community, talking is key.

It's time to revisit the conversations we assumed were done and discover the answers you never knew you needed. It's surprising what you find out when you stop to listen, and the comfort it can bring in realising how important you are too. All the things that we never said should never be without their moment.

parent

/ˈpɛːr(ə)nt/

---

noun

1. a person's father or mother.
    "the parents of the bride"

verb

2. be or act as a parent.

conversations with my parents

When I was twenty-one, I thought that I'd like to be a dad. Then at twenty-six, I had no interest in ever becoming a father, and at twenty-nine, I pondered it once more when a cute baby smiled at me. Then the baby puked. That puke never came out of my top. *Devastating*. It was a beloved long-sleeved AllSaints number that went in the bin. A bold but brilliant over-priced garment. God, I miss that top. It looked terrible on me, but I miss it.

At thirty-three, I resigned myself to the fact that I didn't ever want to become a parent. But ask me again in a couple of years' time.

Part of me thought that I might be too selfish to become a father. I was. I wanted travel, adventure and a small car. I also wondered if I'd ever be good enough at it. And, even in an age of fantastic adoption options for the LGBTQIA+ – *thank god* – I still cowered at that responsibility. Who would trust me with a kid?

Therefore, perhaps I wasn't meant to be a dad. I wasn't even interested in father and son role play. Unless of course it was with Bruce Willis. I might be okay with calling him "daddy." But I certainly did not want to be called "daddy" myself. I recoil at the thought of being old enough to be someone's father. It fills me with dread and, I'm also gay, so ageing is something that wounds me daily. Hourly, in fact. I'm not sure that will ever change.

Obviously, there is a part of us born to procreate. Biological and paternal. Something that, should we be fortunate enough or care to do so, is an incredible thing – and a life-changing one at that.

But parenting doesn't stop at that choice. Regardless of my internal "will I or won't I" argument, even if I don't ever become a father doesn't mean that I won't become a parent.

I often feel like I already am.

❧

The relationship I have with my parents was not what I thought it was. I have read it wrong for over thirty years. But this is how I saw it before recently.

My eyes roll constantly. If you don't roll your eyes when you're around your parents, you are not a child. Or at least not a sane one. Perhaps you're also intoxicated. Good for you.

Basically, you can't have experienced the agony, embarrassment and cringeworthy moment without doing this action. In fact, if that is you, the non-eye rolling type, congratulations, and you may as well skip this chapter.

Parents are designed to be on our case. Say annoying things and torture us in front of our friends. They'll do this in front of boyfriends or one-night stands too. Revealing the truth about your age or real hair colour or the fact that you once farted during your graduation. They'll do it when you don't want them to or when it's a really inconvenient time. You'll hate them for it.

It's a rite of passage.

Uncomfortable and relentless. Just like the effect of a curry the night before your graduation.

As a gay son, I've also come to realise that I've partaken in or endured a lot of extra stuff that I'm pretty sure heterosexual sons would not have gone through. Things on top of all of the other typical child requirements. The GSD: gay son duties.

Most of these things are obvious clichés. For example, I've helped my mum sort her closet hundreds of times. It's a large closet, and every time I go through a thousand pairs of female tights, thirty days later they are back to the state that I found them in. Entangled with random strands of hair. Only there are another twenty pairs. Agony. I've also advised my mum on which angle is best to capture a photo for her dating profile. *Always top down.* Then helped her select which ones to use to hook a new man.

GSD.

Then there was that time that I gave her a vibrator that I had received from a PR event. *I'm a good son!* To which she politely replied, "Someone else no longer wanted it? Well, I don't want it if it's already been used, Daniel!"

Insert eye roll here.

I've advised (insisted) on a bikini wax before a holiday. A holiday that was to be just me and my mum. Me, her thirty-year-old gay son. Cute. Or sad?

Clothes, hair, beauty, pedicures, manicures, boys, music and movies. I might not have even been interested in half of the subjects, but in being gay, I had covered them. I've been happy to do so. It's my GSD.

But I can say as a matter of fact that my straight male friends have not spoken to their mums about the menopause. They have not tied up her hair from hot flushes, nor have they scratched her lower back when she had an itch. We're talking really low, guys.

Being gay changed something in our relationship. Or opened up a wider stream of conversations and activities. I'm not quite sure which.

Then there was my dad. You might assume that it would be

slightly different with the masculine gender. I certainly did. But it wasn't. If anything, he now asked me even more questions.

He'd ask which celebrities were gay, anticipating that I had the answers. *I wish – marry me, Jake Gyllenhaal!* Talked to me about the current music chart and cookery and also expected me to know how to make a cosmopolitan. I mean, I do, of course. It's a valuable skill to have. I can't cook, but I can make a cocktail. He also has spoken to me about my relationships, having a genuine interest in them. Pumping me for details, if I liked them or if I thought it would go somewhere. Two men discussing their feelings...what was this sorcery?

GSD.

Straight friends that I knew rarely discussed this with their dads. They did not share feelings. They barely shared a conversation deeper than their KFC order or which channel the football was on.

I was different.

Of course, these weren't bad things. They certainly weren't the things that made my eyes roll. Far from it. The eye rolls came from long phone conversations when I had only seen them an hour before they rang. Them telling me that I looked tired. *Thanks.* Or them asking me what it was I did for a living, again.

Standard child eye rolls.

But being gay changed our lives. Fact. An evolution of our relationship. Before my eyes, my parents had moulded to the shape of their new son. Learnt to go with my flow. Followed the rainbow.

I did feel a little bit sorry for my sister. She now got conversations about hanging pictures and how to change a fuse. But then again, she had always been better with a drill. Lucky.

In essence, my folks had to re-learn how to parent me. Because up until I came out, they didn't really know me. In fairness, how could they?

My dad recently told me, "I had never known anyone else that was gay. However, I also knew this was my time to learn and finally get to know my son. Maybe I hadn't known you before that."

He saw it as his second chance. But as lovely as it was that I'd become their *Queer Eye for the Straight Guy*, the role I now played wasn't always so easy. For them. For me. For us.

As much as I didn't want it to be, parenting someone who is LGBTQIA+ was different. A new experience. A foreign relationship. A lesson to learn.

And I don't think I ever realised just how different or how out of touch my view of parenting me was.

❧

As far as relationships go, a parent, in whatever guise that comes in, is potentially our first real connection in life. Our first example of forming a bond with another person.

Parents are our introduction to the complexity of relationships, the good and the bad. They are our tour guide around the crazy zoo of life. And, before coming out to mine as a teenager, my relationships with my parents followed the suit of so many other people that I knew. Back when I was a little boy, unaware of who I was, this is how mine began.

It started with need, and probably a hint of annoyance. I cried far too much (just put on *Beaches* or *The Notebook* and you'll see me in action). I was their second child, completing my parents' perfect two point four family life. The "norm."

My mum was a banking clerk, and my dad was an area manager. They had it all. A lovely three-bedroom house in Cambridge, great friends and well-paid jobs. They also had a horrendous brown sofa that seemed to be a feature in just about every baby photo that I've encountered.

When I was two, we moved to Southend, in Essex, the home that I now blame for my wrongly acclaimed accent. *My passport says Cambridge and I'll stand by that.* Southend wasn't all that bad, though, as I started off in life. It had the world's longest pier and open-top bus tours and would also be the setting for some of my most treasured memories in the future.

Growing up, my parents always seemed happy. More like friends, but happy. Which, when they broke up due to a lack of passion, made complete sense. I'd gone from my needy stage, my playful stage, my annoying stage, the moving towns stage, my naughty stage, to eleven years old. There I was, going from the picture-perfect family to the broken home.

At that time, with divorced parents, I was in the minority. A group that, unbeknown to me, I would reside in for the rest of my life. Divorced parents do not make you queer, though. Our parents do set us up, fuck us up and make us up. But despite what some conversion therapists might wrongly claim, they do not make you homosexual. However, my start in life was already different. All my other friends' families still seemed happy, connected and, more importantly, together.

In a moment around the brown kitchen table, in our recently upgraded house, my dad uttered the words, "Your mum has something to tell you both." And my happiness suddenly changed. Of course, I instantly burst into tears (we've already established that I'm a crier) before my mum spoke, but I knew what was coming. As a child you understand atmosphere far more than you realise, and with the constant arguments, along with the fact that my dad had started sleeping in the box room, we understood.

Their own relationship was over.

I mean, the excuse "Daddy snores too loudly, Mummy needs her sleep" hadn't really washed down anyway. My mum snored too. Loudly. On a holiday we went on sometime later, she had woken me up with her snoring when we were in a hotel together. In separate rooms. On separate floors. Yes, okay, it was our mother and son holiday together! Let's drop it now.

So, at eleven years old, surrounded by ugly brown furniture, the fragility of relationships was imprinted onto my mind. And it never was the same again. Thankfully, seeing the reality of relationships around us not always surviving was the best thing that could have ever happened to me.

A blessing.

Unaware of my future and that there was a life-changing moment around the corner, life ahead was going to be tough. I would come up against obstacles, pricks and issues, over and over. But I was more prepared than I realised. Because that huge blow in seeing my parents split cushioned so many more in my future.

If you can survive your bumps, you can be stronger for the moments that matter.

❧

As if life with two Christmases, stepparents and an obsession with Britney Spears wasn't hard enough, finally, I became eighteen. An age to remember. Not just for being able to drink legally, but I turned eighteen just after I opened the closet door to my mum.

Thank goodness I'd had some bumps previously.

You should have seen the look on her face. To this day I'm quite frankly surprised that she didn't know or consider it. *How did she not know?* When I asked her that question, she replied, "As a parent, you just don't think that way. You love them and don't see it. You brush it under the carpet and then have Sunday dinner."

BUT I LOVED BRITNEY SPEARS!

I mean, she also once caught me walking around in her high heels at nine years old while my dad was in the garden planting tomatoes. I'm not even sure why I even tried them on in the first place; I was curious, I guess. They looked far more exciting than my dad's black work shoes. Those were a boring men's uniform. Straight-laced. Not for me.

She didn't tell me off, but she did start putting her shoes away in the cupboard from then on. And there I was, back on stick-holding duty in our tomato patch. I really hate tomatoes.

When I shared the news on my bed at seventeen, my mum wasn't happy about me being gay. She feared I would get AIDS, worried what the neighbours would think and was concerned her second husband would dislike it. He did dislike it, it seemed. I'm not sure he was all that nice, but I finally got my revenge on him when I cleaned his sports car with a kitchen scourer shortly after.

Unfortunately, whether it was down to his toxic influence or my mum's own fears, my relationship with her actually got worse after I came out. (I've often heard it gets better – I hope this is the case for others.) We stopped talking, stopped hugging, stopped communicating. I was actually quite surprised by her reaction. Hurt.

One day, shortly after confessing my sins, my stepdad picked me up from the train station and took me on a "little car trip." His words. *Prick.* We went out into the country lanes surrounding Southend. It was a sunny day, and it was really quite pretty driving in his scratched-up sports car. That's when he stopped the engine and told me that my mum would never accept me the "way I was" and I wasn't to mention it ever again.

Arsehole.

It seemed like he blamed my mum for not coping and claimed to be comfortable himself.

I'm cool with it, but your mum now hates you.

It was one of the hardest things I've ever heard. There I was, in a moment of needing my "original" relationship more than ever, my first guide, my support, which was now on hold. Absent. Abandoning me as I was about to enter a forest full of bears, players and mirror selfies.

So, at the legal drinking age, our once lovely mother and son dynamic shifted. Paused. Drink helped ease this new transition.

Thankfully, despite shitting myself and leaving four voicemails on my dad's answering machine, the other half of my parental unit took it better than I had ever imagined. Having remarried when I was fourteen and choosing me to be his best man at their wedding, he had been a champ throughout my life. I was by his side – or his "best Dan" – as I cringingly quipped through my blonde curtains during my speech on the wedding day.

Please note, to any future best man roles, I will never use that line again. *I promise.*

Debbie was a lovely wife to him and became a brilliant permanent figure in our lives. She is also the reason I can make a killer cosmopolitan and have seen so much of America. *Win win.* So, four years later, after listening to my blubbering voicemails, the first thing they said to me about my revelation was:

"So, do you have a boyfriend? We'd love to meet him."

I didn't have a boyfriend. In fact, a guy that I was seeing had just dumped me because I was too young, and I had naturally assumed my life was over. Never to love again.

In that moment, I really needed my guides. Although one of them was temporarily out of action, my relationship with my dad became stronger. And, slowly, my happiness started to return.

A new chapter began. The rise of the gay son.

❧

Early relationships were so odd. Confusing and ever changing. Fucking fickle too. Mind boggling in fact. They are these foreign things that are often forced upon us before we find the ones that actually suit us or that we want.

They are awkward. Never as straightforward or as organised as you'd like them to be. And my experiences of them with my parents echoed this. But we need these early relationships.

Behavioural psychologist Judi James says that "One thing that no one realises until it is their time is that growing up is a myth. It's something people pretend to do when they have children or get a job." Judi claims that for a young child, parents are omnipotent and always right. Children depend on their parents for their survival, and they grow up believing their "rules" and opinions are both normal and right, which is why this idea of "acceptance" feels so essential emotionally.

We strive for their approval.

I've always been told that we learn a lot from our parents, and this is true. My mum taught me how to make macaroni and cheese – my death row dinner for sure. She did it with this mouth-watering bacon and tomato base. DM her for the recipe details; you have to try it. She also told me to chase my dreams, however grand they might be, and encouraged me to take plenty of risks.

I once dyed my hair blonde and slept with a man that I didn't know.

Not sure that's what she meant.

My dad, the more cautious one, told me to save. Money, memories and myself. He taught me my times tables when I couldn't grasp them and, most importantly, how to be kind. He was very kind. That was the most valuable lesson of all. Something I know now looking back. He appeared to be a hard man, but fair. When I was younger and naughty, he'd chase me upstairs. For some reason I hated being upstairs alone. This lesson taught me that. Now I think that I just hated my own company. Perhaps I found myself too odd.

The truth is, there are a lot of brilliant things that I've taken from their parenting despite moments of absence. Probably too many to mention. However, it's not what we learn from them but instead what we see and don't want to carry along with us that could be the most important lessons we get from our folks. And it's those things that really shape our future relationships. Or ruin them.

Eventually, though, the student will become the teacher. We'll take our knowledge and start to share it however we can. It's inevitable. An unavoidable process of life. And, after some consideration, I'm starting to wonder if I'm becoming the parent. I'll soon be the one showing them how to make the mac and cheese!

Because Judi also mentioned that a survey once showed that we begin to turn into our parents at the age of thirty-five, and at that age we'll have less control over which aspects of them we mimic. *Fuck!* I think I've started early. A scary thought to consider.

But I've come to realise that as we grow up and evolve, we try on the role of "parent" much earlier than we might anticipate. We advise, nurture and guide others. Parents, lovers, even friends. Especially when our own guides have had their absent moments. Distracted by their lives or abandoning us.

In the definition of the word, the reality is that the verb is more accurate than the noun. Because we "act" and continue to act in the position of parent far more than we acknowledge. Like so many things in life, the concept of what or who a parent is has changed and evolved over time. Therefore, it seems rather foolish to see it in such a rigid form as just *a person's father or mother*. Instead, let's see it as influence. An acting example that we set or respond to. Because in truth, a parent is different to everyone, and when you are different yourself, you have no idea how important they might be in who you become.

How you'll act or develop or grow. Or actually, how much you'll teach them in return.

❧

When I was twenty-five years old, my mum split from her second husband. Weeks before, I had heard the way he spoke to her. It wasn't nice. After what seemed like a turbulent relationship, the final straw came in a dramatic finale.

I wish I'd scratched his car more. And slashed his tyres.

After they split, I sat with my mum, a once vibrant woman whose laugh was infectious and who owned any room, and I saw her diminish. Real pain. Despite us having had seven years where we were in each other's lives but not really "in" each other's lives, I'd rushed straight to her side. I'd been absent until then.

I had come to spend a lot of time with my then boyfriend, James, and his family. They were so easy, so open. Plus, they cooked amazing dinners and drank wine on Wednesdays. They were different. Accepting.

Mum had hated that I spent so much time away from home. I don't think she ever realised the reason why. But, as I sat with her after the split, I started to see a familiar face. Yes, she was broken, far more broken than after she had left my dad. This relationship had taken everything from her. Literally. Going after that passion had cost her greatly. Part of me wondered if it was worth it. But because my mum's seemingly toxic turmoil ended, in letting go of a relationship that consumed and influenced her, she could see again. Her attention swung back to her children and friends, igniting distant connections. Allowing me to finally be her gay son.

When I eventually told my mum what her ex-husband had

said to me when I was eighteen, her lip quivered, and she couldn't speak. When she could she said, "I have never had a problem with you and never will." A slight fib. But deep down I know.

Don't get me wrong; I think part of my mum did find having a gay son hard. To this day she still does. She worries what people think, still doesn't want me to get AIDS and hates the thought of the neighbours hearing me say "anal." But she's never loved me less for it. I know that. I just needed reminding that she was there.

It was a lesson for us both.

A reality that people can influence our relationships. Act a role in our lives that can either enhance or damage us. Outside influences challenge those relationships and change them in a second. They can ruin them without warning. Then they can rebuild them just as quickly. And as a gay son growing up, our relationships can really damage the foundation of our start in life.

It's a rocky road when you come out. That butterfly releasing itself from the cocoon moment. The time you needed strength to fly. Support.

The power of outside influence should never be underestimated. Because when that influence rocks your base, it can cause the people you need most to be absent. Your guides.

My parents aren't perfect, but I realise nor am I. Now, I can look back at thirty-three and see that after coming out my relationships got stronger with both of them. Even if it took my mum a little longer, she got there in the end.

I was their gay son, reporting for GSD, and that's how they treated me. Available for laughs, dating stories about my gay, fabulous life and known for drinking in the Two Brewers on a Sunday. I didn't wear dresses, but I had been known to wear rainbow T-shirts for Pride. Occasionally wore concealer to hide bags. Sometimes spoke in a camp way.

And finally, my modern relationship with my parents made

sense. It didn't need a further conversation about it. It just eased over time.

We had an understanding.

Not everyone is that lucky.

Judi James states that rejection of any kind hurts, but when it comes from our parents doing it because of something that isn't a choice, it can feel downright cruel. "We all crave and need unconditional love and our parents should be the ones supplying that stability in our lives."

Despite having sampled rejection myself, I could never truly understand how people feel when they are completely abandoned by their parents for being gay. Until I sat down with Mufseen Reza, a Muslim man who came out to his family at twenty-five years old and a person who felt his relationship with his parents might never ease.

A conversation that opened my eyes to just how damaging our truth can be. As he sat across from me, happy, smiling and seemingly confident, Mufseen told me a story of a double life, painful conversations and an inevitable truth.

"I knew that I'd have to have the conversation eventually. They'd already been looking at prospective matches for me. Women. It would never be an easy conversation, but I didn't anticipate what would come next."

After coming out to his father, his life drastically changed. Claiming that his father would "rather he was dead than gay," according to Mufseen, he hasn't spoken to his parents since. Something that clearly wasn't easy to comprehend.

"They just couldn't deal with having a gay son. It is not in their make-up, their culture, their plan."

Despite continuing to see his family through strained meetings, at the end of 2018, after being forced to sit alone in his room at Christmas so that the rest of his family wouldn't see their "gay son," Mufseen had enough. And this strong, talented man walked away from his family.

"You don't realise the strength and effect a family has on who you are, especially when you aren't the norm. But you can choose you in that equation," he continued.

"At the time, I needed space to understand that who I am matters and being a gay Muslim man is not a bad thing. I love my mum and family, but their life hasn't evolved and mine had. Of course, I'd love my parents to reach out, part of my dramatic exit was to encourage that, but they haven't. I don't know if they ever will. It's hard to deal with, but then you have to look at your life and see the positives. I'm living as an openly gay man. Which is incredible and right.

"Parents do shape our lives; I know mine taught me so much. But we also have to believe in our own teachings. Follow our own truths. I hope one day things will be different. But my parents are not my only mentor, guide or support. You quickly realise the allies are all around us. There are plenty of role models that we encounter. Plenty of father figures."

As he sipped his beer, he remained composed. I had pricks of tears in my own eyes at his reality, but he had hardened to it.

"My parents have definitely affected my life," he commented. "There isn't a day that passes where I don't think of them or wish that things were different. That's why hearing other people's coming out stories is so important. Helping other parents and progressing acceptance in our community is key. That's my lesson to now share. Of course, I still need them. I might not have found it at home, but I have found it in so many others. I've also become to others what I needed for myself. I act in the role people need most."

After the conversation, we hugged and chatted about boys. Naturally. Mufseen is proof that when you are gay, parental relationships, even if they're blood, can change in the blink of an eye. Then stay that way. Stay absent.

When you are a parent and are faced with something different, you can go two ways: embrace it or replace it. Our guides can leave us or change towards us. It's a harsh reminder that blood isn't always thicker than water. Thankfully, for Mufseen, and so many more gay men around the world, they have plenty of other valuable water sources. Giving way for other parenting influences.

❧

So, there you have it; I am the GS.

The token gay of a somewhat accepting family. Sharing the lols but also helping advise the family on what to wear and what not to wear. Often what not to wear. Gok Dan. The gay son. Out and occasionally proud. And now fully accepted. No further conversations required.

Everything about that is true. I was. But as I said, I got it wrong. I made assumptions about my own parents. Stopped having conversations.

I came out. Then they wanted me to talk about my life, one parent sooner than the other. Then they expected me to be a certain way. "Oh, that's just Daniel." Then they required some GSD. To me it seemed that black and white.

But I had forgotten to ask them questions. How they felt.

So, I did.

❧

When I sat down with my dad, he was awkward. We'd never had

this conversation before. Why, I have no idea. So, when I decided to re-open the subject now in my thirties, my dad started speaking. And it all came pouring out.

"Debbie shouted, 'I knew it!' Instantly. But I didn't." He confessed that he didn't really know how to start our chat.

"I realise that this will sound wrong, but my first thought when you came out was, is he seeking attention, was he sure, was this for real? How could a lad with so many girls as friends be gay and not fancy any of them? As a heterosexual man, never having known otherwise, I didn't fully have my head around it. It baffled me."

Having come out, I'd never spoken to my dad about how he felt, other than getting the nod of "we still okay?" and moving forward.

"However, after years of worrying that you weren't interested in sports, worried that you only had female connections, a sense of relief suddenly descended over me," he continued.

"For too long I assumed that to be a man who was accepted, you'd only be able to achieve this through playing sport, being a scout and having guy friends. I was conditioned to know this and think like this. Society reflects this too. Part of me even tried to push this on you. Help you. Or at least that was my thinking behind it. I'm pretty sure you hated judo and going away camping with a lot of nerdy boy scouts. But that's what I thought you needed. I thought, what do I need to do as a father to help my son be normal? Because you weren't normal. Or at least, not how other kids I knew were. What could I do to stop him being an outcast?"

Then I came out. But what was the end of the conversation for me was actually the start for my dad.

"I desperately wanted to understand and for you to open up to me. But you wouldn't. Or couldn't. But when you came out, after letting it sink in, I realised something. My boy, my flesh and blood, wouldn't be an outcast at all. Not any more. It wasn't a route we chose for you, but I quickly learnt that nor did you. Outwardly,

I fought hard to showcase my support. I didn't want you to see my concerns or worries. And believe me, I had them. If you liked fashion, certain music or gay stuff – whatever that was – I wanted to show interest."

This is what I knew of my dad: his reaction, nothing deeper, but then he continued.

"Inwardly, a selfish stream of fears consumed my mind. First, it was, what will people think of me? What will people think of him? I won't have grandchildren. Will I? Will he live a good life? Why's he not into sport? Is every gay kid not into sport? Loads of questions filled my mind.

"Then it was a simple question. Is he happy? I'm not proud to say this, but seeing the way your mum dealt with it, or was blindsided into dealing with it, actually made me fight a little harder. Fight to deal with this myself. Because even if you didn't see it, I did have to deal with it. It wasn't easy. I'm sorry."

All my life I had assumed my dad instantly accepted the initial conversation. I never imagined he struggled himself.

"As a parent I believe that you have a role. You want to be there for your kid, guide them and help however you can. But you also want to be liked. You want your kids to like you. Rightly, or wrongly, I had an opportunity to finally really be there for a son who had never let me properly in since becoming a teenager. Never fully told me about his life or his friends. I realise now that it was because he was scared to do so. Which upsets me actually. I didn't know half of what you were going through. But all I knew was that now is a chance to really be there.

"My mum once told me that a parent's role is to never lose sight of your child. And it's true. But no parent is selfless. Even when you become one you resent your child a little for how your life changes. Of course, you love them unconditionally, but there is a selfish side. I gave up cricket for these kids! But the reward comes in parenting and then the bond you are lucky to have. That was what I was so desperate to retain with you two after splitting from your mum. As your dad, I wanted to be in your life regardless of sexuality."

My dad continued to tell me that he wouldn't have chosen this path for me.

"Looking back, though, if I had the choice, I would have chosen you to be heterosexual. At the time, I would have done anything to give you an easy and good life. Part of me does miss the fact that you weren't really into sport and wondered if this was because you were gay. But looking back I see so much more clearly. I'm glad you feel supported by me and Debbie. As at the end of the day, all I really cared about was your happiness. There are regrets along the way. Things I'd do differently, yes. But the one thing any parent needs is time. Time to let this change sink in. It is a change. I remember your mum asked me after, what did we do wrong? Now I look at you and know the answer was nothing."

My dad became more passionate as the conversation continued. On a subject he thought he had nothing to add to, he found comfort in the chat.

"Having a son who was gay forced me to deal with a situation I wouldn't have had to encounter otherwise. It changed me. It opened my mind to see things differently. I know I was guilty in the past of looking at people and seeing gender, race, sexuality. But now I look at people and see two things. Good and bad. Would I have chosen to have a gay son? No. Am I proud of you and happy that you are happy in life? Yes.

"Do I care that you are gay? Not one bit. I realise you cannot prepare yourself for the hurdles your children might throw at you. I thought you could. I'm glad you came out to us at seventeen years old and didn't have to hide who you were any longer. I hate to hear that you went through a painful time. But I don't see you as gay. Or that you like cosmopolitans and give me fashionable clothing hand-me-downs. Thank you, though.

"I don't actually care what you're into, but I'm interested in it. Hindsight is a wonderful thing, but I think the key really is to trust in your relationships and give things time. Look at the conversation this is allowing us to have. About time you spoke to me about it. Time can be a great thing. I love you."

After speaking with my dad, it was only natural that I should sit down with my mum. A conversation that I similarly assumed would be black and white.

"Daniel, no. I never have seen you as a 'gay son.' I saw you as a son," she said, frustrated that I might suggest I'm different. "I have no problem with it. I love that you want to spend time with me or help me sort my clothes for the eighteenth time. Okay, ninetieth time. But I don't just see you as a label or someone that helps me look better." She laughs.

I smiled and eased into the conversation. *Why hadn't we had this talk before?*

"When you came out, I was influenced by a relationship that I was in at the time. An all-consuming relationship. Unfortunately, I think there were things that were said to us both that caused a separation between us. I don't think I fully noticed it at the time. I assumed you didn't want to talk about it further, so we didn't. You never had a conversation with me about it. Of course, I worried. I worried about all the stupid things parents worry about. Then I worried about AIDS. Then I was selfish. I thought about not having grandkids or a daughter-in-law. Like I needed a daughter-in-law! It's laughable now, but at the time you think like that. In that moment, you think about all the things you are not going to have, and you forget what you do have. You have a healthy son."

As we chatted, my mum paused a lot. Her eyes became glassy and reflective.

"I'm sorry that we had years where it seemed like I wasn't there as much. It really upsets me. But I didn't see it as distance."

When asking if she'd choose me to be gay, she replied, "I think if any parent answered truthfully, they'd choose for their child to have the safest and easiest route in life.

"At the time, being gay was not that route. I'm not even sure it is now. I saw gay men on TV, and everyone would make fun of them. So yes, I probably would have chosen a different way for you. I think my chance to deal with you being gay got taken away from me slightly. Wrapped up in a time of my own journey.

"As a parent you want to do your best for your child. I think you know that, for me, I always wanted to provide, make sure you were safe and encourage you. Regardless of my relationship then, I strived to be the best mum for you. I'll never forget some of the crazy ideas you had. Or the dreams. You were a dreamer. And I parented. However, I left the area of your sexuality to one side. Then I remember when you got a boyfriend and spent time with his family, I got so jealous. Why wasn't he spending time with ours?

"Looking back, I didn't realise the impact of reactions. The consequence of how we deal with things. There is a chunk of time where I know that you feel like we drifted apart. I hate that. I'm just glad we came back stronger. I'm glad you know that I love you regardless."

I pressed her for an answer to how she saw me compared to others.

"I was scared when you said you were gay. I was scared for you. This wasn't the norm. None of my other friends were encountering this. It was hard. But you're brave. I saw that. It is brave to reveal your truth in a world that hasn't fully accepted it. Is our relationship different to others? Yes. Do I see the difference? No. You are just my son. No other label. There was never a question of my acceptance. It should never be a question for any parent. You just sometimes have to give people time. But, if I don't see the difference, why do you?"

After having a conversation, I realised something. Parents surprise us.

I had no clue that my dad didn't want me to be gay. Outwardly he took it so well. But then again, I never asked him how he felt either. For years we had not discussed what happened next.

I was wrong. I am not a GS. I am just a son.

Nervously, for fifteen years, I had performed to a stereotype. Expecting my parents to feel a certain way. I had played a role that I had cast myself in because I didn't want to have uncomfortable conversations. Yes, I do a lot of GSD. I enjoy so many of these things. I assumed they saw me as gay. I worried that's all they'd see. So, I didn't ask. Then I became just that. But I realise now it's not because they expected these things, or for me to be a certain way, but because they tried to adapt. Wanted to adapt. Thank god. I am fortunate that my situation was different to Mufseen.

We're always hardest on our parents. We are annoyed at them and eye roll continuously. This won't change. They're hard on us too.

My dad covered up his feelings to protect me. To this day, my mum still wants me to lower my voice when talking about anything remotely queer when I'm in her garden. She has an irrational fear that people will judge us. They do judge.

In her head, she never didn't accept me. But she didn't make it clear either. Deep down it was never a question, but sometimes we need to be shown the answer more visibly.

What I selfishly never realised, however, was how in coming out, my parents went through their own journey to find their son again. They both struggled.

My dad always advises me, "Do your best in your life. Make me proud. But do it for you, that's all that matters to me." He's right. We are all just doing our best.

Yes, I am a gay man fortunate to have three parents who accept me. Shout out to Debbie. Some people's parents have taken longer, needed time. And some won't accept it at all.

A parent has a huge responsibility on their shoulders, especially when it comes to gay children. They need to swallow any prejudice, support their child and see them. See them and nothing else.

Hopefully they will be those pillars that lift us up, the start of our relationship journey. Our bricks. However, we have to remember that parents are also "acting" in their roles when they first start them. They are learning as they go too.

If we are lucky and patient and make enough effort, our parents will enhance our lives. A parent isn't just a noun, it's a verb – and parents come in lots of fabulous shapes and sizes.

"It can take a constant, conscious effort to make sure we do learn from our parents' mistakes and that we use them as a lesson for change," says Judi James.

Parent or child, perhaps we are all acting a little bit in a role we thought required it. I know I was. I think about how I would act if I have a kid that comes out one day. I know I'd support them regardless. But I'd want the best for them too. The difference is that we need to keep showing that the best is available for everyone. How we "child" also has an impact.

Perhaps I am becoming the parent. I've certainly taught my parents a lot. But parents don't always see their children how we think they do. I was so scared they'd just see me as the stereotype that I ended up convincing myself that's what they did see. The men portrayed on TV. Neither of mine wanted a gay son, but both of them are happy to have one.

Hopefully, you'll be that person lending them fashion advice, taking photos for dating profiles and sharing stories. It's actually an honour to do so. An added bonus. A chance to become closer. But if we are truly lucky, we'll become their teachers. That's our role. Our gift to them. Wanting the best. When you are a little different to what's conventional as a child, everyone has a little more to learn.

We are more than what we come out as. Whether you are a GS, do GSDs or are just an S...they're the student now.

Teach.

It's time to have more conversations...

sister

/ˈsɪstə/

---

noun

1. a woman or girl in relation to other daughters and sons of her parents.

    "I had nine brothers and sisters"

2. a female friend or associate, especially a female fellow member of a trade union or other organisation.

conversations with a sibling

Blame your sister. That's what I was told to do.

I mean, younger me would have probably already tried to blame her for lots of things. We're all guilty of trying to pass the buck, especially when we are little.

I did.

But this wasn't me trying to frame her for eating too many biscuits, as I sat there with chocolate around my face, *young me*. It wasn't me pointing at her when our parents said the TV was on too loud, *young me*. Or for eating all the sweets from Halloween. Yes, I used to be fat. *Young fat me*.

This was different.

At thirty-three, I was told to blame her for the fact that I was gay. During my undercover research for a report on conversion therapy, an unnamed therapist told me that my "close" relationship with my sister was an "influence" in me being gay. My bond, my connection, my ride or die. The reason, or part of the reason, for my difference. My "little problem." Too much feminine influence.

During the "therapy" session I was stunned. He was of course crazy, deluded and dangerously impressionable. I shudder to think of how many people he's talked to and convinced that his brainwashing thoughts are fact. They're not. He was, however, correct about one thing. My sister had influenced me. She'd talked with me, confided in me and brought me down from a ledge several times a week since we were uni graduates. Helping me to accept who I am. Embrace my flaws and not be afraid of the person I was.

The gay man.

Her little gay brother. She influenced me heavily. And I love her for this. But blame? No.

Laura is everything you'd expect a sister to be. Opinionated, thoughtful and always feeling second place to the rest of my friends. Now, we also live together. Not in a cringe sharing-baths, finishing-each-other's-sentences way, but in a convenient and happy one. Being my (slightly) older sister, you'd think that she was the serious one.

No.

She is the one who suggests cocktails before bed, makes me do the swapping clothes TikTok routine and books random restaurants far in advance to pin me down. Because if I was a commitment-phobe in life, Laura was a commitment pro.

Our relationship is good. Great, I'd say. If you saw us now, you'd assume this was always how it had been. It should have been. But it wasn't.

And being gay wasn't a plaster for the issue. In fact, being gay *was* the issue.

❧

Life is a photo album.

When you are young, you have no choice but to have your picture taken. It's part of growing up, and whether you like it or not, your parents are going to film, photograph and Instagram the shit out of you.

Your first step, first burp, first word, that moment you ate mud and even that time that you pulled down your pants in Debenhams. Snapped. Captured forever, and probably in a dusty old brown photo binder in the garage.

Everything was brown.

Photos in cute outfits that are often taken with your siblings, and frequently featuring your tiny willy, flapping about for your mum's friends to see. Note: the tiny willy grew. Cherished moments that are taken with reluctant arms thrown around each other and strained smiles. Documented.

My parents did this and the parents of today are no different. Instead of being in the photo albums kept next to old schoolbooks, however, they're now plastered across Facebook, available for the world to see. Tiny willies everywhere. Lucky us. Moments that your parents think are cute but the rest of us think are quite boring. *Babies all look the same.*

A steady stream of forced pictures. This is life. Or at least, life before *you* have control of the camera. And, as a gay man, I certainly do have control of the camera now. Thank god. Yes, I'm partial to a selfie.

I guess it is a rite of passage that we all have to suffer through. Secretly, or not so secretly, I think I loved the lens. Even back then. I mean, at five years old I had no problem performing a naked sea lion show in the garden with my cousins. Nor did I mind dressing up in someone else's clothes and being caught on film.

Candid photoshoots.

I think I quite enjoyed being something other than myself. Wearing clothes that weren't the standard "boy uniform" and experimenting. Sampling who I'd rather be.

My sister, on the other hand, had always just tolerated camera time, rather than loving it. She didn't realise how lucky she was having pretty outfits, colours other than blue and freedom. Freedom to have fun with what she wore. Because girls could be more flamboyant, more out there and more engaged. Boys couldn't, at least not back then.

And as siblings, we were different.

Opposites.

❥

Girls are lucky. Girls always made pretty bridesmaids, flower throwers or mini versions of their mums. All squeezed into princess dresses, tutus and cat ears. I mean...what the hell isn't to love. Give me a tutu any day. I assumed my sister enjoyed it. Don't all girls enjoy that?

As a boring boy, I was actually quite jealous of the "everyday" girl clothes they got to sample. In my eyes, my sister was the lucky one.

When I was born, my mum insisted that Laura had been excited for her little brother's arrival. She would finally have someone to play with. There was even a cute picture of her looking girly and staring at me after I'd been born.

Ahh.

Doting eyes that were secretly thinking, *who the fuck is this that's come to steal my limelight?* Soon enough we had the obligatory naked bath pictures together, cute matching outfit snaps and messy dinner-time shots. As siblings do.

We even had the happy holiday photos in Disneyland Paris with Snow White. That moment where young kids clutch a stranger's hand who is dressed like someone in a movie but who is, in fact, just a lady in a bad wig. A stranger. Slightly creepy, actually, when you think about it, don't you think?

But as the birthdays passed and we attended more weddings, her in a lovely peach dress and me in a boring black waistcoat, my sister started to become annoyed by her fat little brother. I think her intense frowns displayed in pictures clearly portrayed that she didn't really want me at her seventh, eighth or ninth birthday parties. She certainly didn't want to share her lovely Barbie cake that our mum had homemade for her on her tenth birthday.

Again, lucky.

God, I loved that cake. An actual doll sat perfectly on top of it, with the cake looking like part of her dress. I had marvelled at it for so long that I even missed Ronald McDonald handing out a balloon on a stick. Those balloons were gold dust, weren't they!

The cake was epic! You can therefore understand my disappointment, six months later, when my birthday came around and I got a Thomas the Tank Engine creation. Because I was a boy. Boys didn't have Barbie cakes or fantastic clothes, and they also weren't meant to be close to their sisters. They definitely shouldn't play with dolls or cut Cindy's hair too short, and they really shouldn't want a day shopping with the girls.

SHOPPING FOR FUN CLOTHES.

No, all of that was seen as odd for a boy/brother and, therefore, I began to think that I was strange. Quietly. A strange little fat boy. I continued to become the odd one of the family. Or at least that's how I felt inside.

At seven years old I was even jealous of my mum and sister ironing together. *Ironing!* They would have this beautiful routine. Laura pre-ironed on a tiny board that Mum got her as a gift (I wanted that board), then when Mum ironed the item properly, it was put away. Quite boring really, but as a kid, it was as good as ice cream.

As good as it was going to get.

If I was lucky, I sometimes got to be the folder. A blue job.

A man's job. But frankly I was happy to just be a part of it. I'd fold and my sister would frown at me for taking part. This was her domain.

As my sister grew up, I became the annoying brother who my sister didn't really understand. Hated in fact. Looking at me as if I was an alien. A foreign intruder in her life.

The misfit.

By the time that she came into her boobs at seventeen, we barely spent any time together and had fewer forced photos. For her, I was just an irritation. A fly that required regular swatting.

Go away, Daniel.

If I was caught in her room, she'd scream for me to get out. If I held a Barbie, she'd want it back. *She didn't want it.* When I spilt white spirit over her paint by numbers, I was confined to my room. The result of an over-excited hand reaction that I couldn't control.

Contain those limp wrists, Daniel.

Our life in pictures together hit pause. The shutter closed. Still, something in me wanted her close by and I wanted to be her friend. I needed her. Which perhaps was slightly annoying to be honest. I bet I was exhausting to be around.

It was a feeling of being lost without her. I wanted her near, even if she disliked me. Because she had always been there. In my life from the start, looking over at me in the crib. And there was something in her that I listened to. Older sister. Wise. Had it together.

My idol.

Of course, she was going through her own journey, which I didn't appreciate, and navigating teenage life. Not an easy ride for anyone. Especially not in braces and headgear at night. Bless her. But I wasn't thinking about that. I was just wondering why we didn't click.

As the camera turned off on us, we grew further apart. Were a brother and sister not meant to be friends? Was that the reality?

❧

According to Judi James, sibling relationships tend to be based on animal survival patterns, which is why they can often involve fights, battles and competitive behaviours from a very early age. Judi says, "All children like to be the centre of the universe, and siblings provide a way of teaching us to share but it doesn't mean to say that we like doing so, which is why we can carry resentments and jealousies throughout our entire lives."

Our entire lives!

That was my fear right there. By definition of a sibling, Laura and I were relations, not friends. A fact that, when I was seventeen, was very hard to swallow.

Now, if your sister instantly loved your flamboyant ways and you became fast friends, maybe even plaiting each other's hair, then I'm happy for you. Truly I am. It would have saved Laura and I a lot of time.

Braid away!

But not every siblingship is like this. I wish! We don't all get each other straight away. Some of us compete, some of us dislike each other and some of us never will get on.

TV shows didn't help with this either. Like many things in life, they glorified or heightened this relationship. There were only two types of siblings, or so it seemed, in the glossy world of television.

Two!

There were the ones who loved each other, spent all their time together and even had similar groups of friends. If you were twins as well, then you'd struck gold. Warm siblings.

Then there were the ones who hated each other. Loathed their existence and struggled through forced moments together. Barely raising a smile and preferring to ignore the other's presence. In the really dramatic shows, those were the types that slept with each other's husbands, plotted their murder and definitely did not send them Christmas cards. They might never speak, let alone look in the other's direction. Cold siblings.

And in the colourful land of television, there was no in between. No grey area. That was it.

Disappointingly for me, we were the latter. I'm pretty sure we wouldn't sleep with each other's husbands, or plot a murder, but Christmas cards might have been pushing it. We would never be those siblings that just "got" each other, had each other's backs and weren't just relations, but friends. A situation that, at the time, I thought would last forever.

An entire life of hate and resentment.

Don't get me wrong. She didn't want me dead, and as much as it might have pained her to say, there was unconditional love. Caring. But that was as far as it went.

I used to think that only children had it easier. No one to bicker with or annoy and probably easier on the parents too. I look at all my friends with two kids and see the strain.

Shout out to the parents of multiple kids!

Two brats are a lot when you are also trying to balance Pilates, wine and getting eight hours of sleep, right? But a friend of mine who grew up with no brothers or sisters told me that she often dreamt of having one, as it would have been like an instant friend at home. Someone who you could play with and confide in and who could be your ultimate ally. Someone who would always be there, no effort, no questions. She would say, "It would make life easier. Better." Clearly, she'd seen the good version played out on TV.

At the time, I remember agreeing, telling her it was wonderful to have one and lying about the fact that I didn't really talk to mine. My own sister was off at uni and having the time of her life. She literally had such a cool life. I watched from afar.

My single child friend continued to tell me that I was "lucky," but we agreed that you also didn't need to be blood to be close. "Sisters" come in many forms. A person to instantly be there, no matter what. A friend that was like a sister. Connected and in touch with each other.

And despite having some incredible "sisters" around me, there was one support at home that I never stopped craving. Never stopped hoping for. Never stopped needing.

Little did I know that annoying brothers didn't last forever. A rainbow was on its way.

❧

When you are young, you don't ever truly realise the value of what you have. How can you, when you are growing up? Innocent. You don't know any better.

George Bernard Shaw said that "Youth is wasted on the young." You can only appreciate this quote when you are old. Otherwise, you roll your eyes and say, "Leave me alone, Dad. Get out of my room." Shaw was correct, though. But I can say that now because I'm old.

When you are young, you don't have time to register everything around you. Life happens; you learn and grow. You can't possibly breathe in every moment and realise its importance. Nor can you truly understand how important certain people will be in your story. You'll have moments where things feel important but then realise they weren't at all. The actual important things are seen and appreciated by looking back. And some things are truly important.

I'd have loved to have told my sister first. Come out in my truth. My own words. Part of me wondered if it might have brought us back together. She was the most important person to tell, and this would be our fresh new start.

I knew that.

She would be that person who would tell me it would all be okay. Of course, because she would make sure it would be. That was her role. Our parents would understand, and she would help with that. She would have my back. She'd be my buffer.

My guide.

Of course, she would hug me, and I'd cry, letting out the release. What a fucking release that would be. We'd then probably sit on her bed giggling and she'd ask me what boys I fancied. I'd respond, "hairy ones," and she'd burst out laughing, telling me that stubble would cause me a rash downstairs – something which I actually did find out later on, alone, with the fear that I had just got herpes.

I hadn't just got herpes.

Then she'd tell me that I was never alone. Never would be. Because I had a sister. Because frankly, she knew that I was scared without her. And I really didn't want to go through this by myself.

That would be my coming out story to my sister. Finally, she'd see me as not just the annoying brother, but misunderstood, and everything would click. Perfect. Unfortunately, someone else told her first.

It wasn't perfect.

It wasn't helpful.

It was brutal.

And just like that, I was out to my sister and our intimate moment was stolen from us. Forever.

A moment that should never be stolen.

❧

The year was 2005.

I had just started to explore who I was. Behind closed doors. I realise that sounds like a name for a bad porno. Actually, "bad porno" probably sums up the very dull sex life that I had when I came out. But when I say explore, I'm not talking sex. Okay, I had sex, but I'm not just talking sex.

Without sounding too New Age and radical, I was finding myself. In doing so, I realised that I had never quite understood the implications of living in a small town. Southend-on-Sea, despite sporting the longest pier in the world, was relatively small time. Not a good thing when it came to gossip.

Eugh.

Malicious chatter that I've seen used as an incredibly harmful weapon in our community. Ammunition. We'll come on to that later.

However, while I may have felt like "the only gay in the village," thinking no one else was homosexual, I wasn't. And when I finally found another one, I soon wished that I hadn't.

Bruce Davis was two years older than me. He had tight curly hair and wore cool glasses. He didn't come across scared of who he was and embraced his sexuality while still retaining an element of being a "man." I looked at him in amazement.

He worked in GAP and was openly "out" as a gay man. Gay and Proud. Something I later realised wasn't the abbreviation that GAP stood for. An insult a school kid slung at me once when I was wearing a GAP hoodie. *Ha, ha, you're GAY AND PROUD.*

Bruce beamed with pride and seemed relaxed. It was enviable. You know, that moment you see someone, and you stare in awe of their presence. Their thirst for life. Happiness that shined through their smile and nature with ease.

Perfection. Like how I imagine that I'd look at JLo and the fact she never ages if I saw her. *What is that?*

Bruce shined. I was not shining. Not at that point.

I'm not sure what possessed me, but I needed to reach out. I needed to know another gay man. He was a siren, singing to me, enticing me to crash my boat in his direction. And boy, was I about to crash.

Not for sex – I'm not sure my feelings were of fancy – but as water. He would be an important person in my story. An important moment.

So, I answered that call. Seventeen-year-old me, one summer's day, went into GAP, clutched an over-priced orange sweater that I really didn't want and walked over to him while he was working.

This was it.

My sweaty hands cemented the fact that I'd have to buy the top, regardless of whether I wanted it. And there on Southend high street, in the new GAP store, I outed myself to a complete stranger. A desperate attempt to no longer feel alone.

I cleared my throat.

"Are you gay?"

No answer. Probably not the best opener. I continued.

"I am. I don't know anyone else who is and thought I'd say hello."

It was not cool. Slick. Easy. It was awkward as fuck. He looked at me quickly, smiled and then took the jumper. In his defence, he was working. Also, despite me knowing that he was gay and open about it, maybe I had got it wrong and he wasn't so confident in his skin. Perhaps he didn't appreciate a teenager saying this in his place of work. Even if it was quiet and no one else was around. I wouldn't have done!

I felt bad. I apologised and said that I was new to this. This was out of my depth. After barely acknowledging my blurted rambles, he rang the sweater through the till and put it in a bag.

"Twenty-nine ninety-nine, please."

I stifled a smile and grabbed the string blue bag. God, I used to love those bags. A month's pocket money swung by my side as I made my way to the exit. My eyes pricked with tears.

Fuck off, tears.

After being released from the store that I'd sweated profusely in, I continued walking in the direction of home. Knowing that it was a good forty-five-minute walk. I didn't care, not now; I needed the air. I left the shop with two regrets.

First, I wished that I could have been the cool kid who dealt with this smoothly and effortlessly, rather than embarrassing myself. Second, I wished that I had chosen a blue jumper. I suited blue.

Had GAP really stood for Gay and Proud, I left feeling anything but. Instead, I felt hopeless. If this guy was a gay man, I wasn't sure I liked them. Where was my ally? My friend? A comforting response?

In that moment I felt like they were a breed of creature around the watering hole in Africa that was not fazed by the ones alongside them, fighting for their space too. Others weren't important. As long as they drank freely, they had their place. Fuck the rest of us. He was a lion; I was a warthog.

I knew outing myself to him was risky. He went to the same sixth form as my sister, but I also knew that they weren't in the same group and I naively hoped that he would appreciate how hard that may have been for me. Perhaps he'd even think of his own journey. Stand by his own.

I was certain that we had some unspoken level of understanding. He appreciated my struggle. Saw me sweating. Man, was it a struggle. I was brave. This incident would be between us. That would be the end of it.

It wasn't. Of course, it wasn't. He didn't keep it to himself. I hated him.

Days later, Laura came into the kitchen. I was on the computer, chatting on MSN.

"So, you're gay then? Bruce told me."

My stomach flipped and I looked up at her. This was my sister all over. Direct and asking for facts. She wanted confirmation, no fluff. She was angry. My mouth opened, but words failed to fall.

"Thanks for telling me!"

She left before I could say anything. Before I confirmed. Spoke out. Said sorry. My body went numb. My mouth remained open for what felt like the rest of the day, and I sat in the kitchen of our blended household from our mum's second marriage, feeling uncomfortable and angry. Now she knew. This was not perfect.

Fucking GAP.

I often wonder if he had found joy in sharing that gossip. I wondered how my sister reacted to it and then how she felt after.

I never had the conversation with her after. Did she feel concern, did she know, did he feel bad at all? I bet he didn't. I bet he continued drinking water, taking up space and ignoring the other animals.

The ones that needed scraps.

Me.

❧

My sister had been so angry when she found out. Really annoyed. But not because of Bruce. I mean, that didn't help.

A sister is meant to be someone we talk to, someone who knows our secrets first and then can defend us. The greatest ally. However, she was pissed. She hadn't known my secrets. She hadn't been prepared to defend. You know those cartoons with steam coming from the ears? Words couldn't express the feelings, so a visual was more powerful. Well, Laura had steam.

She thought that this was something that made me more "special." Gave me more edge. In a moment when she was desperately trying to find her own identity, I was out-shining. Even if I didn't feel like it.

She felt plain. To her, I was colourful. I didn't deserve something extra that made me unique in a way that she could never be. *Steam.*

After the forced coming out, I struggled to understand her feelings. I felt quite bad, as I actually just really wanted to be her friend. We both had no idea what each other felt. Because neither of us asked either.

In truth, I didn't want this. Any of it. Not at the time. If this was what being gay was, she could have it. She could have had all my colour, if only I could have given it away. But I couldn't. We can't. *We shouldn't.*

I asked her not to tell our parents, which she didn't. She might have hated me, but unlike Bruce, she had a lot of decency.

She was kind. Really kind in fact.

But in a moment that could have brought us together, we were pushed further apart, and she went off to university as my relation, not my friend.

The end.

❂

I jest.

But there was a point where I really thought that would be it. I had hoped that the one weapon I had in being gay could fix us, plaster over our issues, be our saviour. But gossip beat me to it. There was real damage in it. It was for the most part, an act of hate. An attack on a character.

Judi James says that there is no real template for sibling relationships. "Some start badly but become a source of love and comfort later on in life. Some are always loving and protective and others are always open warfare."

Thankfully, our own war ended. Time healed. We gradually

saw the importance of each other. Seeking comfort in our parents' mistakes, common interests and realising that we actually enjoyed each other's company.

My thirteen-year-old self was doing cartwheels for it. I could imagine him dancing around his Teenage Mutant Hero Turtles bedroom with a hairbrush, singing Britney. Happy.

I'm not sure when it happened. There was no big bang moment. Suddenly, in my early twenties, I had a sister in my life again, and I started to understand the significance of the role. Here was a person that got you and had you. Even when you didn't have yourself. A bond, a union. A crucial part of the LGBTQIA+ community. The warm sibling I'd seen in TV shows.

A sister.

Whether you're lucky to have one by blood or if you have a friend that feels like one to you, sisters are our ultimate allies. For me, it took time apart and being comfortable in our own skins to appreciate the value in what we had all along. I'd love to tell you that there was an emotional moment of acceptance with my sister, that we'd hugged it out and tears were shed, but there wasn't. We never spoke about it. It was a mature understanding that hadn't been there before.

Venus Williams once said, "As a sister, when they're doing something it's your own success, too." And, after all those years, my sister finally saw me doing something.

Slowly she stopped looking at the annoyances and understood me. Related to me.

No longer did she see the brother who wouldn't get off her bed or the dude who hung around her friends when they were over like a bad smell. Instead, she saw the boy who wanted her friendship. The person who needed it. And she wanted it too.

We hung out, attended each other's birthdays (happily) and joined in eye rolls when our parents frustrated us. We went through break-ups, make-ups and road trips across America. Ultimately, I had courage by my side. An unquestionable support.

I thought our relationship became stronger because I was gay. For a long time, I thought this was my superpower. It allowed us to bond, talk boys, compare notes on dates and which character we fancied in *Grey's Anatomy*. Patrick Dempsey of course. What I didn't realise was the "gay" part was just an extra. I had a different superpower. Something my relationship had needed all along.

Honesty.

Because when I came (was forced) out, I gave something else to our relationship. Me. The real me.

Finally.

❧

My relationship with my sister is one of the best. Fact.

She fiercely protects me, and I have her back. But having never had a real conversation about being gay and how we felt, after my coming out, you don't realise how much it's good to talk until you do.

Things should never be left unsaid.

Laura said, "It wasn't that I didn't want a gay brother. It was that I didn't understand why you had to be special. When we were young, we got on and played together, but when I went to high school it changed. I hadn't been the popular kid. I wasn't cool. Nothing exciting defined me. I was a plain girl. So, my friends were important. I was trying to create my own life. You were just there, annoying and wanting to always be there when my friends were about. Or getting in my way. You obviously weren't like other people's brothers. I guess at the time I assumed I'd pulled the short straw."

At a time when we couldn't have been further apart, Laura said getting the news from someone else that I was gay was the cherry on the cake.

"I reacted in a way that surprises me today. Who was that brat? I'm ashamed to say, but my first thought wasn't, how is he, is he okay, is he struggling? It was – oh great, another thing that makes him more interesting than me."

What I never realised, however, was her reaction to the guy who told her.

"As annoying as I found you, I would always defend you. You do that as a sister. Here was a moment that was hugely important, and someone ruined it. I was so angry at Bruce. When he told me, I remember saying, 'Yeah, and?' Like I knew and didn't care. I didn't want him to see it bothered me. He had got such a kick out of sharing that information. The thing is, I bet he never thought about it again, but he didn't realise the impact that might have."

Confessing to always feeling like the boring, generic girl next door who struggled with guys, Laura saw this as another thing that I had and she didn't.

"Of course, I now know that just because you say you are gay doesn't mean you know who you are. But at the time I thought it did. It felt like a personality and that it defined you. I was bland because I was straight – which is mad to say. At the time I thought – cool, you know who you are. Great. And I didn't. It's weird how I felt – thinking everything was about you – because actually, Mum wasn't talking to you and it wasn't really ever spoken about.

"I wish I had asked more questions, but it was at a time when I didn't know gay people or know how to react. I also wasn't confident, so I was more concerned about the impact on my life. I didn't think about anything other than, okay, big deal, move on. I don't think I ever asked you how you felt about being gay – how crazy is that?"

Laura said that she worried her friends would like me more,

that I was more interesting, but then went to uni and had more of an understanding of who she was.

"When I started to have more confidence in myself, I started to be more open to being friends with my brother. Before I'd been so scared to let you in and around my friends, because you had an edge. That's how you came across. I never thought about you getting beaten up, or diseases. I never worried. I just saw you as strong and fearless and someone who I didn't need to worry about."

We discussed living a sheltered life with a lack of knowledge or education around what gay people might go through.

"I didn't need to ask anything when we finally started talking, because you seemed okay. The past was the past. In fact, I got jealous. I did think in the absence of me, who did you have to talk to about it? All you wanted to do was talk to me and do things, but I wasn't ready. Then, when I was, you had this new group of friends and I was a side thought.

"It stems back to Bruce Davis – people knew you and I felt like I didn't. Suddenly all I wanted was to know you. But you'd moved on, rightly so. People would say, 'I love your brother,' and I was like, great, I don't know him. Back then I didn't understand that you didn't get what you needed at home. Hence going out and finding your own support."

The jealousy surprised me, as I'd never understood that before now. I explained that I'd wanted her close for ages.

"You probably felt safe with me as it was an unconditional love, and no matter what, you being gay or anything, I'd be there. I was there. I just didn't show you. In a way that is what a sibling is. Because you feared others might not accept you, but a sister would. The thing is, you say that you envied my 'normal' life, but seeing you live and be strong and know who you were made me envy you."

We laughed about awkward moments and the fact that she,

instead of me, once went as a date to my ex-boyfriend's work party when he wasn't out.

"That must have been hard. You must have found some things really hard. God, that's awful. There are so many things I've never asked. Like how you met your friends, what made you come out, how you felt, who you fancied? At the time I don't think I even thought, so he fancies men? But actually, you yourself have sometimes seen being gay as gross – and I wonder if you push your own fears on it. You didn't talk much. Now, we are so open with each other. But I forget to ask how you got here. Okay, I get a bit freaked if you talk too much about sex, but we talk."

Laura said that she'd never seen me as her gay brother, just an annoying one.

"The reality is, you being gay might have been the most interesting thing about me. In our mid-twenties we just became close. I'm not sure that would have happened if you were straight. You being gay definitely helped; it changed our relationship. Maybe if you were straight, we'd be close in a different way. I've never wished you were straight, though. The only thing I've ever thought is that if I had a straight brother, maybe I could actually meet some guys. I love your friends, but I'm not really their type."

We agreed that we were lucky to have a good relationship now.

"It's a non-wavering support. It's hard to explain. But you are there and forced together, other people won't know what you've been through in the same detail. It's unconditional and there aren't any questions asked. Which actually could have been a downfall too. I only see positives in our relationship and in you being gay. I'm fortunate to have a connection with my brother who is gay and taught me quicker that life shouldn't be sheltered. In having a gay brother, I was forced to educate. It's only a positive to me.

"There have been many times where I've defended you and I realise how much homophobia is out there. Times I haven't even discussed with you. Sometimes I even feel like I need to announce that you are gay on dates or to new friends – I don't know why, but it's like something that I'm checking to see if they are okay with it. Testing the water. Also, I'm protecting you. You want to be the first to say it, so no horrid comments come."

It's strange to hear the effect you have on someone without even knowing it for something you can't help.

"The reality is, if all you knew in life was one community, one race, one gender, that would be a sheltered life. A boring one too. As a sibling we learn, and you've opened me up to stuff. But my role is also to support you. I know you've found it hard to feel normal yourself. I had no idea conversion therapy wasn't illegal until they blamed me for making you gay! It's only through listening and learning – you grow. We grow. There's still a clear fight for minorities.

"I saw you being gay as a privilege at the time. You had something sparkly and new. I didn't ask the right questions, but in reality, it helped us form a closer bond. If anything, I feel like I have to remind you that you are the same as everyone else. Being gay is normal. Having a gay brother is just wonderful."

❧

Labels are the things that we give out. Handing them over to make other people feel comfortable. At ease. What I never realised is that mine – being gay – was so misunderstood by my family.

A label that was outed before I revealed it.

At the time, my sister saw it as something extra, something that defined me. A gift. A privilege. But what we often don't ask ourselves is how we feel about that label.

A sibling isn't an easy relationship to have. It's hard work. I'd always hoped to have my sister close, and we went through a journey to get there. But I realise that the support that our relationship brings is unquestionable. Someone who gives us unconditional support, whether we realise or not. Because when you are different, and others might not accept you, the importance of someone who does is vital.

As a gay man, we often reference the many "sisters" around us, standing by us. And in this modern day, a sister, in any form, is a necessity to us. Unconditional support. Family. They are one of our toughest critics, will showcase annoyance when warranted and won't mince words.

A loyal defender. You'll get on their nerves, misunderstand each other and be jealous.

We all see labels differently. But mine (sister) now happens to be a friend – turns out she always was. A reminder that I'm not alone and someone has my back even when I don't realise. The next layer of my foundations. A rock for future relationships. A mirror to showcase our worth and tell us to accept ourselves. Our pick-up when we are down. Someone to finally ask questions when the label feels uncomfortable.

Harsh at times, but essential.

And also, a reminder that just because you are the gay brother doesn't mean other people don't have their own stuff going on. Sometimes we need reminding of that.

We are all special, even the plain. Don't let anyone take that from you.

Thank you, sister.

friend

/frɛnd/

---

noun

1. a person with whom one has a bond of mutual affection, typically one exclusive of sexual or family relations.
   "she's a friend of mine"

2. a member of the Religious Society of Friends; a Quaker.

verb

3. INFORMAL add (someone) to a list of friends or contacts on a social networking website.
   "I am friended by twenty-nine people who I have not friended back"

4. ARCHAIC befriend (someone).

conversations
with a friend

Stand-up comedians are incredible, aren't they?

To stand on stage to an audience with the sole goal to make them laugh takes courage, talent and balls.

I would hate to be a stand-up comedian. Imagine the pressure of delivering. To be funny. To make people really laugh. To perform.

I'm not a stand-up comedian. I don't think I'm funny. If someone asked me to crack a joke, my mind would be blank. I'd go red. I know this one inappropriate joke about salad cream and that's it. That's my repertoire. One joke.

However, I often feel like I'm a one-man act. Performing. Especially to my friends.

Shane, a friend who I've known for years, will start any interaction by saying, "Go on then, son..." This is his way of asking for my stories. He'll pump me for gossip, dating tales and details. It's my job to deliver. Not to let him down and give him the routine. My act. He always claims that his life is *boring* and that I'm always *doing something*. He is engaged to be married, living back in my hometown and enjoying what he would call *the simple life*.

Go on then, son! I deliver.

My girlfriend Sarah will hug me whenever she sees me, then straight away say, "Tell me a story..." Sarah wants escapism. I live in London; she lives in a small seaside town in Essex. To her, my life is vibrant and colourful. She wants my one-man sketch to make her smile. To be honest, she's impressed by any story that goes past 10.00 p.m. Her fixed bedtime as a married mum of two kids with a full-time job and no lie-ins for five years.

Tell me a story... So, I indulge.

Holly, budding business owner, mum, wife, all-time life-smashing superwoman, tells me that I'm always too busy for her. I am. Often trying to pin me down for dinner, she wants a front row seat to the show. "Your week looked fabulous on Instagram, I laughed so much...what on Earth happened in that hot tub?"

What... I share.

I crack jokes, tell stories, bad and good dates, anecdotes of pole dancing in Soho, drinking cocktails on rooftops and travel.

David, a dad, husband and CEO, has gone grey because of the stress of his life. He feels that he never goes out any more and asks me to indulge him.

I entertain. Performing the act.

I do this a lot. Any time I'm around my friends. It's become my role.

There are so many (bloody incredible) friends who I could reference in this scenario. People whose lives don't feel as spicy, sexy or glittery as mine.

Their lives are fucking awesome, FYI.

Friends who want my stories. Not because they want to spread gossip, bitch about me or mock me, but because these are friends living their lives at what seems to be a more accelerated rate than mine.

I'm the tortoise. That's my pace as a single gay man.

These are true friends who have already got their shit all

together. All figured it out. Smashing adulthood. Not like me. Angels. Just interested in their friend. People who see me for who I am and accept me.

Gay. Single. Career focused. Likes a cocktail. Not got it together at all. In bed after 11.00 p.m. most nights. Failing adulthood.

People who I bring my one-man band to and perform for. A party trick to fill a gap. To fill a void. Part out of fear, part out of habit. And part because my life has always felt a few steps behind everyone else. I needed an act. One that I've rolled out since before I came out. My comfort blankets.

But one that fills a gap that, unbeknown to me, was filled ages ago.

Having always feared that I'd lose the "audience" if I didn't perform, I forgot that I no longer needed to. Even if I'm gay.

We don't always have to perform, at least not to our friends.

❧

"We often make lifelong friends from sheer proximity, i.e. the kid at the next desk at school or uni, or the one who lived in the same street or worked in the same office, and finding new friends can be more challenging than we expect," says Judi James.

Forming friends was, at first, an act of convivence. People near you, around you, classmates, kids pushed together by their mums. Forced friends that may or may not stick.

There is a time in everyone's lives when they'll wonder, *do I have friends?* Real friends that challenge you, help you and accept you. Loyal, protective, people who add value to your life. People who want to be there, not just because you were neighbours. Preferably someone other than your pet rabbit, Snowy. Or the school caretaker. (That man was just creepy.)

Your people.

I used to wonder if I'd ever find that person who would finish off my sentences because we were so in sync. Knew what I was thinking before I'd said it. And had my back. No matter what. Someone who didn't mind that I was different. Odd. Accepted it, didn't challenge it, appreciated it.

A friend.

Perhaps they would even throw a punch for me. You know, when you see friends defending other friends in movies and one throws a punch for the other. That's a good friend, right? I needed that person. The ride or die. The ultimate forever friend.

But doubt filled my mind. Consumed my thinking, worried my brain, lost me sleep. I doubted if I'd ever find a connection that strong. Someone willing to throw that punch. To be that person. I mean, who truly deserves the level of friendship that Kenan and Kel clearly had? That Tia and Tamara were blessed with? That four out of five Spice Girls have today? Goals.

Could people who aren't the same as the "norm" have that?

Growing up, I wondered just how valuable some friendships that I slowly obtained actually were. Convenient or real?

I desired to keep the *good* ones close. Work on the bad ones. Ultimately, having as many as I bloody well could. A mission to find friends. People who were there. And lots of them.

Quantity, not always quality. If you had lots of friends, people would leave you alone, accept you. Even with a lot of time spent wondering if some of them were really my friends, I always wanted more. Sure, they could be challenging and exhausting; our relationships can be tested a lot at times. Some won't last. Some you'll miss. Many you'll hang on to for too long before realising they might not have been friends at all. Despite this, armed with my doubts, I still wanted lots of them. And I even clung on to some that I knew weren't great. Weren't really friends at all.

After coming out, by nineteen years old, I had a brilliant sea of friends and foe before me.

Do I have friends?

I had assumed spotting the difference between them would be the tricky part. Who really would be there, would throw that punch, have my back? It wasn't. In fact, when you start to realise your own needs and who you are, you quickly learn that quantity isn't all it's cracked up to be. That quality is far more superior.

True friends weren't hard to discover. Not really. They revealed themselves in acts, not just words. Support. Sometimes it won't even be a huge display, but a moment that cements why you are friends. A look, a gesture or even a memory. Solidifying that they are one of your people, no doubt in their minds. They are your person. You are theirs.

So that when you ask yourself that question, when you are low or feeling downtrodden, after gaining so many "friends" throughout your life, *do I have friends?*

You can answer with ease, clarity and confidence.

Yes, I do.

Because Judi James was right. Finding the new friends is challenging. Breaking the convivence, the society moulds, striving to find like-minded people or allies. But when you do, it's easy to spot the difference.

Despite fearing that I wouldn't find any myself, I did. Let's face it, the boy next door was never going to be my lifelong buddy. He had his head in car bonnets, smoked joints and played Crazy Taxi... I listened to Britney and took selfies.

Do I have friends?

The question became easier to answer as I found more confidence in who I was. For too long I obsessed over what people wanted in a friend. Never really thinking that it could be what I could offer. What I brought to the table. But learning that there really were friends for us all, real friends, was a brilliant moment in life.

A saving grace.

Yes, we all struggle with the answer to that question for a while. School, uni, work: it will crop up throughout your life. At first, I strived to control it, searched to find the friends. Which worked to an extent. We do need to seek out different friends, find our tribes. But actually, I wish I'd just relaxed. Lost control. Sampled differences. Found quantity and then quality. Lived. Because I realised that you should be yourself, without apologising. People always shine through. Friends always shine through. Let them find you. Let them see you. Let them appreciate you.

Friends.

People who you'll love for a lifetime and who you'll laugh through adversity with, and you'll change into the person you need to be while they are by your side, holding your hand. Or not change. Just develop. Grow. People who remedy that feeling you had when you were younger, when that question rang around like an alarm in your head, hurting your confidence. Making you cling on to people who really weren't friends out of fear you wouldn't have any.

Do I have friends?

Because the answer is never about how many you have, it's about who you have. And soon enough, you'll have the tools to say it.

Yes, better friends than I ever imagined.

❧

Part of the definition of the word "friend" is frustrating. It references a list of people on a social media site. Our friendship lists. Showcasing our clan.

If you aren't on the list...

The list actually comprises people who clicked "add friend" or responded to a friend request. Growing your friends. Now part of the definition of the word. Eye roll.

I think it's clear why I find that frustrating. It doesn't surprise me, but I strongly believe that it shouldn't be part of defining this word. These people. Our friends. Our real list. Because that list isn't public information, nor does that number matter.

Like I said, I used to want loads of friends for myself. In fact, I cared so much about that list. A superficial figure that means absolutely nothing. But absolutely everything at the same time.

I had been told a number of times that as we get older, our pool of friends gets smaller. "It will happen, Daniel!" friends would say. Family members would agree. Older colleagues suggested. Apparently, we stop caring about numbers, focusing more on quality. Quality people in our lives, not the list on social media. Not the likes. Not the shares. Not the gratification that you are worthy of their friendship. Of course, I refused to believe this at seventeen years old. That would not be me. It couldn't be me. I didn't want that to be me.

I enjoyed having multiple groups, multiple people and a healthy number of head counts at my birthdays.

"Plus one? Yeah, bring them along."

"Your cousin is in town? Of course, she can come along."

"Oh yeah, bring Bob. Love Bob. Who's Bob? Sorry, what's he called? Marcus, yes he's welcome too."

"The more the merrier."

And I was merrier. I was happy to be surrounded by people. Happy to have numbers, adding to the list, daily. It wasn't about what everyone else thought. I'm sure it looked that way at times. But it was for me. For young me. The seventeen-year-old. Then the nineteen-year-old. Then the twenty-five-year-old.

After you go through life scared that you won't make any friends, fearing they can't and won't be themselves around you, quantity felt good. It felt healthy. It felt comforting. Surrounding myself by lots of people felt like acceptance. Birthdays felt better, Facebook figures looked healthier. People saw me as normal and popular and, most importantly, they wanted a bite of the action. The more friends I had, the more I did, the more new people I would meet.

Quantity felt good.

As my list grew, I clung to every single one of them like a glue gun to a drag queen. Social media helped with this. When it first blew up, how many "friends" you had suddenly seemed incredibly important. It was important. It was no longer a matter of hearing about your life and what you were doing; it was about seeing it. Online. Figures were facts. Figures meant friends. Popularity. I needed this.

Poke me Great Britain, I'm ready to have more friends.

Despite the majority of those five hundred people not really knowing anything about you, they were a status. A symbol of your popularity. They mattered. It was an online CV of likeability that had moved from Myspace to Facebook and then later to Instagram, Snapchat, TikTok.

Until the next.

Pictures, check ins, likes = numbers. A new and improved recognised and logged stage of friendship.

Drag Queen. Clinging to the glue gun.

It wasn't that I'm greedy; I was happy for friends to mingle with others. I encouraged this. If you were ever at my birthday party (and let's face it you probably were – I invited everyone), you'll understand that I worked the room. I would say "hello," mingle, introduce people, keep drinks refilled. My step count on any one birthday was probably bloody incredible. I put in the time and distance. There was something that I adored in new friends meeting old, seeing people connect and no one being left behind. Everyone deserved a friend, or five hundred.

It was a list that mattered to me. The me who clearly had my priorities wrong. It didn't last, though. You cannot sustain five hundred friendships. I can barely sustain a handful. Turns out, there is a timeline of friends lists.

In your teens, you want as many friends as you could have. In your twenties, you want to find new friendships along your own journey and explore different ones. In your thirties, you start to cull your connections (a fact that I can't quite believe). Then in your forties, I'm told, you regret some of your cull, clawing back. In your fifties, you reignite lost associations. And apparently, in your sixties, you repeat the cycle. My mum currently has more friends than I do and is one of the most popular speakers on Clubhouse.

Another app. Thanks for telling me, Mum.

The circle of friendship life. A journey that matters more than you realise at the time. Lessons.

In my early twenties, I had assumed that dwindling numbers was a sign of a decrease in popularity. A decline in friendships or relevance. It wasn't. It was just an increase in the ones that mattered. Of course, I refused this way of thinking for a long time.

Clinging on to the list!

I was scared to embrace something that would lose quantity.

High school had been about grabbing any friends who accepted me, thankfully forming some lovely connections, and then afterwards I was desperately wanting to find as many gays as I could add to the list. But, gradually, I cared less for Facebook – I rarely even remember it's there. I've come to terms with past friendships that have distanced for various reasons and accepted the facts. Because what we gain is momentous.

And because I'm in my thirties cull stage!

As we age, as we move through our decades and change, those who stay with us are the ones we need. The ones we continue with. The hands to hold through the shit times and the relationships we need to preserve throughout.

My lesson was to focus on the real list in my life, not the online one. A lesson we only learn in time. But one we don't realise at first.

◉

The one-man act started when I was thirteen. I had ten chubby fingers and nothing much to give other than my personality. And even that at times was testing it. So, I fanned out my fingers and allowed girls in my class to press one down, then I'd sing.

I was a terrible singer. Still am. But it made them laugh.

"Sausage fingers Dan."

I liked hearing them laugh. My routine was making them giggle and I liked it. It felt good.

Before high school, making friends wasn't an issue. In primary and junior school, I felt wealthy in my friendships. But that was before we learnt to judge one another. When it was acceptable to have lots of girlfriends as a boy and not have to answer questions for it. Blissfully ignorant to sexuality, genders, difference.

Children.

My first actual friend was a boy. Not so strange on the outside looking in, but for me as I grew up and witnessed how uncomfortable they made me in later years, it's odd to say now.

A boy!

I couldn't tell you his name. I just remember he was nice to me and we hung out. Played together without killing each other. Our mums were friends, so in turn we were too. He was my first friend because back then, boys were meant to play with boys and girls played with girls. Pink was pink. Blue was blue.

So, I had a boy who was a friend. He was kind. He let me play with his toys, shared them and made me feel at ease. I remember because I didn't ever dislike the times we spent together. I enjoyed it. I didn't have any dread hanging out with him, like the feeling that I got when I was older and around boys. There were no inhibitions. Opinions and judgements weren't formed. We were too young for that yet. Innocent. We just were. Friends. Not deep, just sweet. Played together, no questions asked.

I wonder what happened to him. I wonder if he had known my sexuality at the time, understood that I wasn't like him, if he would still have played the same. Would he still have been that kind?

Maybe he is gay now. Perhaps he does drag, or is bisexual, or has his own story. Perhaps he's just a nice lad.

I miss that innocence. That all-accepting fresh canvas that doesn't ask questions but just plays. Relaxed, kind and easy. The way a friendship should be. But that naivety doesn't last. Soon enough we develop opinions, see differences. Become ugly in our opinions.

That was my fear. A developing fear as I grew up, that if people were aware of my true self, would they still be relaxed and see past a thing that shouldn't really matter?

Could they?

But it did matter. Being gay – it changes things. Changes friendships. You may as well have a stutter, or an obvious visual defect – something showcasing your difference. Because knowing that you aren't the same as the people you are thrown together with creates an immediate fear.

Do they know? Do they suspect? What do they know? Are they okay with that knowledge?

The more aware we are of our fears, the more others see them. The more they spot the mince or catch a glimpse of the real you.

So, after the innocence of youth, when people can ask questions and form opinions, you needed to bring something else to the table.

Detract from the pink elephant that was growing in the room.

❧

Judi James says, "We tend to have different friends for different reasons. Old friends for the memories and shared experiences and a longer understanding of who we are, friends we see to have fun and friends we turn to when we need support or advice."

Growing up, I really did assume that I was the only gay in the village. If you did too, then you know exactly how odd that feeling can be. How alien and alone it can make you feel.

My true first friendships were with girls. *Sorry unidentified young, kind boy from my youth!* It wasn't that I purposely tried to find females. Or that they were the easiest option. It just happened. They seemed like they were kinder. More forgiving. At least that's what I came to realise. After finding some who didn't point and laugh at me, to my disbelief, people who wanted to actually hang out with me, even after school, and who *chose* me to be at their birthdays, I felt at ease with friends.

Not convenient but actual friendships.

I discovered that I could relate to this gender a lot more than I could my own. And, at the time, I felt like I needed forgiveness. I felt like I had to apologise for the different, odd boy that I was. Girls were more forgiving. These girls were my comfort.

Perhaps it was also the fact that it was unlikely that I was going to sleep with them. Or the fact they saw me as less of a man. Non-threatening. But it was easy company that just clicked. That made me roll around the floor with laughter and develop fond memories and that encouraged my opinion when I had been scared to speak. People who told me their secrets, and friends who I shared a few of mine with too. We found each other. *Thank god.* A group of around ten girls and me. A fat, curtain-parted-haired boy with ten chubby fingers, and my girls.

I became a GBF before I even knew what that abbreviation meant. A role that I played before I also hated the term.

GBF is an out-dated and ridiculous label given to gay people who become best friends with straight people. It should no longer be used unless the person in question is happy and comfortable with it. No one should be seen as just a label.

At the time, it was a comfort blanket that I sampled throughout the duration of high school. One that the girls didn't really realise they'd given me or knew that I felt uncomfortable with.

First, a silent branding, then made clear by the revelation that I was, in fact, gay.

GBF.

A position not of power but of acceptance. A role that at the time you take, not because you want it, but because it might give you a sense of belonging. And I was craving that.

Weren't we all just looking to belong?

So, I took it. Unaware at first. However, the gay best friend was complicated for many reasons. Here they are.

There's often only one of you at the time that you get the title and there is no crown, FYI. Therefore, there's no one else to bond with on the same level as you. No other LGBTQIA+ person. You are still alone to a degree.

Then there is the issue of how you're portrayed to others. Not to the people who call you the GBF, but the ones who see you amongst the friends. Amongst the girls. You're typecast. *That gay one.*

Sometimes (very often) your name will be forgotten. It does not feel good.

Oh, you're her gay friend, nice to meet you.

Then there is the internal issue of not enjoying the title yourself.

God, I feel so singled out right now.

Regardless, finally, you have a group. Some people. The makings of a list. But you are branded in a category that you aren't (necessarily) comfortable with. Labelled. Forever.

That was high school. Labels and clichés. A wave you had to surf. We all did. Again, high school movies didn't help this. They fed into categories, stereotypes and boxes. So, the GBF was typecast as an image I quite frankly hated for too long. A "bit part" in the lives of the real people, lucky to be included and even luckier if they had a speaking part.

I disliked this.

I wanted a speaking part. I wanted more than just a speaking part in fact. A role. Not the supporting act. The main event. Not just a friend. A best friend.

Unfortunately, for me, this was the uncomfortable truth you had to live through. Thankfully, though, this evolves. And my own girls saw me as more than this. We move from high school and we grow. In turn, we outgrow labels. You find your comfort levels within the friendships you form, speak up more, and find that you'll still be a best friend to someone, but you'll be a friend who happens to be gay, with much less obvious branding. And it feels better. Way better than just the GBF. Because you finally have a name: your name, and people use it.

My ten girls used it. They knew my name; they fought for it. They still do today. They didn't know for sure if I was gay at the time, but they were people who didn't question it either. They didn't need to. They didn't care. *Gulp.*

My first real friends were a group of girls who probably saved my life. Had they not have been there, by the side of a young gay boy getting bullied, I dread to think of where I would be. And now I look back and wish I hadn't cared so much that they were girls.

Who fucking cares?

I wish my younger self knew this. Or had a glimpse into the future to know that it's okay to have just girls as friends. To be accepted. Because at the time, while younger me was so thankful for the friendships that came with that title, he desperately wanted to be seen as more than just the gay boy. More than the GBF.

Do my dad proud.

As the years moved on, my girl group grew to include their male partners, who now have also become my friends. I dropped the GBF title – they didn't care that I was gay – but my life as one still showcased our differences.

I had my girls, but I realised that I also needed my guys.

❧

Can you be friends with the opposite sex?

I'd always assumed that as a gay man it would be incredibly easy to answer this common question. For obvious reasons. I would almost fight people to say, "*yes*, we can all be friends with the opposite sex, or the same sex, without there being any sexual undertone." Get with the programme. Friendships can exist regardless of the gender. Again, the definition states, "a bond of mutual affection, typically one exclusive of sexual...relations." So... *of course, you can be friends!*

Then I came out.

At eighteen I started discovering this new breed of species, *the gay men*, and I started to ponder the question a little deeper. Can you *just* be friends with the gender you are attracted to?

I wasn't so sure. It no longer was an easy question to answer.

Of course, there were clear (to me) people I could be just friends with. From my side. There were people who found my "just friendship" easy too, from their side. But was it always from both sides? Were we both feeling the same?

Friendship, unlike the definition suggested, was not exclusive of sexual relations. Not always. And especially not for gay men. Or so it was the case for what I witnessed. The definition has once again let me down.

Confession: a handful of my friendships started with sex. No, I will not divulge who. They know who they are, and we've already put away that memory in a dark place never to be opened again. Granted, maybe it was just a hand job, but something sexual had happened with a handful of my now friends where a "hard on" came before friendship.

When I worked in a call centre at nineteen years old – *didn't every gay boy have a job in a call centre as a teenager?* – I did a spider diagram with my colleague, illustrating how my gay group became friends. An entangled web. A group consisting of around twenty-eight members (yes, I wanted quantity back then) had met through a collection of one-night stands, mates of mates and hook-ups instead of teacups. Dicks before drinks. Sex before friendships. Slowly, through a web of connections, friendships were formed.

A group.

Some were strong, some not so relevant and new ones hopped in out of the blue. Friends who were sexually attracted to the same people. A try-before-you-buy group of guys who were linked sexually and that I had hoped all used protection.

Not all your friends will have a sexual connection, but in my gay world, a lot started that way.

❧

The gays.

A term coined by my dad to identify the different groups of friends I had after coming out. He once told me that he was actually jealous of the connections I had in my life.

Envious.

He shared this when I was nineteen years old, a little more comfortable in my skin, out and growing a lovely group of gay mates.

One night, two of my friends picked me up from his house dressed as lifeguards for a fancy-dress night out.

Us "gays" were addicted to fancy dress.

The whole group donned *Baywatch* outfits with the very short red bottoms, first names on the tops and everything you can imagine becoming frisky lifeguards. Basically, a slutty version of ourselves. Shorts that showed your bum cheeks and yellow tops that cut off the circulation from the tightness.

Nipple-showing tightness!

These were outfits that screamed confidence and acceptance. Which was part true. Probably part of the reason that my dad assumed I'd always been comfortable. But this was another act. Like so many other chapters are. Because when united with "the gays," that is exactly what we were. Outwardly strong and confident. With numbers came strength. Unbreakable. A group of people that was formed from the web of relations.

Loners, past GBFs, awkward nervous ones, casual drug using ones, party boys, fuck boys, geeks, nerds, older, younger, different.

Friends.

It was an unconventional group of misfits that finally fitted, and it felt so good. The feeling you get as a gay guy who didn't before have gay friends and finally gets them is euphoric. Finally, these people relate to you. To your struggles, your past, your fears. United. But looks were deceiving, and when you aren't all together, that strength is weaker. That confidence dips and you are back playing the minority.

The gays were only strong together. The projected person my family saw was an Insta vs reality situation. An iceberg that they only saw the tip of. That's why, at nineteen and growing up, the gays became so important to me. When we weren't all together, strong, in fancy dress, I wasn't the same. Not one hundred per cent the confident person I was with them. I realised this was an extension of family.

Judi James says that "We often try to define friendships in

family terms, suggesting we are striving to produce our own family unit with them."

The gays. People who weren't blood but could understand how I felt. Relating to an awkward start. The chosen ones.

Frequently, RuPaul says that in the LGBTQIA+ community we get to choose our family. Many of us search, find houses, find groups, find acceptance. It's a truly unique and positive message. He is right too. We get to choose. Unfortunately, a lot of people do this because they received unacceptance before acceptance. Some families will never accept them, and their friends become that family. For me, the gays did feel like a slice of family. A web, but a tight one. I actually turned my nose up at the fact a lot of the gay friendships were formed through sex. It disheartened me a little. It seemed on the surface that finding each other was a basic formula of sex or someone your mate had sex with. Don't get me wrong, some of these people have become lifelong friends. I'm almost glad for those awkward one-night stands for that fact. I'd be lost without them. But in my group, sex connections came first, and I feared this was the only way.

Could you be friends with the gender you fancied?

As I got older, other connections were established before erections.

Rejoice.

But, in the gay world, even if you are meeting "new" gay friends, often eyebrows raised and questions were asked.

Oh, who is this new gay then? You banging?

Even to this day, if I start hanging out with someone new who happens to be gay, my other friends will ask if I'm dating, shagging or considering them...

For some reason, gay men, intelligent or otherwise, have to answer questions in their own community when they have new friends. Find new people. And looking back at how my connections were formed, I understood why.

Now, in my thirties, I realise two things:

- Gay mates are made through sex or people who have had sex with mates.

- Gay mates are also made through interests, loneliness, work, exercise and whatever else connects you.

"The gays" were a new chapter in my hetero-norm life. I was fresh out of high school, sampling tribes and people. A rite of passage, perhaps. And not one to be disheartened by.

Yes, I realise now in my thirties that we'll always answer questions, much like heterosexual women and men have done about their friendships for decades. Often, I believe there might be a blurred line between friendship and sex between two people who fancy the same people. But good friends become family. The web, however entangled, forms and helps form you.

When I discovered friendships with people like me, *my people*, I started to accept more of who I was. Forgave myself for being different. I learnt a lot from the relationships with my friends. New and old. And continue to do so.

Quantity is no longer as important, but "the gays" have grown through new connections. I've been fortunate to make new friends within the LGBTQIA+ community that I now cherish and learn from. If you are fortunate to have both friends and family, then that is wonderful.

I do.

But so many don't. So many of my friends don't. I am lucky. I appreciate that. But even with that support at home, I realise you need those people who connect on a new level with you. I needed that at nineteen years old; I need that still today.

Our friends become substitutes for a variety of things over the course of our lives, supporting the areas we have holes in.

Family, like-minded friends, partners, kids.

But it's through them that we discover ourselves. Each one revealing a new piece.

First came the girls, then the gays. Helping me grow. Accept.

Friends will help you get there, but they won't carry you to the finish line. That's down to you.

❧

London's Borough Market has always made me happy. Its aesthetic is so pleasing.

Cobbled streets leading you to stalls of vibrant and fresh produce. People bargaining, sampling and buying food. Bustle and laughter and patter. Conversations around future plans. Dinner arrangements inspired by what you see. What you taste, experience.

The market is alive with people, conflicting smells from different cuisines and temptation to try something new, everything new. It makes you feel alive. Spontaneous.

If you have time, not caught up in the trappings of modern life like your phone, route-planned direction or work worries, then you taste. You'll pick the stall that fits your mood and desire. The cheese lies out in slabs in front of you. Mouth watering at the texture of one, the softness of another. You sample one. Then get recommended another. One is far too smoky. Another has chilli hiding amongst its crunch. An unwelcome surprise in an otherwise smooth look. You'll whittle it down. Go through the good and the bad. Enjoy moments of each, for different reasons. It's a process.

So much choice, right? But you make a choice. You find the

best fit for you, for your needs. The one you seek there and then. Whittling it down. Have a smaller group of cheese. But a strong selection.

A process of life. This is how we find our group. This is why it gets smaller. Trial and error and reward.

Finding our cheese.

●

Birthdays are a fantastic indicator of friends.

I'm not talking about quantity any more.

As superficial as it seems, who shows up now, who speaks up and stands out, matters. The people, not the head count.

Birthdays have always been this. When we are younger, they hold a popularity status. As we grow older, they retain this in a new way. We still are popular, but richer in who likes us. Birthdays do this. They remind us of who is around us. Who shows up, and continues to show up? No, we do not and should not need birthdays to see this, I know. But they do provide a good barometer that says a lot. I think birthdays are how we can accept the rollercoaster of friends and the decrease in numbers. Because when they turn up, you feel fucking amazing.

At my thirty-first birthday, I finally got it right.

I had a balance of friends and a great venue, and people I actually genuinely cared about attended. The ones who didn't weren't an issue. Not any more. I'm not talking about real friends who couldn't make it – everyone has a pass. But the ones who weren't there weren't required.

People from my work turned up, surprising me that they might want to share their time outside the office with the "extras" in their lives. Friends from school. Straight mates. The gays. New gays.

LGBTQIA+ people. It wasn't the largest group, but it was a group I was fortunate to have. And it made me smile.

If you are nostalgic like me, you'll take a moment on a night like this to look around. You'll see who made effort. You'll see how far you have come. Because when you are different, that group right there is gold dust.

I'm not saying that only those who were there are all that matter. Because that's not true. Life gets in all our ways. There are people I love who couldn't come for valid reasons. But effort shows us value, whatever form that comes in. Effort is the definition of friendship. We put it in and take it out.

After that birthday, I realised my friendship group would change.

Drag queen clinging to the glue gun.

It pains me to admit this. It pains me to come to terms with this. Imagine, if you like, that friends are the stamps in our passports. We've been to many places where we don't have stamped evidence. Travelled across borders and through airports and not obtained that inked symbol verifying it. The proof.

Occasionally, however, we do get proof. We go to places and get stamped upon entry. Yes, it's far rarer these days, but when it happens, we always smile. Stare at that stamp and admire it. That stamp is a representation of our real friends. Not a *list* on social media, but a refined group that you can count on. That is the important thing.

Through travelling to lots of places, destinations and towns, we meet lots of acquaintances but only truly obtain a small passport of friends. Far more valuable than a stamp in every port. I've realised that not everyone will be our friend. They won't be imprinted, permanent in our lives. Some will disappoint, some will be fleeting and some you'll wish you hadn't met. Regret.

Friends will take stuff from us, and we'll take different things from them. Some will be greedy. They'll be best friends, friends with similar views to your own, strained friends and enemies. People you kept close. Daggers now in your back.

They'll even be people you wish were your friends. People you feel drawn to. People who you think would make brilliant friends. *Dolly Alderton, call me!*

But the real friends are the ones who stay. Stand still. Wait. Show love in dark times, laughter in sad moments and strength when you are weak. Valuable relationships.

And if you're lucky, permanent stamps in your life that never expire.

❧

Alex was one of the girls.

She accepted me for being gay and had me at her birthdays, house-warmings and even as her man of honour on her wedding day. A friend for life.

So, we had a conversation about it.

"You know my memory is terrible, right? I don't think I ever saw you as anything other than you," she said.

Alex has been my friend since we met in high school. She leads a very different life to me, but she's been a listener, a travelling buddy, a fighter and a caring friend to me. Alex, along with several other girls I grew up with (shout out to my girls), has been there. Through it all.

"It's weird, as it was such a huge moment, but I can't really remember how I viewed you before you came out. Before you told me you were gay. I remember thinking, this is just Dan. Friends with a lot of girls. One of us. Move on. Growing up, I think we led very shielded lives in Southend-on-Sea. There wasn't much representation of LGBTQIA+ people available to us. I literally knew no one else that was. I didn't even know you were, to be honest.

"In fact, the first time I heard *gay* being used or referenced was when it was hurled your way as you walked down the corridors at secondary school. Before that, I wasn't truly aware. Not of what a gay guy was, did or felt."

As I chatted to Alex, who said she originally assumed a gay man was "airy fairy and had a camp voice," I realised just how different our school experiences were.

"I feel like in school, everyone goes through an element of bullying. But for you, yours was out there for everyone to see and something you had to deal with on a daily basis. But after the school bell rang, we zipped up our bags, I went home to my life and you went home dwelling on all of the new insults that you'd received. Thinking about it now, I think it was very much an out of sight, out of mind experience. When it isn't happening to you personally, you don't fully appreciate the effect those words have on the people they are directed at."

Apparently, it wasn't just me ignoring the obvious when it came to my sexuality.

"You never gave anything away. I was thinking about this before our chat, as looking back you could probably tell the signs that you were gay. But nothing was obvious at the time. You never would comment on fancying anyone or say either sex was hot. You kept conversations like that out of the equation. In fact, when I think about it, I realise how much of yourself you might have held back. You were just cracking jokes, making me laugh and being a friend. But maybe deeper stuff was going on that you masked. Glazed over."

When I finally came out to my friends, they were supportive and there for me.

"You shared what you needed to share. I realise this now. You almost led a secret life, even when you came out. I think that coming out wasn't a bursting-out-of-the-door moment, but it was a progressive realisation that you had come to. I don't remember a huge defining moment. Because we were there on your journey, I think that's what we went through too. It just organically happened.

"But once out, you just got on with it. You didn't dwell or tell us how you felt. You didn't say you were struggling or felt anything but normal. Terms like GBF were slung around, and because of your tough exterior, we didn't know better. I think it was more others who referred to you as that. But to us girls, it never was about highlighting the difference. Had you told us more of what was going on inside, I think we'd have understood that not all was the fun and jokes that was being portrayed. You weren't just that happy, fun boy. It's actually fascinating talking back through this – god knows why I didn't just sit you down and ask more."

As a mother now herself, Alex said that it's incredibly important for her children to grow up around different ethnicities, backgrounds and communities.

"It's paramount to who they become. I think having you as a friend encouraged this, but society moving to accept everyone and highlighting people's struggles just confirms these feelings. We had no representation when we grew up and I think, or I assume, there is more today that is assessable. People need to learn. I want my kids to be rounded and good people. Educated and aware. That only comes from growth and learning from others. Something we didn't always have at school.

"There might be more exposure in 2021, but I'd imagine this isn't enough. We can keep doing more. I think of bullying and what you went through. That must have been tough. I wish you'd told us more about how you felt. It's hard because you held back, which is weird now when we talk about everything. I see how scared you were. Friends are there to pick you up and fight. You have to let them."

Fight is exactly what she did. As we grew older, Alex defended me more times than I remember. Batting off insults and homophobic slurs like she was Lara Croft raiding a tomb.

"As your friend, I had perhaps a deeper sense of protection. Here is a friend, someone you care so much for, being verbally attacked for who they are. That carries on past school. I would be angry and outraged if anyone spoke about your sexuality negatively. When you love a friend and know their goodness, you defend them. It's instinct. You were different, even before we knew you were gay. Something was different. Unfortunately, difference when you grow up sticks out like a sore thumb. I didn't see you any differently than I saw the other girls. However, I realise those on the outside looking in saw a boy in a group of girls. That means we had to defend you from the start."

When asked if we'd be friends if I were straight, Alex fell silent for a bit.

"Do you know, I don't think I can answer that. I honestly don't know. Even in today's world, straight men and straight women being close friends raises eyebrows. Which is crazy. I look back at school and think of sleepovers, all the fun trips, laughter, evenings, dancing, and wonder – would that have happened if he was straight? I don't think it would have. It's actually not nice to think about. As a straight girl, navigating high school and then life after up till now, what I get from you is honesty. You give us so much. I get this man who is my friend, who delivers honesty to me. I'm not sure if that's because you are gay or just know what I need as a friend. I don't think I'd like life without that honesty, to be honest.

"I don't think I see your sexuality. I don't think I have seen it for a long time. I never saw you as gay. But I probably did in the back of my mind think, I have a gay friend. For so long, you stayed a few steps behind, vibrant, but behind. Now I look at you and think you're running in front of us. I don't see you behind at all. If anything, I miss the younger you. You now have so many people to please and spend time with due to finding your own tribes, which is fantastic, but to me you weren't different, but just a friend.

"Friends are family. You protect them no matter what. Listening to you chat through this has made me think of how much we think we do for each other, but then our own lives get in the way. We forget to check in and ask questions. I'll never fully understand the struggles you went through, but I've never been afraid to fight for them.

"One thing I will say is this: I sometimes have to remind you to tell me about your 'other' life. I think you sometimes hold back as it feels like a different part of it, but I don't see it like that. I just see the whole you. Perhaps my life is viewed with open eyes because I grew up with a different sort of person as my friend. I'm thankful for that, to be honest. If that's the case, I think that's pretty damn important. I don't see an act... I see you."

❧

"The fact is that we need friends, and we need real-life friends rather than the virtual ones on social media," says Judi James. "Friends force us to hone skills like empathy and to listen and understand as well as talk. They help us cope with our emotions and moods and now that it is common for people to live away from the family unit rather than stay in it, they provide the emotional support and security that we need."

When I was younger, I wanted to fit in so much. A goal. Having girls as friends at the time seemed like it only enforced my difference. My weirdo status. I loved them but I feared that they also highlighted a part of me that I wanted to hide. I felt like I should have more.

Now I realise that I'm the only one who really cared about

gender. Cared about difference. I'm the only one who was truly uncomfortable and thinking about it too much.

Everyone else just went home after school.

This was just my journey. For too long I worried about my sexuality being an issue for friendships. Put on an act to help give me a little more shine. Muted different parts of my life for different audiences. Stood on a stage and performed.

If I gave the laughs first, they wouldn't laugh at me.

What I didn't see was that they stuck around. True friends encourage us to be better, make us better and guide us. They are there regardless of your difference and to remind you that it doesn't matter.

They don't see sexuality as a label.

Your real ones aren't thinking about if you are gay or their GBF (if they are, ditch them); they just love you. And they are so important.

I grew up thinking that I was still playing a role, the GBF I disliked so much in school, but I realised that the trauma from my past made me worried that was all I'd ever be. So, it stuck with me.

I'm glad my true friendships started with girls. They bloody well rock and they accepted me when no one else did. Because as you grow up, gender rules dissolve and you are just thankful that those people were there to hold your hand.

Your friend. By your side. Your person.

My act finished a long time ago. I'm no longer "performing"; I'm friends with people who are just interested in me. As I am in them.

As a gay man, finding other LGBTQIA+ people was just another incredible next step in my journey. An added valuable addition to my ever changing "list." Many of those friends have found an extension to their own lists via Twitter and other social media. A supportive online community.

We are in a brilliant age where technology can help anyone

feeling isolated or alone. People online whenever we need them. I no longer look for quantity. I did this to fill a void and surround myself with people to fit in. Now I focus on quality.

However, despite that timeline of friendship changing, dipping and spiking, I realise it doesn't decrease, it just shifts. In my late twenties/early thirties, I've formed some brilliant new friendships, opening my eyes and experiences. We shouldn't ever be closed to making new ones. They help us grow.

I don't think I would have survived without the people I've met on my journey. My friends. I think I would have died without the girls, the gays, the work buddies, the family. The importance of them will never go.

There are no rules to follow; we can make new ones and we should. Friends help us learn.

Do I have friends?

For too long I was seeing the "difference," when the real ones just see you. And that's a beautiful thing.

Who cares how friendships are formed? Sex, GBF, boy next door, work, bad dates...

Do I have friends? Yes, thank fuck.

body issues

Dear Body,

You used to be fat. This is a reminder.

Okay, chubby. Yes, you used to be chubby. An overweight child who would sweat in the creases of his stomach. You hated that stomach. And the second one that sat below it. Round. Rotund. Tubby.

A ball-like shape with sausage fingers. Not chipolatas, but the good type of sausage, the thick and full ones. You were thick and full. Those fingers would never see a ring on them. No one would put a ring on it. I mean, how could they? Those fingers were fat. Who would want you?

You didn't want to be chubby. I know you weren't eating your feelings. You were eating crisps, chocolate, macaroni and salad cream. Heaven knows you loved that bloody salad cream. These were not your feelings, though. But then again, you did not know your feelings. Not really. Because you didn't know yourself.

All you knew was that current moment. You could only see as

far as the fork you raised to your mouth. The future was a question mark.

Puppy fat.

That was what they called it. Protecting you as you grew. Boy did you grow.

You'll lose it.

Would you?

And then you did. You became skinny. Well done.

"Too skinny" as a guy once remarked after sex. You were once "too fat" and now you were "too skinny."

For god's sake, body. Get it right.

When you started to go out, you worried. You worried if you'd fit in. If you were the right size. It wasn't an option to be ridiculed for yet another thing. You'd come out; you needed to look good. *You can't be gay and fat.*

I mean, how could you get fat again when you are gay? The pressure alone is a diet in itself.

No, you must keep an eye on it. You have that shape that will easily gain weight. You know this.

Be strict. Be hard on yourself. Be cruel.

Exercise.

Because that's what we do, right? We exercise. Not for health. But for the body on the cover of the magazine. *Men's Health. Gay Times. Attitude.* That washboard is what you are striving for.

Put down the fork.

Those models do not eat a whole pasta bake in one sitting, Daniel.

Put down the fork.

When they are hungover, they have fruit. They go for a run. If they're hungry, it's a protein bar. They do not eat wine gums with frozen chocolate buttons. Those delicious, sweet sandwiches that give you a sugar high. They give you sugar thighs.

Stay focused. Get the body you want.

Be tough. You can't be fat again.

Round. Rotund. Tubby.

Slim and toned is sexy. That's all anyone can see as sexy.

Stay fit.

You want to be fuckable, don't you?

Focus.

No more pasta bakes.

Single. In a relationship. Single again. In a relationship again. Single. Single. Slim.

Stay slim for the next one. They'll only want you slim. You have a holiday coming up. You want to post a Thirsty Thursday photo, don't you? Breathe in. Go to the gym.

Don't relax.

You're happy with your body, right? You used to be fat, remember.

Thin is healthy. Thin is sexy. Thin is who you are. *Aren't you?*

Yours truly,
The Inner Gay Body Fear x
PS, every body is gorgeous, fact.

bully

/ˈbʊli/

---

noun

1. a person who habitually seeks to harm or intimidate those
    whom they perceive as vulnerable.
    "he is a ranting, domineering bully"

verb

2. seek to harm, intimidate or coerce (someone perceived as
    vulnerable).
    "her 11-year-old son has been constantly bullied at school"

conversations
with a bully

Dodgeball. Do you remember that game? The adrenaline that pulsed through you as you ran, ducked and dodged a soft ball that was being hurled your way.

A game. A child's game. Only those balls weren't soft. *Please.* When a person with the strength of an ox threw one your way, if it hit you, you were going down. Thrown by those kids who were built like houses and seemed to have eaten their vegetables and then some. The ball may as well have been leather. Hard. Whipping your skin. And you were the target. Pure fear. That was what it was: all-consuming fear as you ran away.

Dodgeball was the activity in PE class that allowed the brutes in the school to have an open invitation to hurt you without consequences. Visibly bruising you with no threat of detention. No repercussions. A thinly veiled act of harm. And that's what they did.

Repeatedly.

Targeting the weak, aiming and striking. Not once, not twice, but as many times as the down and out would take. The weak. The different. Balls flying everywhere at them as they lay helpless. A game designed for bullies. Providing a vehicle of delivery without being completely obvious. A disguised attack. Obvious to you but an innocent game to everyone else. Especially the teachers.

A child's game.

These bullies became dangerous, silent assassins. Your kryptonite. Playing *their* game, and you were the prize.

Eventually, though, we grow up. Right? We stop throwing balls and start throwing insults, and the game continues in another form. The bullies. They were everywhere. Sad but true.

I had hoped that I'd have left mine back in high school. Skulking by the bike sheds, in the gym dodgeball hall or hiding in the toilet, waiting to flush my head down the loo. Mean boys who hated me for being me. Intimidating anyone as they saw fit. Because they could. Making lives difficult. They were bored. Perhaps they hated themselves too. Lurking everywhere.

But the game doesn't end. It changes. They don't just stay in school. They seep into adulthood and other areas of our lives. The difference is, as we grow up, a bully learns to camouflage. Finds a new disguise. You might not even recognise them. You probably won't. Hell, they might even look like your friend. Be your friend. Or what you thought was your friend. They might become a presence, a voice in your head or an abusive person in your life. But they're there. And if anything, the bully out of school is potentially more dangerous to us than the one we used to fear the most. The one who you held your breath around. Prayed that they didn't see you and ignored you, didn't call you *gay boy*, again. You didn't even know what a gay boy was. The one throwing the ball.

Bullies.

Everywhere.

❧

Vulnerable is such a fascinating word. It's one of the few expressions that is both weak and incredible at the same time. Yet, for a long time, I only saw vulnerability as a weakness. A curse of far too much emotion. Boy, did I have a lot of emotion. Wasn't that just part and parcel of being gay? I'm sure my mum thinks so. My ex-boyfriend told me that too. *Bully.*

Throughout our lives, we've been encouraged to develop a "thick skin." To take things on the chin, rise above obstacles that are thrown our way and not take things to heart. Become a rhino. Because if people see your vulnerability, they've got you exactly where they want you.

Fucked.

School, for so many of us, is a rather depressing start to life. An anxious stream of awkward firsts.

Exams, making friends, discovering yourself, sexuality, discovering your penis, dealing with nasty people, discovering yourself again, discovering sex.

Sure, it's a time of growth and exploration, but it's also a time to blend in. Sink into the crowds that suffocate us and try not to stand out for the wrong reasons. Because as soon as you stand out, you are the target. The red dot.

I had never fully understood the target on my own head. Partly because I'd survived a fantastic run throughout primary and junior school, and partly because nothing can really prepare you for high school. Brutal. Unbeknown to me, it didn't actually matter what haircut you had or what your sexual preference was. It didn't matter your height, weight or shoe size. It didn't even matter the tone of your voice. You don't realise this at the time. You focus on all your insecurities and issues. You think that's why you are the target. Those things are part of the reason, of course. But actually, none of that mattered. Not really. In high school only one thing was required, even if you are different. Even if you are gay. Confidence.

For those that lacked it, life was about to change.

One of the perks of having a sister and pretending like you were an easy-going brother, when you were really a closeted gay twink in waiting, was being able to watch all the rom coms.

"Go on then, I'll watch *She's All That*, if I have to."

Let's watch Freddie Prinze Jr in his glory days, with pecs that popped and a smile that would make you drop. *Oh, if I have to...*

Secretly I loved every colourful moment of jocks strutting around the screen, fighting for the girl and watching those high school clichés play out in front of me. Bliss. Escapism from the confused life that I currently lived. Envy, jealousy, desire, all rolled into one. God, Freddie was hot. Yet despite having watched just about every teen movie you could get your hands on, I can confirm that Drew Barrymore does not set you up for real life in high school. If anything, she has set us up to fail. She had it easy.

While high school loosely resembled parts of those classic teen movies, in reality, it was a ruthless and an unfiltered version. Like most of those movies, each school would have groups. Those cliques and the "mean girls." Those athletic types and the smokers at the back of the field, puffing on death sticks.

(Didn't teachers just love calling cigarettes that?)

In school there were clear places that you'd slot into and other places that you wouldn't even dream of going. You'd need confidence and maybe a passport for those places. Much like the sorting hat in *Harry Potter*, you had a category. A team. A house. Your place.

If you excelled in PE and woodwork, then you were cool. If you shone in maths, science and history, you were a nerd. Probably wearing glasses and your backpack too high. And, if you were male and were good in drama, performing arts and English, then you my friend, were gay. These were the rules. Guess where I was?

As much as I flirted with different subjects, tried my best in PE and pretended to burn my pencil on the Bunsen burner like the other "cool" guys, my subjects found me. The stereotypical rainbow-loving ones forced me into the limelight. A limelight I wasn't ready for.

I'd love to say that these subjects were the only things that made me a target, but unfortunately, there was also the issue with my voice. It wasn't until high school that I realised that it was a lot higher than the rest of the boys around me. It sounded fine when it was just me and my sister. But in high school, it even beat some of the girls.

"Your balls haven't dropped, Harding!" Mark Evens heckled at me one time after maths class. Okay, twenty times after maths class. He was relentless. He'd heard me answer a question (incorrectly, I wasn't a nerd) and then sniggered at the back of the class while rolling a death stick. The teacher had ignored him. *Yeah, thanks Mr Brian, really got your students' back.* From that moment on, I stopped putting my hand up in class and instead put it down my trousers in an attempt to coax my balls to drop.

Desperate.

It didn't work. Just in case anyone wanted to try. It's actually quite painful. Don't pull your balls. Although, some guys like that.

To be honest, if Ursula the Sea Witch had been available, in that moment I'd have let her have my voice in replacement for her deeper one. I was a fish out of water. A poor, unfortunate soul. I'd have done anything.

That was when I started hating the sound of my own voice, amongst other things about me. A fact that, looking back, makes me extremely sad for my thirteen-year-old self. Chubby, curtains and camp.

Judi James says that bullying is any behaviour that feels

intimidating or threatening. "It's not just actual violence, it can be verbal or even being stared at or laughed at. The favourite excuse of a bully is that it was 'just banter' or 'just a joke.'"

And I felt like the eyes were on me. Because when you are in high school and hate something about yourself, it's hard on other areas of your life.

So, there I was, in school, staying quiet and trying to rub off this new and confusing target on my head. Unfortunately, it only grew.

❧

My friend Darren once asked me, "If you were presented with a Neo-type proposition and could take a blue pill to be straight, would you?" Take the gay away. Rid yourself of that high-pitched dolphin voice...

Thankfully, when he asked me it was years after my high school experience. I'd lived with my insecurities for a long time and also couldn't have imagined going down on a woman ever again.

It's a no from me.

But had he asked me during a time when life looked bleak, I'd have been asking for a glass of water to accompany the pill. Ready to swallow for the first and last time. Because I'd have done anything to be normal. Anything to avoid the bullies. The relationship I feared the most.

❧

I hate to stereotype. Mainly because I think as we grow older, we break those pigeonholes constantly. Redefining what is okay, what is normal, what is offensive. But looking back I was what you'd assume a gay kid would be.

I was the gay, camp (sometimes fat) kid portrayed in terrible teen comedies that focused on heterosexual norms. The odd one out. It was a fact that everyone seemed to know. Everyone but me. Like some strange punchline to a joke that made everyone else snigger while I had to pretend that I got it too. I didn't. I had no fucking clue who I was or what was happening in my pants.

Every day after school my mum would pick me up and asked me how my day was. Eventually I started getting the bus to avoid this question. *My day was okay.* I survived. Her bubbly, bright boy – yes, it was a puppy fat period – was there, but his light was dimmed. Maybe even off. Thankfully, she didn't realise. My dad however would press me two weekends out of three and every other Wednesday, which is when I saw him during their divorce arrangement, asking who I hung out with, who my mates were and if I liked anyone.

Agony.

I'd later in life come to love his interest in me, but in those moments, I wanted the ground to swallow me up, or make me into one of the other school clichés that didn't have issues. I didn't have any answers to tell my dad. I'd have loved to have had an answer. I bet the jocks at home were answering their dads' questions easily.

Smashed it at footy today, scored two goals and then went to Carl's house after school to watch Man U. Wicked game. Can I have a beer?

Their father would smile proudly and say, "Well done, lad!" handing them a Bud. I found football boring and, at the time, I hated beer. Much to his frustrations, I managed to dodge my dad's questions and do the teenager shrug. Even that was hard for me. You see, I didn't really want to shrug; I wanted to talk. I was desperate to.

But as my target grew, so did the attention it received. And, despite keeping my head down, with it came the bullies.

ꗠ

"It is a myth to say that all bullies are cowards and that you should just stand up to them or give as good as you get." Judi James says that bullies come in all shapes, some bullied themselves.

In the past, bullies who are portrayed in movies and TV shows have been a very stereotypical breed. Much like the LGBTQIA+ community. I think it's time we changed this, *FYI!* Usually over-weight, often not the best looking and typically dumb, that was their typecast. Their role. Now, this type of bully exists, of course, I've encountered them. They usually can be actually laughable and aren't always that scary. Idiots who follow rather than lead. But much like how TV has evolved and shown a more diverse representation of our enemies over the years, a true bully comes in all sizes and levels of intelligence.

Yippee for the gay boy.

To an extent, everyone will get picked on in one way or another at some point, especially during school. But if you're lucky, it will be fleeting. As a "gay boy," it's likely you will be bullied, and it's probable that it won't just pass by easily.

I'm sorry.

My first insult came less than a week into high school. I honest-ly didn't even know what "gay" was. Nor did I know the other words that were flung my way over the first two years of school.

Faggot, poof, queer, gay boy, dick licker, uphill gardener, arsehole bandit, fudge packer, dairy queen, snake charmer, dirty dicker, shirt lifter.

The list was endless, and I swear every week a new creation was formed. Although, I'm now happy to report that I am indeed a snake charmer and proud. Back then, the imagination of my peers was something to be admired.

In school, you learnt fast. I quickly came to understand the main meaning behind the words. All of them led to one conclusion.

Freak.

But despite everyone branding me with these insults, quite frankly, I didn't know if I was an uphill gardener or just struggling to find the bush.

Usually I'd shrug them off, walk past, as my heart raced in my chest and I shrunk a little bit smaller. Sometimes, I'd have a small fire that burned in me and let out a desperate "Leave me alone, Lewis Horsham!" No witty responses lived within my mind, and instead, I wanted to just block them all out.

Be invisible.

Unfortunately, my vulnerability shone through and the vultures seized further opportunities. Soon enough, it wasn't just their words.

●

I've never been a violent person. In fact, I hadn't ever thrown a punch until my friend Dawn once took me to KOBOX last year. In the sweaty underground room, I wrapped gloves around my hands and loosely attempted to punch a hanging sack of sand. At first, I was weak, effortless. But as the class progressed, each throw I swung with more conviction and gradually I felt a sense of release. However, despite the decline in the stress levels, even if Donald Trump were in front of me, I still couldn't imagine physically hitting someone. Hurting another person, impacting them. And perhaps that's because it happened to me.

You always remember your first time. When someone pushes

you with force and punches your cheek, it's hard to forget. That blow takes your body completely by surprise and an internal alarm rings around your frame as the shock ricochets. Every limb goes limp. Every muscle tenses. You helplessly stumble backwards, attempting to stay on your feet as a ripple goes through your body.

Then you fall.

In movies, there's a reason why the sound of someone falling is heightened. It gives that dramatic effect that they have been hurt. That they have suffered at someone else's hand. *Thud.* Boy, does that sound happen.

When it happens, you think, *did they deserve it? Who knows?* It's really only the person throwing who can offer the reasoning, but they got it. Deserving or not. And once you are down, there on the ground, the hardest thing to ever do is get back on your feet.

"Stop looking at me, faggot!"

I remember being shocked and scared. Wondering if I was about to get beaten up like the school nerd does in a teen movie.

Would my head go down the loo? I know I have a pea-head, but could it even fit? Would I drown? Am I about to have a punctured lung? Never to breathe again.

It happened when I was fifteen years old. If I had been wearing glasses, they would have been torn off my face and stamped on. They'd have then watched, laughing, as I scuttled around in front of them. Bullies always laughed. I say "they" because I quickly discovered that a bully always needed an audience. Their following. Alone, bullies aren't the giant ogre who performs in front of their friends. Surprisingly, they are human and sometimes actually smile. Together they are a pack. Watching.

So, I was punched. And it was awful. Bradley Dalston was a school bully. Annoyingly, he was also probably the hottest guy in my school. Yes, later I realised I probably would have had sex with him despite his temper.

Damn you, Bradley, and your sexy smile, incredible arms and dimples.

Of course, the rest of his pack, his minions, offered insults to be part of his crew, but Dalston was in charge. Top dog. In control.

I didn't know it at that moment – I had a lot of horrid years ahead during high school – but he would be the start and the end of my high school bullying. Little did I know that I'd come to understand this ogre more than I ever thought I would. When you look up from the floor, at your lowest, all you might see is hate, but that's not the whole picture. It never is.

I quickly came to realise that although it wasn't my fault that I was being bullied, despite constantly wishing I was normal, it also wasn't entirely theirs either. Sure, I didn't deserve to be punched. Even if I had a face that people had called "punchable" (an ex-boyfriend said this to me. Bastard. *Bully*). But to these school bullies, I was odd.

A target.

As much as "different" frustrates me in a variety of ways, it was also true. A fact. Something I once hated and now, in my thirties, cherish. We were all uneducated. There wasn't enough inclusion or information. This is still a continuing problem today.

At the time I was at school, I can't remember another kid who was branded "gay" other than me. Later I found out that there were over fifteen people who came out as members of the LGBTQIA+ community after we left school. A fantastic and colourful collection of people who didn't reveal themselves at the time. Or couldn't. So, for the most part, I was alone in my community. Odd. Different.

There was a ginger kid who had a high voice like me and a floppy hand. Someone called him a *poof* in passing once. But that was never verified. There was also a rumour he'd got a teacher pregnant, which quickly became the focus instead. I think he planted that rumour.

Smart man. Why didn't I think of that deflection?

Perhaps wrongly, regardless of the pregnant teacher rumour, I steered clear of him. I worried if people did think that he was gay, then they'd also think we were a couple. They'd see me with him and a new rumour would begin. My head would be down another toilet. I actually really fancy ginger people. Ever since Bradley in EastEnders, then Bradley's dad, Max, and Daniel Newman. But that's now. Now I like a hot ginger with abs. Then...then I didn't know what I liked, or who I was.

So, I steered clear of anything else that was different. I was discriminating because I was scared. There I was, obviously mincing in school corridors, befriended by girls and excelling in drama class. Thinking I was keeping my head down. All because I desperately wanted people to ignore me.

Could I just be invisible, please?

At first, I assumed that my relationship with bullies would be forever awful. That I'd never survive school, I'd never fit in and I'd never be popular. I didn't accept that my difference was part of who I was, whether I understood it or not. And bullies helped me start to see this.

When the finger is pointed at you, it's hard not to have a look and enquire.

◦

I look back and don't recognise that scared boy. Worried about opening his mouth. Fearing what would be slung his way next. Because it can't not affect you.

Judi James says that being bullied makes us feel helpless and fearful. "It erodes self-belief and self-confidence, and many bullied people begin to believe they were picked out to be picked on because they are weak."

And it did make me feel that way. But soon enough, people got bored of slinging the same insults.

As we moved through the school years, being called "gay" rolled off my back like lube down the inside of your leg. If it was said, I'd barely even blink. Often, I wouldn't even notice. I'd come to accept it like it was part of my name. My identity.

Gay Dan.

Then one day, walking down the corridor, someone nudged past me, called me a *faggot*, and Bradley Dalston shouted, "Oi, leave him alone!" Out of nowhere I'd stopped in my tracks. I felt like a superhero had just protected me from a burning building and I would survive. I'd be okay. My enemy saved me. Dalston smiled at me and kept walking. Later he apologised for anything he'd done or said. He said that he was showing off. He had a heart after all. He said that I was a *cool guy*. I wasn't. Not really. But I forgave him. Without a question or an issue. He didn't have a reason for bullying me, nor did he have a reason for stopping. He just developed an understanding. Educated himself.

From that moment, I heard fewer insults and started to get on with life. My penis verified that I was, in fact, gay, revealing itself in some of the most annoying moments. Mr Munday in PE, Mr Walker in music. And Mr Bromfield in French. *Bonjour to the Eiffel Tower in my pants.*

It turns out, the bullies had been right all along, but I had needed to find my own way. Of course, I didn't tell them that.

By sixth form I loved high school. Found my flow. So much that I chose to stay. My relationship with bullies in school was hard and painful, and there were moments I wanted to die. But with it came growth and my very own layer of rhino skin. An epic layer of skin. A skin you need to survive the rest of life.

❧

The bullies we encounter now are not the ones from school. Those were easy.

They are now the bosses who are pushing us in a direction we don't want to go, or the client that rings you at 10.00 p.m. and demands a response. The rude person at the bar who ignores you and then laughs. They're the emotionally harmful boyfriends who make us think one thing or manipulate, make us doubt ourselves. They're the person who called you fat, not verbally, but with their eyes. They discriminate, intimidate and encourage others to target you.

All around us. Sometimes obvious and sometimes in disguise. Playing a game. Adult dodgeball. People who want to make us feel small. Insecure, belittled. People who make us second guess ourselves. Make us regress. Scared. We can't escape them. But thankfully, they bring out our light and make us face facts. They make us fight for pride.

Be proud.

Most of them think they are still hurting us like they did in school; some are, but if anything, they are pushing us to be more present. Accept who we are. Because we also bully ourselves. We torture ourselves about our bodies, stare into mirrors and frown at the people looking back. Call ourselves names and drag ourselves down. Put ourselves through conversion therapy to stop being gay, hate our voice, hate our face, our reflection, our walk.

We are all bullying as adults. We need to stop.

❧

As we know, bullies come in all shapes and sizes. They can be the kid at school, the person from work, the neighbour, the ex, or they can be you. Confronting your bully isn't easy, so when I sat down with Spencer Cooper, who is a self-confessed past bully, I knew it would take me back.

Back to dodgeball.

"Gay is no longer an insult to me. I am gay. I'm happy. But it is to other people, and too often it is weaponised."

Spencer doesn't like the fact that they were a bully. In fact, they rarely discuss it, but that was a title they held and a role that they played. A part of their journey.

"Gay was a negative. It still is for so many people, and that's how I saw it back then. At school. My negative. My difference. I might not be your obvious school bully. Certainly, to look at now you'd assume anything but. But I was. I have been. During school, it was my job to convince everyone that I was straight. It was *the* most important thing for me to do. I constructed a girlfriend to fake who I was. To squash rumours. Detract attention. Because the attention was on me. They were like policemen attempting to get my confession. I got wind that a group of guys at school were going to take me to the bathroom, strip me and make me confess to being gay. I was terrified. Here it was, my greatest fear about to be realised. So, I had an act. Become tough, become mean, become the bully."

Spencer knew their truth earlier than others might have. But they also weren't comfortable with that truth. They weren't ready to accept it.

"I lived a life where I held my breath. I didn't relax, didn't say too much and never said anything out loud to give it away. Before I even realised what I was doing myself, I'd been so downtrodden, endured so much hatred, I became numb. I pushed back."

Spencer confessed that even though they had "friends" around them, they realised the toxic comments slung their way weren't loving.

"Bearing in mind I grew up in North Wales; no one was gay. If they were, they weren't confessing. All the hatred I received, all the insecurities I had, suddenly started to manifest and I became the bully I hated."

At first, Spencer started with simple insults. That quickly turned into verbal abuse that got out of hand.

"In the moment I didn't know that I was bullying. I now realise that all bullies feel this way. They don't see what they are doing as an attack. Their words aren't affecting them, so they don't realise the hurt they are projecting. Despite having been through it, I didn't either."

Spencer started to target groups that made them feel low. From name-calling exchanges with girls they were friends with, to others who stood in their way.

"I felt like I had become a hero. A strong force that was powerful. I was low, so I used this to become a person I hated. And I did hate that person. Deeply. We were the mean kids at school, became those stereotypes, but also did it to each other. I thought at the time that I had friends, my people. Looking back, I don't think I did. It all came down to survival. I did what I did to survive, make friends, be popular and detract. It was a decision. One I have to live with."

Despite feeling horrible, Spencer used words to hurt others.

"I had everything to lose, so saw this as a way of retaining friends for myself. I couldn't be that boy going to school just to be knocked down. I needed to be more."

Spencer continued to verbally bully throughout high school.

"Bullies do it to survive. Most of it is mindless and trivial, but for a lot of them, they are meaning nothing personal, uneducated and perhaps a little lost. They desperately want to be popular. Want the crowd or people to laugh and follow them. Bullies want respect and think this is the way to gain it. It's not, but bullies are stupid."

Taking a while to accept who they were, Spencer prefers not to regret and look backwards.

"I think of the names slung my way. Names that broke me, broke my character, made me change, and I now realise they've made me stronger. They had to make me stronger. They were only ever insulting to me because I didn't accept it. The words were weapons because they hurt me."

I asked Spencer if they regret being a bully.

"I don't have regrets. I wish I didn't hurt people, but that was a time and a moment. A year ago, I received a message from someone I bullied. They said that they had developed an eating disorder, that they couldn't come out because of fear, and I was gobsmacked. I had done that to one of my own. Bullied someone who was part of my community. It shook me. That is not okay. That will never be okay. I feel horrible and I'm thankful the person and I got to talk it through. I had a second chance, and it was time that I used it."

Once having been the underdog turned aggressor, now Spencer is supporting the underdog.

"I had the chance to give back. To do something and redeem myself. Gay is no longer an insult. It will never be that way to me. I'm a nice person now. I stepped up and owned up. Addressed my issues and why I bullied. I have a platform. I have a voice. I now support our community every way I can. Bullying when you are different means you have so much to lose but everything to fight for. It can turn people into the worst parts of themselves. Unfortunately, not everyone learns, grows and changes. Our bullies are still around us, in a way; older bullies make us more alone than when we were children."

Spencer believes that people who bully as adults have an understanding of what they are doing. It is no longer mindless; they know the power in their words.

"People might think that the LGBTQIA+ are an easy target. I used to think that, but we are not. We are fucking strong and don't need to bully to showcase that. What we endure doesn't erase us; it makes us grow, fight, support. The noise for our community is growing. We must continue to speak and educate and not let this happen. It must stop with us. Tell our stories, our struggles, our truths. Show the world how beautiful we are. We will always be lower on the priority list, and I still get intimidated and worry I'll get beaten up for the way I walk, or dress. I'm still that insecure gay kid.

"But I won't be locked away, or lie about who I am. I will dress how I want, wear make-up, be myself – because a bully does not like confidence, and that's what we have. I once was a bully; now I'm refusing to let people do that. To anyone. We all have choice."

❧

I'm still vulnerable and that's okay. No, actually, that's bloody brilliant. But I realise that I need to stop bullying myself. Dragging myself down. Shouting insults in my head at the things I dislike about myself. That's the real bully. The one that we don't need. Not ever.

Stop. Pause. Reflect.

It turns out that the bullies that live outside of our heads will only help us. Yes, they are awful at the time it's happening. It can cause immense pain, suffering and damage. But it can also spark something. They point the finger our way and force us to confront ourselves. To work out a way to feel comfortable.

Our community faces bigots daily. Discrimination, bullies and prejudice against us. We haven't left them in school. However, our bullies give us the opportunity to speak up. To accept ourselves and strive for others to accept us. We need our inner bullies to be comfortable in ourselves. Oddly, they help us.

They'll tear us down, but they'll help us discover things we didn't want to face. Confront. They'll push us to be proud. Find our pride and then parade it through the towns. Because bullies hate our confidence. They hate our pride. Ultimately, we need to educate them. Show them. People are different and that's brilliant.

So be proud. They helped us get there. They make us visible when they're trying to make us the joke. Laugh. They give us more than they realise. Idiots, but hopefully people who don't know better. If they do, they shouldn't underestimate us.

We are different. That is a gift.

straight

/streɪt/

---

adjective

1. extending or moving uniformly in one direction only; without a curve or bend.
   "a long, straight road"

2. properly positioned so as to be level, upright or symmetrical.
   "he made sure his tie was straight"

adverb

3. in a straight line; directly.
   "he was gazing straight at her"

4. in or into a level, even or upright position.
   "he pulled his clothes straight"

noun

5. a part of something that is not curved or bent, especially a straight section of a racecourse.
   "he pulled away in the straight to win by half a second"

6. (in poker) a continuous sequence of five cards.

conversations with a straight man

Straight. I've come to hate that word.

It's one of the most common colloquial terms used to describe someone who is anything not remotely associated with the letters LGBTQIA+. Square. One line. Not a bend or curve in sight. *Well, lucky them.* They were the fortunate. The favoured. Adam looking for his Eve. Living life exactly as it was designed for them. Going forward. Not looking back or veering to the left or right. Undistracted. The lucky ones. Or so I thought. A breed of human (straight male) that I likened to the male gorilla. Big and in charge, sitting there in the centre of the cage as the main event, and usually eating. Always eating. And burping. Let's throw in a burp and a beard too. A Barney from the Simpsons type of man. Someone who, for me, was an unapproachable human. Nothing like me at all. I didn't burp for a start.

We were not similar. This type of man was a "real" man. I was not. And this is how I viewed the straight man: an evolution of my school bully.

A type that I studied from afar as they sat there with an air of arrogance. Power. They oozed it. A creature that would rather turn their back to you while eating a bamboo cane than look your way. They would never look your way. Even when your camera was poised and you just needed one to turn around, just one turn! Nothing. Arrogant.

I was not worthy of their time. I was not straight. I veered off to the left. Or the right. Or both. And despite not realising that I was this way until I was seventeen years old, I had never really recognised myself as a straight man even before this. That wasn't the cage I was in. *Ever.*

Because even with a fleeting "girl" phase, unbeknown to me I wasn't that species; I had multiple bends and curves. It wasn't ever a straight line.

❧

Frankly, the zoo is the perfect way to look at categories. Boxes.

Now, I realise that some people hate zoos. There are some very good arguments that these places aren't always the best home for animals. Some clearly do not cater for their needs or will breed them for all the wrong reasons. And I get that. Zoos are questionable. But they're also kind of magical. They house different species of animals all in one place. Under one roof. Thousands. Animals from across the planet. Merging Africa with Asia or bringing in a world from underwater or soaring through the sky with the birds of prey. Variety. Colour. Animals from different backgrounds, separated only by their cages. Close, but not together. Rarely ever together. Else, of course, they might eat each other. Turn this beautiful picture into chaos.

So, behind bars and cages, they can only glimpse at other creatures. They are aware of them, but they do not mix. They can't mix. That's life in a zoo. That's sometimes how I view life outside of a zoo too.

I was in a cage, surrounded by other cages with people in who I didn't recognise. People I didn't understand. Didn't think that I could ever be friends with or interact with. Different species. Perhaps they wouldn't even want to be friends with me. *I can be annoying at times.*

My zoo of life was open, but we were all caged. Boxed in. Pigeon-holed. Labelled. And the most foreign enclosure to me, more so than any other around me, was that of the straight man. Perhaps bred out of fear from the bullies, but there in his own cage. He was not in my cage. Our cages weren't even next to each other. There were far more similarities with the straight woman, to be honest. Sure, we shared the same air, but that was it. That's all it was. Our lives weren't meant to cross over.

Straight men had always had the power in my eyes. From the boys at school and beyond. Much more power than us. There was no common ground.

❧

The first straight man who I encountered was my dad. Or perhaps the doctor who delivered me. Then it would have moved on to family, friends, teachers, and then as I got older, the boys from school, college and so on. All straight, because that's what I grew up to believe. Although, I'm now pretty sure some of them resided in our community.

Welcome.

None of whom I actually ever branded as "the straight man," but rather, just the normal men who weren't like me.

I was not this breed. I was awkward, "bubbly" and disliked football. They interacted freely with ease. They knew football chants, match scores and how to pull a pint. I did not.

Growing up, the concept of "straight" and "bent" had been lost on me. I just believed that I was on the outside looking in, regard-less of labels. An abnormality. All I saw was the shopkeeper who I nervously handed over twenty-eight pence to for my chewing gum (remember those cheap prices? A Freddo was 10p!), who always put his glasses on to look at me. The bus driver who smiled at all the school kids but then frowned at me. The library assistant who seemed to always shush louder in my direction.

Okay, I was quite loud.

And the policeman with the grey moustache. With his hard hat sitting high upon on his head and his lips pursed ready to tell me off. He scared me, or maybe turned me on, I'm not quite sure. Ready to arrest me. Put me back in the cage that I'd strayed from.

Men. Real men. All of whom I watched from afar. Unrecognis-able throughout my teenage years. Different.

This is what I saw. Of course, when I came out, got older and more comfortable, I realised that I may have been the person put-ting the straight man in his cage. The zookeeper. Tarnished by the bully, now branding every straight man as the same. But perhaps I had the keys all along. However, hindsight is a valuable thing, but it's not realistic. At the time, these men scared the shit out of me. I feared their difference. But this zoo-like creature wasn't just the cocksure school bullies, or the lad who I saw on my paper round who shouted "bum boy" weekly (yes, I was gay and had a paper round like "other" boys). I also washed cars and rode a BMX bike. *I'm so masc.* It turns out, they weren't *just* the villains in my play. The carnivores in the zoo. The bad guys. The ones to fear. These men were so much more. Sure, as I grew up, they'd felt alien to me, and I might have misunderstood some of them.

But we aren't all able to fit into a cage. They weren't my enemies. Even if they felt like it at first.

In my teens, I'd always felt like their eyes fell on me. Burning a hole in my head. Like they had a superpower and could detect my *gay.* My difference. Even if I had lowered my voice, had worn less vibrant clothes or had practised my walk. Tried to dumb down the mince. My nerves would surely reveal me. Out me. They'd notice the difference and the jig would be up. We weren't the same. So, I felt like we couldn't ever be friends or allies.

Could we?

❧

According to Judi James, "normal" is a constructed lie to allow humans to exist in extended societies. "We dress 'normal' to show we are one of the pack and we behave 'normally' to survive life in that pack. But it doesn't mean that is how we really are in our true selves."

When I was fourteen, I went to my first rugby game. The Saracens. My dad, my uncle, my cousin and I poured into the stadium along with cheering fans. Hundreds of people, already drinking, perhaps already drunk. It was 11.00 a.m. The smell of beer filled my senses, and I turned up my nose at its stench. It didn't smell good. Not to me. It smelt like it was dirty. Gone off. The type of drink that would leave a bad taste in your mouth and give you bad breath too. *Vile.* I didn't think I'd ever come to like beer. Beer was a man's drink. A straight man's drink. The crowds all headed to their pull-down plastic seats and I went with them in unison. I was nervous. Not excited in the slightest. To be honest, I couldn't tell you why, but something inside of me feared this environment. It didn't feel comfortable to me. It felt hostile. Foreign. Cheerleaders came onto the pitch and performed a routine. I smiled as they flipped, contorted and shook pom poms to a cheering crowd. A crowd largely of men. Men with bellies and tops that were too tight. Manly, aggressive and intimidating.

The Barneys.

After the cheerleaders, there were female assistants painting rugby balls onto the sides of children's cheeks to get them into the spirit of the game. My cousin and I got ours done. *Looked cute, itched like hell.* Had this been my selfie stage of life, it would have gone straight on Instagram with a "living my best hetero life" hashtag. Then the game began. I sat watching, hoping for something to click. As a fourteen-year-old boy, I wanted to connect with my breed. I understood this much; I just didn't understand why I wasn't. When the crowd cheered, I cheered. When they groaned, I groaned too. It was a pantomime. I was the perfect junior spectator. My dad looked down at me and smiled.

The Saracens won that day. Apparently, they played really well. When we drove home, I clutched the programme in my hand. The guy on the front holding the ball had such muscular legs. They were really incredible. My dad asked me if I enjoyed it, and I replied, "Yes." I think I did, actually. We continued to go to games after that. Not as die-hard fans that routinely went, but ad hoc, whenever my dad and uncle wanted to. It became our treat.

After three games, I asked my dad for a rugby top. I started to enjoy the atmosphere, understand the game a little more and enjoy the different routine the cheerleaders had constructed every new match.

My nerves, however, never went. It was the lion's den. Straight man territory. Uncomfortable, because I wasn't one of them. Even if I didn't know why. Unavoidable, because I didn't know this then. I had the kit, but I didn't play their game. All the gear and no idea.

❧

After coming out at seventeen, my awkwardness didn't really ease. I still felt odd amongst groups of straight men. An imposter.

When girlfriends got partners, I worried they'd be the straight homophobic type I'd encountered in my youth. I feared that they'd think I fancied them.

Sometimes I did, FYI.

By accepting that I was gay and telling people my truth, I felt like I had only verified my difference to the other species. Outted, no longer in hiding. Trying to fit in. No longer would I be allowed at a Saracens game. The itchy face paint would now *really* burn my skin to the effect that churches have on us when we walk into them. Melting like the wicked witch in Oz.

This was my new truth. I had to accept it. Straight men's superpower was also now heightened. They'd see my clothes were different; my walk, as much as I practised it not to be, was gay.

Or so I was told.

My wrist wasn't limp, but it didn't need to be. They knew. The jig was up. Nightclubs had a strict limit, no under eighteens. But there were areas of life that felt like there were just as strict regulations against me. Football matches, pubs, men's clubs, strip joints, car garages, gyms, locker rooms, school. My gay card did not let me into these places.

Until...I got rid of it.

❧

Men. Minus the straight, or gay label, we're all the same species.

Unbeknown to me, there was a collection of straight men who were comfortable in their own skin, knew who they were and didn't turn their back on you. Gorillas that actually turned for your camera shot. Yes, they had no curves, but they also had no problems with people who did. It was a fact that I finally discovered in sixth form. Seventeen years old. Because before then, I wondered if I'd ever be friends with the hairy lump that sat behind the glass.

Granted, due to poor representation in movies growing up, I had assumed that if you were straight, we would not be friends.

Movies have a lot to answer for!

First, I naturally thought we'd have nothing in common. When my stepdad bought a season ticket to Southend Football Club for the whole family, I viewed this as more of a punishment than a pleasure. I'd sit there as the gorillas beat their chests around me and heckled the referee. I detested football. Why you'd want to spend Saturdays here I didn't understand. But it wasn't just football. Apparently, straight men also played golf, stood together at parties while the ladies were cooking and drank beer, not wine. Beer made the men belch and wine made the ladies laugh. I wanted to laugh. I wanted the wine. Second, of course, was the small fact of the opposite sex. I couldn't comment on Sarah Jayne's breasts in our chemistry lesson. Nor did I care to choose a top female teacher to "bang" in our woodwork class. Straight men did. It bonded them. Had they been commenting on these women's style, haircut or smell, I'd have certainly chipped in. Jasmine Gardner in our German class smelt of white roses on a Sunday morning and had hair that bounced with the beat of her step. I personally disliked tight curls on a girl, but I forgave her due to the beautiful scent. And there, in my small mindset, I had resided in those two points as my reasoning that I'd never be friends with this breed.

We had nothing in common. No reason to mix. I knew I'd survive, of course; I had friends and I was okay. Mostly. Until I met three boys. Three boys who changed my mind and gave a newfound hope to my seventeen-year-old twinkling self. Boys, not bullies.

Lewis, Lawrence and Anthony. Suddenly, in a room where I was invisible to straight men, I was seen. It wasn't a moment where I was talked over, reached across, mistaken for someone else, spoken through or avoided. Invisible. I was seen.

It was 2005.

"You're Dan, right?"

My heart raced and I scanned the room behind me. I wasn't with "my girls"; I was alone. I was either dead, dreaming or in someone else's body.

Who on Earth is speaking to me?

Anthony was short, with muscular arms and a cheeky grin. A confident and charming lad. While he waited for an answer, I realised I wasn't dead or dreaming. I was mute.

Talk, Daniel. For Christ's sake!! Say anything.

I then smiled and mumbled through an awkward first conversation. Cracking a stupid joke and asking which A levels he had chosen. Jokes were my cover. Then, just as I feared, the conversation was drying up, and Lewis walked over and held out his hand, which I shook.

I just touched a straight man, and he didn't wince.

Shortly after, he was followed by Lawrence, who just kept laughing at Lewis's stupid jokes. Lewis told stupid jokes. Unaware of what was happening, I laughed along and chatted with the boys. Perhaps this was a horrid prank and reality would set in, but I didn't care. Maybe I was being Punk'd. Ashton Kutcher was about to come out and the sketch would end with my gay head down the loo. They'd move on, I'd move forward. It didn't.

There, in our sixth form common room, three straight boys who had to go back a year due to poor grades saw me. Yes, I fancied Anthony. Yes, I fancied Lawrence. Yes, Lewis tried to be funny. But that's beside the point. It really didn't matter. These were heterosexual men, two who liked football, all of whom liked beer, who all enjoyed my company.

Pinch me.

Soon I was invited to their birthdays; Lawrence even started cutting my hair and Anthony would throw his arm around me in a brotherly way as we walked to the lunchroom.

God those were good arms.

If I was asleep, I didn't want to be woken up. Granted, it wasn't always comfortable, but it was a start and a key moment that, unbeknown to me, would ripple into other areas of my life.

For so long, I had been branded. One of the girls, poof, gay, fag, bum boy. Never had I been Dan or Daniel to them, nor did I have an identity. Quite frankly, the examples before these kind guys made me feel like I wasn't allowed one. I was gay boy number one. That's it. The side part. And I didn't question that. How could I question the main attraction? But suddenly, the gorilla vanished, and the glass enclosure disappeared. I was out of my cage.

After all those years where my own identity hadn't fully formed, or couldn't grow, it started to come through. Perhaps I had no real clue who I was, but with the help of three straight men, I started to discover a more comfortable me.

Our group became a merge of my girlfriends, who had seen me through a lot of rollercoaster moments, and the boys. Part of me knew that I was still seen as one of the "girls," an effeminate addition to a group, but part of me also knew that I wasn't the same as others. And I started to embrace it. Finally, the uncomfortable extra became Daniel. Not straight, with bends.

Disappointingly, now, I don't really see or speak with Lewis, Lawrence or Anthony any more. Our groups disbanded after sixth form and they went off on their own adventures.

When we do bump into each other, it's always tight hugs and fond memories. Anthony throws an arm around me and Lewis cracks a joke. They were my start. My saving grace. A relationship formed with a group that I'd at first felt distant from. Allowing me to go off to uni with a confidence that I could make friends with people who weren't just girls or gays. No longer did I limit myself and confine people to cages. If anything, they set me and everyone else free.

The zoo was gone.

Shortly after sixth form, I walked through a red door into a shared kitchen of fourteen people, knowing that the majority, if not all, would be straight people. University. But I did it, with open eyes. Yes, it was like I was going into the Big Brother house for the first time, shitting myself about the characters that stood beyond the door, but my past allowed me to open that door. Had I not experienced that relationship, that acceptance, gone through that journey, I wonder if that boy would have been strong enough to open it. Push through.

You see, their relationship probably came easy to them, but to me, my three straight man school friends were precious. Unforgettable. Powerful in a way that I didn't know they could be. I never knew how much I needed it.

❥

The other day, my mum rang me.

I was in the middle of constructing a sentence on my laptop and decided to answer as I'd missed/avoided her last two attempts of communication.

I was busy!

She told me a story about her recent trip to the supermarket. How she had forgotten what it was that she needed in the first place and how suddenly she'd spent an hour shopping for things she didn't even know she needed. Including blueberries, AA batteries and ice cubes. It was a very long story, but I listened. After she'd taken a breath, two hours later, she asked how I was. I reminded her that I was, in fact, working and then instantly felt bad for being so short. Knowing that she was clearly craving some conversation, I decided to ask her a question, which I didn't really need an answer to, but asked anyway.

"What do you think about straight men as people?"

For a second she went silent. It was slightly out of the blue, to be fair. Then I could almost hear the cogs whirring in her head as she was thinking for a moment about her answer.

"Are you going to quote me in something you're writing?" she replied.

She'd become sceptical since I had become a journalist. Then she gave me her answer. "What is a straight man?"

In her asking a question back, I got all I really needed to know. I realised to "others" that they wouldn't wonder about their relationship with straight men. Wouldn't consider their sexuality as a part of their identity. They didn't see that label. But because people saw a part of me (gay) before I even came into a room, open my mouth or even so much as smiled, I saw their labels. They were out there for me to see.

My "difference" was linked to who I was, and it was hard for me not to see the other tags that people wore. I grew up in a world where I assumed the straight man was homophobic. It's all I knew. I'd only had the bullies.

If men weren't gay, then they probably didn't understand me, didn't like me, didn't see me. The reality was, I stereotyped them because that's all I had to go on. It was a bubbling irrational fear built from a life spent worrying about being different. My own insecurities projected onto them.

What is a straight man...?

After the call ended, my mum wrote a Facebook status about her shopping trip and the fact that she now had too much toilet roll if anyone needed extra. My phone then notified me that my mum had liked five of my recent tweets on Twitter, including a topless selfie.

Cringe.

I texted my mum to say that I loved her and vowed to stop posting torso pictures on Thirsty Thursday.

I still do.

Having relationships with people who aren't family or of the same sexual preference as us is a key part of our make-up. An important part of who we are. We need to learn. We need to push open red doors. We need to get out of our own heads. Not every straight man is homophobic.

I'm very happy to report that, in my early thirties, I have an array of friends that includes straight men. A lot of them, in fact.

Colleagues, friends, neighbours, friends of friends.

Actually, some of my best friends are heterosexual. A fact my younger self would wince at.

Daniel, really? Are you okay?

But I was glad. Varied relationships round us, rather than limit us. They help us with our own bends. Yes, I still have anxiety around straight men; I'm pretty sure a lot of gay men feel this way. They were often the perpetrators of bullying and it was hard to not assume they were all the same. I mean, so many see me as just a camp gay guy...

I've had homophobic comments, endured conversations that were completely out of my depth and felt instantly outed over and over, when I'm the "different" one. But it has got easier.

They aren't all the same. Some are brilliant.

❧

At twenty-seven years old, I met Adam.

We were work colleagues before we were mates. Which, at the time, other than my friends' husbands and a few extras along the way, was the main route through which I found straight friends.

Because there's no app called *I'm a Gay Man, Find Me Straight Friends to Make Me More Rounded.* And I'd actually question the straight men who went on an app like that. Unfortunately, it's a pretty realistic bet that it would turn into a hook-up app, rather than a find-a-friend platform.

So, work became a breeding ground for new relationships. Don't get me wrong; I wasn't searching for a straight friend. I didn't have a tick list of demographics or people who I wanted to connect with. But I would be lying if I said I didn't want one. I enjoyed different company. And Adam became this to me.

But how does the gorilla really feel?

❧

Adam *did* not want to chat to me. Let alone about our relationship.

"I have nothing to say. I've always been okay with gay guys," Adam started.

This was not the point of our chat, though. I knew Adam was open minded. Confident and comfortable in his own skin. He claimed to always have been. This is why I wanted to chat with him.

"My parents encouraged us to view the world through open eyes. Not be restricted by the judgement of others and accept people. I knew this from a young age."

He'd clearly had a brilliant upbringing. He was kind, caring and straight. At times I'd look at him and see a typical straight man. There were many traits he shared with that breed. Football loving, beer drinking, straight talking, no feelings discussed... But who were the minority?

"Gay is a word that is slung around. I've used it myself a lot before. It's a word used to shout during a footy match, 'give me the ball, you gay!' A term that for the most, isn't used offensively. Or at least not by me. Never by me. A friend at school came out to me shortly after we'd gone away to uni. I'm not sure why he couldn't tell me before. I'd have been fine with it. I think fear made him wait. Made him not reveal who he was. The real him. He was scared. I appreciate that. He did it when there was distance between us. He didn't want to face it."

Adam thinks that people bully due to a lack of education and poor upbringing.

"If your parents aren't showing you to accept and representation isn't available, people who are different are easy targets. You are different. I'm not sure why people bully, or shout words at those who aren't like them. Maybe they are like them themselves and that's why they do it. Mask their own truth. Thankfully, my school experience wasn't coloured with seeing this first hand. I've heard and done stories about people that have had an awful time there."

As an award-winning national news photographer, Adam has visually told the story of countless individuals from all walks of lives, showcasing their truths.

"To be honest, I'm flattered if a guy fancies me. It's a compliment if anything. I strive to find beauty in everything and can appreciate a handsome man when I see one. Hell, I'll photograph them if I do. It isn't a threat. Sure, no one, no matter gender or sexuality, should push it too far. Cat calling, bum pinching, intimidation. But I think most people are respectful. I'd quite comfortably strip in a locker room with you as a gay man and not think twice."

When explaining to Adam my experience of being bullied for being different, he shook his head.

"I don't get it. I don't know one friend who is homophobic. To be honest, if they were, I wouldn't be their friend. I have no time for racism, discrimination or abuse in any form. What I realise, however, is my privilege. I'm a straight white man and I'm privileged. Yes, I've been through things, but I've not had the additional barriers. That is what I'm starting to see as we chat. I can't imagine walking down a school corridor riddled with fear that someone is about to shout a name that puts fear into you. It actually makes me angry."

Adam assures me that straight men are not all pricks.

"We just aren't. I'd actually call myself a 'typical' straight man, as you put it. But I don't think that person is what you once feared. You see us in a way that is like a them and us. But I don't think the majority of people would view it through those eyes. Or at least I'd like to think they don't. Do you seriously think people care if you are with a man or a woman?"

I respond, "Yes."

"Wow. Then I was wrong. I have a lot more to say than I first thought."

Adam pondered the subject further and then we resumed our chat.

"I can assure you, those guys hurling abuse are not going home thinking about you. They aren't thinking about what they said, how it hurt or the impact those words have. They don't care about you. That might sound obvious, with the words they are shouting, but what I mean is you could be anyone who is different.

"The majority saying those things aren't homophobic. They'll grow up, will probably be nice and will probably have friends who are different. Some may even realise they are gay themselves. At the time, they are uneducated. Perhaps not the right guidance or knowledge. But as they grow, as they do educate and listen, if they continue to slur to shout, to intimidate. Then they are a breed that aren't nice people. They don't deserve to be the straight privileged man.

"But that isn't all of us. I wish I actually could go back and tell all young straight men to stand up for the minorities. To use our privilege and help. I think sport has a major part to play in this. Especially in football. If a footballer came out as an openly gay man who was a brilliant talent, that would help. Sport has a huge influence over straight men. People in and out of school not only need to see the more effeminate representations but they need to see men they can relate to as well. That would help bridge the gap."

But what if that never happens?

"It's got to happen. Surely, we are on the cusp of a Premier League footballer revealing his own truth. Breaking the taboo. People often claim that sport unites us. So, this might just be the answer. I'd like to think in schools right now, bullying for being different is less than when I was at school. But I don't know if that's true. When kids are faced with difference, they react. But for those couple of bullies who are directing it at you, there are hundreds of people who feel no hatred towards you.

"I realise now they are the ones who need to speak up. Use their voice. I should have used my voice. I will use my voice. As you get older and meet people who are different, you are educated by spending time with them. I appreciate you might feel awkward in that situation at first, or worried it will link back to your early experiences – but the majority of straight men are open, or probably feeling awkward at first too."

When I asked Adam what he gets from our friendship, he responded instantly.

"An open mind. Having people in your life that are different sexualities, backgrounds, people, just makes you a more rounded and better person. It's a proven fact. You teach me lots."

I realised the more we spoke that Adam didn't see an issue. He saw that people were rude but didn't think that people were deliberate. Which might be the problem.

"Until today I haven't thought about the issues around not seeing the other point of view. Bullies aren't thinking about the impact. I guarantee. They also don't think they are bullying. They don't see it. A truly comfortable straight man doesn't care who you are having sex with. I promise you."

As we finished our conversation, Adam apologised to me.

"You don't really appreciate what others have to go through until you talk about it. This is a good thing, Daniel."

❧

Judi James says, "Like animals, we often use pseudo-sexual re-motivational techniques to try to diffuse any type of attack when we are in a competitive group or in a group with people we don't know well." Deceiving to confuse others of our true sexual orientation. Sending people off the scent.

I did this. I do this. It's a survival technique. But here is the truth.

I like beer. Ask me to a rugby match, I'm game. I placed so much power in straight men that I didn't see the actual positive power they possessed. When one is kind, accepting, open, it helps you to accept yourself too. Just because we grow up thinking all of them might be homophobic from a scarred past experience doesn't make that the truth. We are more than our labels. Other people might not see the tags that you see. Some matter more than others, and that's a personal thing.

I still worry when I walk into situations. Will this be the good breed of them, or the negative? Will they hate me for being me? But they might be feeling out of their comfort zone too. The simple fact is this: the relationships that take us on a journey help us open doors and are key to other relationships in the future.

My relationship with straight men taught me that I didn't need to hold myself back and I could be friends with just about anyone. Sometimes we need kindness. The Adams. More than just the label I thought they were.

Sometimes we just need three wise men to help you see it. And that's a fact that I like to remember.

sex

/sɛks/

---

noun

1. (chiefly with reference to people) sexual activity, including specifically sexual intercourse.
   "they enjoyed talking about sex"

2. either of the two main categories (male and female) into which humans and most other living things are divided on the basis of their reproductive functions.
   "adults of both sexes"

verb

3. determine the sex of.
   "each bird would need to be individually sexed"

4. INFORMAL present something in a more interesting or lively way.

conversations about sex

Awkward. Uncomfortable. Rushed.

How was your first time?

All I can remember thinking was, *this needs to happen tonight.* It has to be tonight or never. This is the one shot I have. If it isn't tonight, the night that I had prepared myself for, planned for and found courage to do this, then I'm not sure I'll ever do it. I'd chicken out. Dream up an excuse, put it off. Find any reason not to go through with the amazing act of sexual intercourse. Because it is amazing. But not tonight, at the age of seventeen. Not my first time.

At the time, I wasn't excited. Not at all. The complete opposite. I'm not sure if I'm in the minority saying that, as I assume most people are excited for their first time, but I wasn't. I was scared. Terrified.

Would I be good? Would it be good? Will I get AIDS? Will I enjoy it? Will I do it right? Does my body look good enough? Am I fuckable? Am I ready? What role will I play? What role will I like? Why isn't this simple?

You know, the standard questions that rang around my head, weighing me down and adding to the growing anxiety I was experiencing. Fear. All-consuming fear. I was shitting myself. Up until this point, porn had been my only real reference for sex. The only available example of gay sex, how it happened and what you did. An instruction manual available on the internet. Easy and accessible. So accessible. It was a hot example of how sex could be.

Cody Cummings. Paddy O'Brian. Griffin Barrows. Josh Moore. Billy Essex. Jason Domino.

I could go on. They looked amazing. Looked like they enjoyed it and made me want to enjoy it too. They had hooked me in and made me want a piece of the cake. A bite. A crumb. I mean, it would be rude not to.

Sex looked great. But porn was not real life. I knew this.

Daniel, this is not how it will be. This guy is not Cody Cummings.

Bad acting, terrible storylines and meaty equipment that looked like it had been digitally enhanced.

Surely the camera has enlarged that.

My equipment was not as big as theirs. Not even close. I'm not even sure I'd want it that big. I'm not sure I'd want theirs that big.

Would I?

Then, there were their abs. Beautiful torsos that looked just as good standing as they did when they were sat down. Literally when they sat down!

How? How on Earth does that happen?

Even with hours spent in the gym, rowing, running, squatting, mine was not like that. Nothing like that. I was not a porn star. In truth, I didn't feel like any sort of star at all. I felt like a fraud. This was not my comfort zone. I was out of place, naked in a bedroom.

So, just before my first time having gay sex, I had drinks. Multiple drinks. Which, as a seventeen-year-old, meant that I was drunk by the second one. Not slurring, or passed out, but tipsy. (Hot, right?) On my way. Hazy. But calmer than I was without its influence. Because I, Daniel John Harding, who wasn't even out to my family yet, was about to lose my virginity to a man. Can you lose your virginity twice?

A man!

He was a man too. An older man. Not a boy, not a young twenty something, but a man. A full-on working, suit-wearing, car-driving, briefcase-owning man.

Phwoar!

Thirty-four to be exact. Seventeen years older than me. Double my age. Also, a father to a two-year-old. Single. Handsome. Horny. He's done this before. I knew this. Perhaps he's done porn. He's confident enough. This would be my first time. My moment. My cherry pop moment, to be exact. The beginning of my gay sexual experience. An awakening. Someone once described it like that in a movie that I watched.

So, this is mine. There I was, awake and ready. Ready after one more drink, perhaps. This was happening. This was what I'd waited for. Was the man special? No. Should I have waited for someone special? Perhaps. Nonetheless, there I was, ready. I wish I had another drink.

As I lay on the bed, moments from starting, it dawned on me: I wasn't ready at all. Not for this moment. It wouldn't be magical; I'm not even sure it would be enjoyable. But there I was. Ready, but not ready.

Did I need a porn star's confidence to have a good sexual relationship? Why was sex easy for everyone else?

❧

Freud believed that life was built around pleasure and tension. He also believed that every bit of tension we had was due to a build-up of libido (sexual energy) and that all pleasure came from its discharge.

Growing up, sex might as well have been a swear word in my household. It wasn't a discussion that was on the table. Not accessible. We weren't that family. It wasn't something that I learnt about from a young age. Or that I spent very much time thinking about. I'm not sure I thought about it at all really. Blissfully ignorant as to where I – or babies – came from. Birds and the bees. That's all it was.

You know, when you get a really bad introduction to a place, or a person, and you instantly dislike them. That was sex. I did not like sex. School was my first introduction.

Awkward. Uncomfortable. Rushed.

Never before had I put a condom on a banana. Ever. Of course, I wanted to. Who doesn't? Having seen it being done in thousands of American movies, I assumed that this was the norm. This was what you did. A classroom stifling laughter as a condom flings off the banana and lands on the teacher's head. She then continues to write on the chalkboard, unaware, until the eruption of laughter becomes too much, and she screams.

Detention!

We then witness a girl and a guy kept behind after school for the disruption. A punishment that only just builds their growing sexual tension until it finally explodes when they sneak off to the janitor's cupboard and do it.

"Do it."

Sex education in the movies. The start of our journey. The introduction. Of course, the girl probably ends up regretting it, becoming pregnant and annoyed that she hadn't mastered the condom on the banana trick. Poor girl. You see, this is why you need the banana moment. This is why it is important.

However, this was not the case at Shoeburyness High School. Not in 2002. Sex education lessons were more about diagrams than trials. Forms of contraception, STIs and long uncomfortable explanations about why we shouldn't be having intercourse.

Don't do it, it's dangerous. End of the matter. Now, maths…

It was a subject where there were no thrills. Literally. Dry, boring and not desirable. Doing exactly what the teachers had hoped, making us not want sex. Absent of any bananas, aubergines or cucumbers. That's what I remember. But I'm older now; my memory is hazy. There was something I'd forgotten.

What I had somehow missed was that back then Shoeburyness High School did in fact have a sex education part two. One involving a vertical white apparatus, a friend recently since informed me. A more engaging, active and stimulating part of the education. The UK's answer to the banana. A boring version. But our very own condom moment.

My good friend told me that in ours, the class clown, Thomas Max, had chosen to put the condom over his head to blow it up instead, only to break it and leave a rather severe red line around his forehead, struggling to remove it.

Classic. So sex ed.

A scene much like the movies had painted, but one that I'd blanked out. Gone. Either I was absent or couldn't remember it at all. Apparently, there was even a competition to win a trip to the GUM clinic with your captain condom creation. A creative way to encourage positive sexual health. And still, nothing. My mind fired a blank. But this was not old age. This was something more. My mind had blocked out the awkward episode entirely, because unlike Thomas Max who had probably already had sex or grown up in an open household, I wasn't sure that I'd ever have a use for a rubber johnny, let alone know what one was. This moment was clearly too prickly for me.

Awkward. Uncomfortable. Rushed.

So, I filed it away, blanked it out. I bet younger me hated that lesson. Wouldn't have been useful to me anyway. Sex education didn't teach you how to have gay sex. But I can imagine young me received a "bum boy" remark during that lesson, regardless.

It wasn't the first time I'd quickly moved on from the subject. At ten years old, my dad showed me a condom. He did so reluctantly. We'd just watched a movie that mentioned them, and he had attempted to give a small explanation as to what they were and why they were used. Brief and dull. So dull, in fact, that my sister and I had forgotten about them instantly. The talk had completely gone over our heads. Which was probably part of his plan. It was also pizza night, which helped distract us. Condoms had no place when pizza was present. Fact. I had all the pepperoni that I needed right there in front of me. A feast.

The topic of sex was just not as sparkly as it perhaps should be. The allure wasn't there. It wasn't pizza. It scared me more than it aroused me. I'm sure teachers and our parents designed it this way, helping us lose our hard ons forever. Avoid teenage pregnancies, STIs or additional issues.

You have enough issues, Daniel!

They also had a lot of terrifying tools to help us never want it. Words. Or weapons.

Chlamydia, gonorrhoea, syphilis, hep B and genital warts. Clinic!

Even that last word made me wince. To be fair, it still does. Diseases you'd be sure to get if you have sex. Especially if you have sex without a condom. Don't have sex without a condom. Don't have sex.

It was implied that disease would be a certainty if you had sex. Plus, you'd be a slut. You'd be an absolute slut if you had sex. Don't have sex. Boner gone.

So, the swear word became the least interesting thing in my mind and faded amongst more important words like dinner, cinema and holidays. At least it did for me. This was lost on me. Perhaps I was destined to be a monk. Would I look good as a monk? I was just a young, non-sexual human who was getting stranger by the day. A freak.

As I grew up, I didn't actually see the importance of sex, and part of me assumed that it was just a part of my difference. Part of my oddity. A product of whatever it was that was separating me from the "normal." Perhaps I just didn't want to face it. I'd considered that I would never really have a relationship with sex.

I'd be okay with that; I had pizza.

❧

Fellow students loved sex. Louis Farmer would always tell everyone how much he masturbated. At fourteen years old, he'd describe how much he came each time and how he could probably do it ten times a day. Maybe even twelve! He'd hit his face and the boys would laugh and the girls would call him gross. He was gross.

Looking back, I now feel sorry for his penis. It must have been red raw and chafing in those nylon school trousers. I hope no girl experienced the horror of seeing it like that.

Gross. She'd have been scarred for life. Never to return back to the scene of the crime. What a crime that would be. He had a lot to answer for. I bet he had a tiny willy. Of course, at the time I had no clue what he was talking about. The only fluid to come out of my "equipment" was urine.

One day, shortly after Louis had over-shared to the class, I sat on my bed. I decided to see what the fuss was about. Louis couldn't be the idiot having all the fun. I had recently watched Elizabeth Hurley in *Bedazzled* and thought that she looked so incredibly pretty. Her hair was perfect and her figure in that red bikini, flawless. She also had this cherry-coloured red lipstick, which made them plump and really matched the whole ensemble. I'm selling it, right? So, I laid back and thought of Liz. Nothing happened. It stayed soft. Lifeless. In naivety and despair, I had no clue what I was doing, or if, more likely, it was broken. I was broken. Damaged goods.

Oh god, I had broken my penis before I had even started.

Perseverance wasn't my strong point, and when I heard the front door downstairs open, I gave up. Mum had bought donuts. That night I opted for a sugary ring instead, pondering if sex could ever be as satisfying as that deep-fried treat. I wondered if sex could feel just as good as other things. What was I missing?

Some might of course argue that donuts are just as good as sex, or better. But as my mouth devoured it and left me with a sugared lip, I had no clue how good sex could be. I wondered if I ever would.

Looking back, had I understood the different categories that we can place ourselves in, I probably would have identified as being asexual. I was subconsciously chaste. Unaware of my own desires and who I really was. A strange in between that was unexplained. Society wanted me as one thing, but I couldn't perform in that way. So, I was in no man's land.

❧

Judi James says that "sexual attitudes and the importance of sex probably changes depending on the person and it probably changes for each person throughout their lives." The more we grow, the more we experience. The more we find ourselves. She says that sex sounds like the simplest, most natural thing, but of course that simplicity is made complex by our own emotional responses, or our expectations or desires in terms of a relationship.

Thankfully, my penis wasn't broken.

Hoorah!

It was just confused. After coming out, I realised that the problem had been in my head and not in my pants. I finally appreciated what Louis Farmer had vulgarly over-shared, but not twelve times a day. I'm not sure when sex found me, but it did.

As I grew up, I experimented with girls, then boys and then

realised where my desires lay. Sex was now on the table. Enjoyable, interesting, desirable. But it was still a swear word. Sex.

My cherry was popped, ready or not, and I realised the relationship that we have with sex is just as problematic now as the first time we take a bite. That tipsy boy waiting on the bed at seventeen years old. It started as an average first encounter that we can only hope gets better. Our first rodeo. I had wanted to get it over with so that I could just pop my man cherry. Be done, move forward and enjoy it forever more.

Once I'm past this, I'll relax. Surely. I'll become my very own porn star.

The mounting pressure to have sex in the first place had been, frankly, hideous. All my new friends (gay guys) were sexually confident. Or so it seemed. And so they told me. Gay men are over-sharers. Would you believe? But for the majority of my first time, during and after, I was worried that I was slowly contracting AIDS. My mind raced thinking about the condom ripping, wondering if I was bleeding onto my sheets and also hoping that I was clean enough. And worried that I was crap at giving head. Standard gay sex thoughts.

God, I hope the sheets are okay. How would I ever get these bed sheets past my mum? Fuck, is that the front door? Not donuts again!

All the while clenching, bobbing and wincing in pain. Real pain. First time pain. Because that's what the porn shows don't display to you: the pain. And it was bloody painful. This was not porn.

My sex education lessons (or lack thereof) at school had failed me. The reality was, if you aren't a heterosexual man or woman, then finding out how sex works – what happens, the good, the bad, the uncomfortable – will all come down to you and you alone. Teachers in classrooms aren't going to prepare gay men for sex. Perhaps they feel they can't. They don't discuss it and so we struggle, we experiment, we mess up. We do it on our own.

First time sex = a lot of thoughts and not a lot of fun. Disappointing. Which, when you think about your virginity and about how you're told how precious it is, is a complete bummer. This one "thing" that we give to one person. A treasure. And it is. Was. It is precious, important and significant. But in truth, you don't realise that until you are older, sitting at a desk and writing about it. Missing it. Our cherry, popped or otherwise, is bloody important. Because once popped, the relationship we have with sex can be an odd, intimidating and toxic beast.

Sometimes sleazy.

Sometimes horny.

Sometimes erotic.

Sometimes awful.

And there is no going back. It can't be undone.

Pop.

❧

You can't talk about sex and not talk about disease. Or at the least not think about disease. I can't.

As members of the LGBTQIA+, our history with sex is a rollercoaster. A ride with dips and turns and deadly drops. Deadly. You only have to look at the eighties to understand why we might consider sex to be a dirty word when it comes to "us." Because it was. You can understand a little why our parents shared concerns about us dying, or why others might think gay sex is seedy. It can be.

There was a time when society was programmed to think that way. We were shamed. Publicly gay men were considered these sexual people who were promiscuous, were dangerous and spread disease. Demons. Unfortunately, some people still do see us like that. Some of us are like that.

In 1984, an epidemic broke out and gay men were blamed for,

and at the centre of, a new deadly virus. Fingers were pointed our way. Adverts were on every channel with tombstones that had AIDS scrolled across them. There was a witch hunt, and we were the witches. If you watch those adverts now, you'll gasp. They're low budget and terribly dramatic. But they worked. It would seem crazy to think of a time like that. So ignorant to the reality of the situation. So quick to blame. To stereotype. A pandemic... But then you only have to look at the more recent Covid crisis to understand the fear that comes with something so new.

Unknown. Scary.

And much like the disease, AIDS, being gay was considered a relatively new and unknown "way" to be back then. Not the normal. Different. Not an accepted "choice" and often seen as a dirty one at that. My mum gave birth to my sister during the crisis. "Everyone was so scared. It was an unknown virus and people lived in fear from it. We just didn't know better. It was known as the gay disease, so that's what you thought. Something gay men had and would die from," my mum shared.

Men were dying and people knew very little about the cause. A devastating epidemic. A time of judgement. A time that had consequences and ripples of its own. It still scares us today. These were uneducated tales of fear. And while I can't even begin to understand the pain, confusion and dread that people must have been living with during that time, I can see why they were scared. I would have been terrified. To be honest, I'd probably never have had sex. I'd even have been scared to do a Louis twelve times. At that time, all you could do was trust experts and doctors to find a way through an unstoppable disease. A new label, a heavier one on our community. Linked so heavily to sex. Our sex.

Would they?

Could they?

Will they?

So, a community that was already largely kept behind closed doors became a focal point for such hatred and fear. A community that forever got pigeonholed with sex.

Seedy.

Dirty.

Different.

⬩

Sex education had failed us. It failed us then, and it continues to now. The ripple that came from the eighties is still felt today. A time that forever changed our relationship with sex. But it is something that needs updating. Educators need to listen, to realise, to do their jobs. And some are.

Thankfully, a combination of education and medicine allowed people to understand AIDS and HIV more factually. To share truth and reasoning.

TV finally came to our rescue too. Just look at the impact Russell T. Davies's *It's a Sin* has had. People around the world are understanding what happened and where we've come from. In more recent years, the breakthroughs in PrEP and anti-viral drugs have been phenomenal. We no longer have to fear a disease that killed so many people, because it is in our control if we use the tools available to us. Much like sex should be. We can control our narrative. It's truly remarkable how far we've come. But the hate that came from that decade and the fear it produced lives on. I think it will for a long time. I feel it.

⬩

Sex as a gay man is not as straightforward as it is for heterosexuals. And it never will be.

Are you negative or positive, when was your last check-up, are you on PrEP, do you do BB, are you undetectable? Are you top? Are you bottom? Do you only do oral? Can we discuss rimming?

When it comes to us, sex is always a discussion. It's frankly hard not to think about sex when referencing someone of an LGBTQIA+ background. The mere term that describes the differences – sexuality – has the word right at the start of it. Because that's what sexuality is: the relationship that person has with sex and how it differs to others. Ours is different. You can't escape the label or the status, even if you try. So, you live with it. Alongside it, keeping it in mind and navigating it however you see best. It's exhausting at times.

If you have a good relationship with sex, then you will get regular check-ups, use protection in whatever form suits you and will be considerate. This, at least, is the hope. That relationship will be tricky, let you down at times and, if you are like me, will still have those moments.

Awkward. Uncomfortable. Rushed. I'm not a porn star.

Unfortunately, not everyone has a good relationship with sex. Some have a very bad relationship with it. Seedy. Dirty. Stereotypical.

There was a nightclub in Basildon, Essex, called Colours. It was trashy – one pound entry and probably needed a coat of paint – but it was fantastic. I loved it. In my early twenties, every Friday, my friends and I would get dressed up in casual going-out clothes – jeans, T-shirt, trainers – and head to Colours. The place to be in Essex. We'd have had pre-drinks somewhere first, arranged lifts, trains or taxis and got there for 9.50 p.m. After 10.00 p.m. entry went up to five pounds – we were broke. Two drinks were also five pounds. So, we got there for the cheaper entry. You can understand why. But Colours was also seedy. It was a nightclub that had seen a whole host of activity. Snogs with men who were wrong for you.

Drunken dancing and swinging round poles. And a blow job from a stranger in the toilet, or a fumble in the dark corner where bouncers turned a blind eye. Or worse.

I hadn't personally planned the blow job in the toilet. I never really had interest in "public" sex and also, the fear of just about everything was always on my mind.

Awkward. Uncomfortable. Rushed. I'm not a porn star.

However, one Friday, after multiple vodka and lemonades, I went to the loo to relieve myself. A cubicle always felt less intimidating and so I queued and got in. I had clocked the man with nice arms who looked at me as I came in. But I'd needed a wee. And that was my focus. So, you can imagine my surprise when I zipped up and turned round to see him standing there. He smiled and started kissing me. His arms were huge, so the twink in me went with it. Next thing I knew, he was on his knees. He had amazing arms, so I went with it. Before I knew it, I was on my knees and reciprocating. Did I say he had amazing arms? So I went with it. He then zipped up and left me to stagger back up. I left one minute later, knowing full well that the line waiting would have known what had just happened.

Awkward. Embarrassing. Rushed. *Was I a porn star now?*

My friend Lee teased me that my face would probably light up from the fluids in UV light. Cringe. Shortly after, I went home. I raced to the bathroom as my parents slept, unaware, washed my face nervously and then scanned my mouth for cuts. Knowing that I used to bite my gums, my over-active mind raced with fear that the stranger had just cum into not only my mouth but also my blood stream.

This was me. Worrying constantly. Thinking of every worst outcome. Sex was fun, but it scared me. From that moment, fear lived inside of me and every sexual encounter that I went through rang like an alarm bell. From hand jobs in the back of cars, to sex on my best friend's sofa with a guy that I liked, and beyond. After (and sometimes during) each encounter, I'd scan my mouth, lips, arse, and check if I was alright. I needed that extra check. But every day I lived in fear of it. Clinic visits to reset, breaks in between partners, months without. Sex scared me.

Of course, I didn't stop, I was young and enjoying myself. But even though I wore protection, was as careful as I could, each time I had sex I was sure my status was about to change. Hanging in the balance. My relationship with sex became one of love and hate. An abusive relationship of fear that was completely exhausting. One that always resulted in needles.

I hate needles. I know that is a common thing to claim, but I really do hate them. When I had my TB jab back in school, I fainted as the needle punched my skin. I vaguely remember being thrown straight onto a crash mat and Cianne Daily shouting, "Daniel Harding's fainted!" while bursting into laughter as I laid unconscious. Then on a blood test at seventeen years old, I punched the nurse accidentally. And at twenty-five, I collapsed after receiving my jabs for travelling. Other patients had to step over me. I hated needles. And I still do. My friend Darren once said to me, "You'd think you'd be used to a little prick by now." But I wasn't. Needles were not fun, even if they were necessary and saved lives. Which they do. And the worst needle of all was the one that determined your status.

The HIV test.

In a recent straw poll, forty-two per cent of people had their first STI check-up between the ages of eighteen and twenty one, and shockingly, twenty-one per cent claim to never have had one. Never!

I had my first one at eighteen years old. I'd put it off for too long. Justifying my way through the short list of sexual interactions I'd already had and resulting in the conclusion that I was "clean" and okay. (Clean is a completely offensive word and only adds to the shame around STIs. Shame that I wholeheartedly disagree with.) However, I assumed I was this status and so desperately wanted to be "clean." In truth, I was terrified that I was wrong. Was I the dirty one? There was that Spanish waiter who I'd sucked off after meeting him in PizzaExpress. We'd exchanged numbers secretly in the toilet and been texting. He'd seemed nice, friendly and horny. What more did I need at eighteen? It wasn't sleazy, or terrible, but I worried. I worried through my auntie's wedding the following day. Worried the night I went out for food with friends. And you couldn't even mention pizza to me. Pizza. My food love! Then I got a text message. I didn't know the number and it was hard to trace back then. But the message read:

I THINK YOU SHOULD KNOW. THAT WAITER FROM PIZZA-EXPRESS HAS HIV.

In eleven words, my world came crashing down.

Hanging in a balance.

This was it. The logical side of my brain was telling me I was okay. I'd Googled: I'd not done anything unprotected and the odds were in my favour. The irrational side of my brain was screaming that I had AIDS and the ads that I'd seen from the eighties were playing on repeat in my head. Tombstones falling into dust. I couldn't eat (especially pizza), I couldn't focus and I couldn't sleep. Nor could I tell anyone. I was embarrassed to speak with my parents, especially after my mum expressed her own fear, and I didn't want to come across as a slut to my friends.

Was I a slut?

Even though, in hindsight, I wasn't alone at all, I felt completely isolated and scared. So, weeks later I dragged my somewhat skinnier body down to the GUM clinic and prayed even though I wasn't religious. As I was gay, I was probably going to hell anyway. Here comes the needle. A small prick.

The man delivering it was called Peter. I still remember him to this day. His bedside manner was impeccable. A natural ease of care and a kind smile. He had round-framed glasses and wore a checked shirt. He also rocked a moustache. Peter knew I was nervous. It was hard not to see that.

"It's my first test," I quivered.

His smile was warming, and his presence made me feel at ease. He asked me my sexual history, how many people I'd had sex with and the sexual acts I'd partaken in. I shelved my embarrassment and shared with this stranger.

Did I wear protection? Did they wear protection? Did we rim? Did I swallow? Did I know their status?

Surprisingly, I answered all his questions with much more ease than I imagined I would have. He was like a kind policeman who you wanted to confess everything to. There was no point in lying; these were his exact words. Which was true. Then he took my blood, a nurse took what looked like a cotton bud to my bottom and then the nurse pushed a scratchy device into my urethra.

Something that doesn't happen any more – luckily! Yes, I'm old.

Afterwards, I sat back on the sofa in front of Peter and I told him that I was terrified. I told him sex scared me. He reached for my shoulder and told me not to worry too much, reassuring me that if I was telling the truth, there shouldn't be much reason to worry.

Was I telling the truth?

I replayed my short-lived sexual adventures of the past year. Cringing at moments like I was watching a home movie. (I will never be doing a sex tape, that's for sure.) He had told me that results can take up to two weeks, and I gulped. Then he said, "Sex should be fun, Daniel." The words went over my head. How could it be?

Every day after, I woke and dreaded any noise or vibration

that came from my phone. On day fourteen, I rang for my results. Recited my date of birth and waited. A second felt like a minute and knots inside me twisted.

"Negative."

He said it so quickly, clearly and directly. Then went through every STI, repeating the word after. It felt like I'd just received the best exam results you could ever imagine. I thanked him and then vowed never to have sex again. I wasn't sure my nerves could take it. These nerves stuck with me.

Of course, I broke my vow. I was human, young and got irrational boners at men in tracksuit bottoms. God, I miss those days. Those moments of embarrassment when you are in a supermarket, or at your desk in school, and it just happens. You start to get hard. Thankfully, Elizabeth Hurley had become my Achilles heel and repeating her name in my head usually allowed me to go soft.

Thank you, Liz!

But I did go forth and learn. I practised safe sex and had check-ups. Each time it was just as scary as the last. Each time I went through a rollercoaster of emotions, fears and outcomes. Unfortunately, the result wasn't always what I wanted. An ex had given me gonorrhoea and blamed me for it. Another had syphilis, which I had to get a jab for, even though my test later came back negative. It was two unnecessary jabs in my ass that resulted in me collapsing and convulsing in shock on the clinic floor.

I hate needles.

But STIs were a real factor when it came to sex, and for me, a huge influence in the relationship I had with it. So, I could not think of sex without thinking of disease.

Now, in the gay community, sex is everywhere. It's on your phone, in your bar, in a club or at a random house in London with twenty people who are HNH and ready. If you want it, you've got it. And, while sometimes this is great, especially when practising sex safely, it can also lead to addictions and other issues.

Sex can be both a pleasure and a curse. I've had friends, who shall remain nameless, who have fallen down the sex rabbit hole. Fallen so hard, in fact, that I'm unsure if or when they'll ever come out of it. They followed that rabbit, drank the potion and are fucked. Literally. I've heard a lot of people marry up sex and drugs. A Britney and Kevin concoction. Wrong on so many levels. Chemsex is just that. A relationship of two indulgent things that can be so good and so bad.

This is a "scene" in our world that doesn't really help the common misconception around all gay men being "sleazy." It's a scene where sex happens, inhibitions are lost and protection is often over-looked. A scene of drugs and drama.

Of course, with PrEP now in place, the risks are reduced, but the effects are still there. My said friend once went missing for four days. Resurfacing after a "party" and needing two days off work. I loved my friend, cared about him deeply, but I saw the toll these parties had on him. He told me once, shortly after, that he wanted to block things out. Block out noises, life and issues. Gently, I told him that I thought he should seek some help. He had an unhealthy relationship with sex, and it had fallen way past pleasure. Soon enough, the ripple effect this also had on the relationships around him started to come into force.

I once was due to meet him at Westfield Shopping Centre. Three hours had passed since he'd sent me a photo stating that he was on his way... He lived ten minutes from there. Finally, a voice on the Tannoy announced that the shopping centre was closing. Every inch of me wanted to wait. I feared that he'd been mugged, then I feared that he'd been murdered. He didn't answer his phone and, after the last time, I knew better than to ask his family. So, I went home. I told him via message that if I hadn't heard from him by 10.00 p.m. I'd call the police or his parents. I was genuinely worried. At 9.45 p.m., I got a text. He was fine. He'd explain later. There wasn't a sorry, there wasn't a concern for my worry. "Later" came three days later, and after coaxing it out of him, he told me that he'd gone to a hook-up, which led to a party. He'd known he was meeting me; I even had a coffee with his name written across it. But that coffee had gone cold, and slowly, so did our friendship.

Sex was the devil and angel on our shoulders. The good and evil that we had to decide on, daily. Our relationship with it now is stronger than it ever has been, with the ease of "dial a dick" on our phones, on our apps, and at our fingertips. Perhaps some use it to numb pain, block out the world, while others enjoy it. However you "use" it, finding a balance with your relationship to sex is just as important as paying your rent each month. If you don't, you could be left in an undesirable situation.

I still check in on my coffee cup friend and hope he gets the help he needs. I'll still wait till the shopping centre closes, just perhaps not so confident that he'll turn up next time.

❧

A nurse once said to me, "The first step to good sexual health is education." She said this to me as I shook nervously on her clinic sofa. I'd fallen in love with a guy who had HIV. He told me two months into dating, in part fear and part requirement. He was honest with me, didn't let us go further before I knew. Every part of me considered walking away. Considered running away. I met him in a Nando's after he had told me in person a day before. Having been in shock (and scared) at the revelation, I'd gone home straight after. There, in between peri peri chips and Portuguese chicken, he told a more composed and reasonable me all about it. Allowed me to ask the questions I needed and offered me his knowledge. I was twenty-six years old. I'd completely assumed I'd leave that chicken date with a plan to just be friends. The Daniel I knew couldn't take this information. I wouldn't be able to date a guy who was HIV positive.

Are you mad?

But as he chatted, patiently, looked at me with an honest face, I was drawn to him. It wasn't perfect, but there in a chicken shop we found a flavour we could agree on. Our sex life took a little while to get off the ground, and this poor nurse had me on phone calls, on her sofa and in her inbox, constantly. But it was worth it. When his lip bled during kissing, I went to see her. When his semen went over my skin, I went to see her. And when we had intercourse, safely and using protection, I went to see her. And she told me to educate myself. So, I did. I read, I listened to podcasts, heard people's stories and spoke to doctors. I spoke to my then boyfriend and we taught each other.

Soon, I stopped seeing HIV and saw only love. Me, a person who never thought I could, stopped thinking and started feeling. We were careful, protected each other and protected ourselves. It wasn't perfect; it was often hard, but it was also okay. Sadly, we separated for other reasons, but we both took a lot from the experience. Finally, I'd found a way to be comfortable with sex and my relationship with it benefited from it.

Perhaps sex didn't have to be scary. Not if you educate.

❧

I'm now thirty-three and realise that sex is incredible. And it has been many times throughout my life, despite my fears. You groan, you moan, you orgasm. Repeat.

It can be brilliant for our health, mental well-being, positivity, destressing and bonding. It can be exciting, interesting and intense, all in the same moment. You can explore, experiment and see what works for you. In our community we are so sexually explorative; there are no limits. Within reason. Yes, it's addictive, it can go wrong and can often be uncomfortably messy. But sex is a part of us, a massive part of who we are, our relationships and our passion for life.

Freud was right. It can be our muse, our defuse, our outlet and our fetish. But when it's healthy, consenting and there's love between you, it can be bloody brilliant for everyone. Now, with anti-viral drugs, PrEP and information widely shared, it can be completely safe and you can be in control.

I'm still that guy.

Awkward. Uncomfortable. Sometimes rushed. Not a porn star.

But I've learnt that sex can't be viewed in the dated terms of the eighties. We can't be stuck in our heads to enjoy it. We can't live in fear. We should learn, of course. But we should relax too. Enjoy.

And it can't be viewed through the eyes of an international porn star... Or can it?

❧

Having always thought of sex as a swear word, I never thought I'd be able to speak to someone so frankly about it. It was a conversation I didn't want to have. I'm uncomfortable in this conversation.

But I shouldn't be. We shouldn't be. And so, I finally did have the conversation. With a porn star. Because who better to open my eyes than someone who partakes in sex twenty-four seven. I'd never truly spoken about sex until now. And I should have.

Jason Domino started work in porn at twenty for money. He was very open about his reasons and his journey.

"Sex has been like a relationship for me in itself. But that relationship has changed in nature."

Before becoming comfortable with who he was, at nineteen, Jason put himself through conversion therapy, as at the time, he thought that was his only option to live a normal life.

"I was trying everything I could to not be who I was. I had to go through therapy that made you watch porn and drink sickening substances. It doesn't work. I'm a gay porn actor. Don't do it. It's damaging. I realised it was unnatural to not be loving yourself. It took me a while to accept it and process the years I denied it. All of us have grown up with the fear of rejection because of who we are sexually. Each person has their own journey in processing. I feel like that's why a lot of people enter the male sex work industry. You do something so different to what is expected of you, breaking the shackles and going almost against it. Accepting yourself and... rebelling."

When did sex become an important part of who you were?

"I thought, rather than running from who I was, I needed to embrace it. Sex is part of us. The therapy was brutal and framed it like I was sick and could get better. But it showed me the opposite. It still happens, which is awful."

In his early twenties, Jason got into a relationship with someone who had extreme depression. In turn, he needed money quickly to help them.

"I was aware of sex workers' rights at the time. I started to do porn to elevate myself. But there is a perception of glamour and it isn't glamorous at all. I used it to gain status and help myself. In turn, I made money and it happened to help me get out of the bad situations I was in."

But did you have to have confidence to be a sex worker?

"When you are working, it's a job. You adopt a persona that carries you. Fake it till you make it. With sex, your dick is a barometer, though. There is only so much you can fake. Only so much confidence. If you have financial, mental issues, even if the camera is on, sometimes you can't perform. You have to listen to the body when it comes to sex. That's important in any part of sex. Viagra doesn't just magically help. It's deeper."

Before being a porn star, like many of us Jason told me that he had watched porn.

However, he heavily linked shame to the experience, saying that watching it almost felt wrong, naughty and something that he thought others might not be doing. However, we are doing it. But what's it doing to us?

"As a society we are so uncomfortable talking about porn. As a worker, I'm aware I am making a fantasy. It's escapism and that's how we have to see it. It's not educational, even if you are new and young, watching it for the first time. It's not meant to glorify and glamorise sex, it's meant to help you escape. Release."

We both agreed that porn had a huge place in our story. It helped us when we feared no one else was like us.

But for Jason, being a porn star has helped him and others more than he imagined.

"Unbeknown to me at the time, my first porn experience was with someone who had HIV. Which led me to create something that mixed porn and education – something we needed."

In 2016, Jason, along with others, bravely created Porn4PrEP.

"Along with factual interviews, I performed on camera, unprotected, but on PrEP, and had sex with someone HIV positive. A condom-less scene with a top who had a high viral load at the time. A first ever. We got invited to the UN to discuss it, it got so much awareness. Because there isn't good enough sex and relationships education. Our education misses out so many important lessons; it still does in schools. And our community is different in how we have sex. The stuff we learn in a classroom isn't going to help. Porn, like Porn4PrEP, gives a fairer, realistic lesson, especially in sexual health."

Jason said that if we are taught in a show-and-tell way, it develops a clearer message.

"How we teach it isn't right. No wonder we have fears, doubts, unanswered questions. No wonder we turn to porn."

As someone who lives and breathes sex, I was interested to know how it affected his life.

"Having a secret over you hurts you. I've learnt that from my past. When you are open, accepting, embracing, you can use those past memories and damage and have positive experiences. So, I don't lie. There is a stigma in being a sex worker, but if you can be open and proud, then a lot of those stigmas disappear. I didn't have the patience to lie. It wasn't courageous, I was just done with the hiding. People erase people's kindness, especially when we are seen as one thing, but also doing incredible things.

"Porn4PrEP, porn stars helping communities, housing the homeless after earthquakes, part of Stonewall, helping parades, using their platform to normalise our community. Sex workers help us more than we think. Sex work shouldn't be seen in this negative light. We aren't one dimensional. We are more than sex."

Jason told me that as a sex worker, it is just work; you separate it.

"Sex for pleasure is that. Not work. I'm professional and you can enjoy different parts of the work side, but sex for work is different to sex for pleasure. The two are different. In porn you are filming uncomfortable angles, with multiple people, stopping and starting over hours. There is paperwork to sign, things you have to do, and on top of it, you have to show the right face and perform."

However, he said that as a person, it's hard to be a sex worker. If Jason wanted to get another job, he'd most likely be fired if his past career was discovered.

Jason was and always will be defined by sex.

"Although there are incredible things in place and we do have rights, porn unions you can go to if there is discrimination, there is a long-term stigma. I don't regret; I'm content and comfortable. But no matter how glamorous it looks on screen, we are an invisible community. Visible as a product, invisible as people. It's not the porn's fault, or our sex lives, it's society. Our perception of sex."

But Jason lives in the now; he doesn't regret. Porn helped who he was, helped him realise sex between men wasn't a negative but instead brilliant.

"Sex is brilliant for gay men. It's not just reproduction or something we had to do. It's passion and well-being. Gay sex used to be illegal; we still live in a world where it is in some countries. But as a community we have a unique experience with sex. There's a freedom, a pick and mix. It's allowed us to explore sex as a community. Like window shopping and sharing dick pics, open relationships and other sexual desires. It's allowed us to question sex from a world view and do it our own way."

Jason said that sex is so important to him as a gay man. It helps him cope and relieve anxiety.

"I breathe freer because of it. The light is a little brighter. The smells are a little bit better. It's easy to spot joy in the world after sex."

But can it be negative?

"Sex shouldn't be a dirty word. There's homophobia linked to 'our' sex, though. But I don't think we should ever look at sex as a negative. Addiction, porn addiction – all sounds negative. But nothing to do with sex should be cured. Obviously, we have a history with STIs; lots of people went through a horrific time. But from it, we have learnt. Yes, we have to be safe. We've been through difficult times. I don't want to reduce anyone's trauma. There is also chemsex and substance abuse, which is so common in the gay community. But we can't see sex negatively. We have to be smart."

Jason said that he thinks we have a different relationship with sex as gay men.

"I think we have a healthier relationship with sex compared to heterosexuals. We are liberated from the cultural expectations around sex. Something so freeing in that. I also think that sex can change our lives. Sex education from an earlier age, for all communities is important. It will allow us not to weaponise it but understand it. Make it normal. Enjoyable."

As our chat came to an end, I was in awe of Jason and his outlook on sex.

"Money is often a driving factor in becoming a sex worker, but sex work isn't a bad thing. It's enjoyable, taking care of people, and it's also a form of activism. Sex isn't bad. Yes, I'm a sex worker. I have rights. If you are one, you have to be safe and make sure you use all the organisations at your fingertips. But my relationship with sex is healthy. Pragmatic. I have a partner, we are open, but you can do this as a job and have a normal life. Through sex I've found comfort in my sexuality and come to terms with it. And through it, I continue to educate and help. Sex is more important than anyone thinks."

❧

Sex scared me. But only because I didn't understand it. And so, my relationship with it was moulded by that. But it isn't dirty or scary or shameful. Like the sex advisor once said, "Sex should be fun, Daniel." We shouldn't fear it, over-think it or judge how others do it. We shouldn't run with fear or refuse to educate ourselves on it. We all have our own way.

In speaking to Jason, I realise now that sex is what can help us all. And finding a way to enjoy "our" sex allows us to enjoy life. Which is just frankly aubergenius. Yes, I said that.

a letter of complaint: a gay and their phone

Dear Phone,

I am writing to tell you that I'm turning off your ring tone. And vibrate too.

Don't you even try it!

Your constant notifications are proving too much. I'm sucked in, consumed, and I fear an addiction has formed. In truth, I'm breaking up with you.

We are over.

Okay, we aren't over. That was harsh. Please don't run out of battery. We are just taking space.

Frankly I can't keep up. WhatsApp messages, WhatsApp groups, Hinge, Tinder, Bumble, Grindr, Instagram, Twitter. Not Facebook. Facebook, I'm over you. TikTok, iMessage, emails.

You just don't stop. You're relentless. I can't stop.

Do you know, I've not watched something on TV from start to finish without checking my phone for over a year now. That's terrible. I need to disengage so I can engage. Okay, a slight fib as I went to the cinema and didn't check you. But the anxiety I experienced when I did was through the roof.

Why am I so obsessed with you?

This has got to stop. Yes, I'm single. I fear life is ticking away at an accelerated speed and every moment matters. But what about the moments I'm missing? The times that I'm spending looking down and not seeing what's in front of me. Obsessing on the online society we live in. Do not even start me on the selfies. Your constant reminders about storage space are enough prompts. I know I take too many.

What am I scared to miss? What is this FOMO I'm feeling if I don't check social, don't upload a picture or boomerang a round of drinks?

Who needs to see it anyway? Does it make me young?

Why do I need to tweet my thoughts on pineapple upside-down cake? Who really cares?

One hundred and thirty two likes, that's who.

Anyway, I'm sorry, but we need space. It's unhealthy. A digital detox. Goodbye Grindr, goodbye Hinge, goodbye Insta...

No, I won't delete.

I will just not use. I'll resist taking a photo of the roast dinner I made. Even though I spent time on presentation. I can live without you. Or involve you less.

I must. This can't go on. I'm obsessed with you.

Yours,
My Sanity

love

/lʌv/

---

noun

1. an intense feeling of deep affection.
   "babies fill parents with feelings of love"

2. a great interest and pleasure in something.
   "his love for football"

verb

3. feel deep affection for (someone).
   "he loved his sister dearly"

4. like or enjoy very much.
   "I just love dancing"

conversations about love

In one of my favourite moments from *When Harry Met Sally*, Harry describes the feeling of wanting the rest of your life to instantly begin as soon as you realise you want to spend it with somebody. This sentiment has stuck with me.

Love was not on the menu. At least, not for me. Not for our community. Yes, we could feel it. Do it. Want it. Need it. But it didn't feel attainable. Not available for order at the time that I realised what it actually was. Have sex, sure, that's behind closed doors, just not love.

Love.

Love was not for us. It wasn't seen as a priority for "our kind." We were undeserving. So, it didn't become a priority for me. It was a heterosexual thing. Man and woman. Woman and man.

I pined for it, but it wasn't the top of my to-do list. And when I thought about love, I thought about the actress Meg Ryan. For a long time, Meg was a poster girl for all forms of love. Passionate and explosive and desirable love. The characters she played always embodied the love that we all seek. That I sought. Pure. Honest. Inconvenient. Love.

I was in New York City in a steak restaurant ten years ago. I can't remember why, but I was in a bad mood. God knows why, actually. I was in NYC on holiday, eating beautiful dinners and sipping exotic cocktails with people who I loved.

What the hell was there to be grumpy about?

The hostess sat us in a booth and gave us menus. To our right, seated next to us, was a lady and a man. On a date. She had tight blonde curls and uncontrollable laughter. Infectious. We ordered steaks, red wine and a breadbasket that could feed a church. The woman's laughter continued through our appetisers, main course and flowing drinks. Then she stood up. I assume to go to the toilet. Or to leave. And we saw her. Meg Ryan.

Actual Meg Ryan.

She slung her jacket around her, throwing her head back again during another bout of laughter. A genuine smile taking residence across her face. I bet it was always there. My bad mood dissolved. I smiled. The rest of the dinner we chatted about Meg, her movies and the fact that an actual Hollywood movie star had been casually dining next to us.

MEG RYAN!! WTF.

Ten years on, we sometimes chat about "that time." And I can still hear her laugh. I can't comment on her happiness, but that was a laugh of love. A love for life, for experience and a joy for whomever she was with. Meg was love. She'd had love. Was in love. Acted in love. Felt love. To me, she oozed it. That was love.

Gradually, I started to see love as more of a priority.

If I could love like Meg, I think I'd be happy.

I thought I'd laugh just as loud. Feel just as good. Love should always be on the menu. Because I wanted what she was having. A slice. A portion for myself. Find my laugh. My love. Meg had it, didn't she... Why couldn't we?

But "we" couldn't openly until 2005, when the Civil Partnership

Act came into force. Enabling same-sex couples to obtain legal recognition for their relationships. How romantic. Then marriage was finally recognised in the UK in 2013, when Parliament passed the Marriage Act, introducing marriage for same-sex couples in England and Wales. The world finally allowed us to love. Which was good, because, as my favourite quote suggests, you want the rest of your life to begin as soon as possible.

And I was itching for it to begin.

❧

Pretty much everyone I know finds love hard to define. My glam friend Clare repeatedly tells me "we can't control it," and to just go with it. But when put on the spot, if you had to describe what love is, I bet it would take you a while. Go on. I'll wait.

It's one of those complicated subjects that's hard to talk about and even harder to explain. I struggle with this constantly. Talking about hate, however, I find really easy. Too easy in fact. I'm clearly a messed-up man.

I hate fish, touching eyeballs and talking about death. I hate it when the tiniest noise in the middle of the night becomes an orchestra to your ears. I hate not being able to find the words to describe my feelings. I hate take-off and landing on an aeroplane. I grab the arm rest and once even grabbed a stranger next to me. Poor woman. I also hate when your ears pop and stay popped for what feels like days after you've flown. I hate sleepless nights and the fact that pizza isn't healthy. Why? I hate that Scream mask Halloween costume. Why would you wear it? Awful.

I could go on. I could fill this chapter with hate. It's incredibly easy to point out stuff that I really don't like. In fact, I've got it down to a fine art. When scrolling through profiles on Tinder or Hinge, I can easily point out what I'm *not* looking for. What they are lacking, why we wouldn't be compatible or why they wouldn't fancy me. Hate is easy. It flows. It seeps out of me like lava.

But what I love? Well, that takes more thought. It's tricky. It takes consideration, contemplation and looking deep inside yourself to reveal often uncomfortable realisations. Putting yourself out there, open to rejection or hopefully, an erection of love. Exhausting to think about. Love is a huge revelation.

I've often been told that love and hate are strong words to use. Use them with caution. Which is true. They are. Powerful. So, when it comes to love, I really have to consider if what I'm experiencing in that moment is love, or just like. I like marmite; I don't love it. I like frozen chocolate buttons; I don't love them. I like the thought of marrying Jake Gyllenhaal; I don't love him. I mean, I could, but I don't...yet. I like Fridays after work, the feeling after I've worked out and when I get a match that I fancy on Tinder. But do I love those things? The jury's out.

Because can you honestly answer that unavoidable question, *have you ever been in love?* Go on. I'll wait again.

❧

At seven years old, I told my mum that I loved a girl called Ayucka. She was a fellow student in my class and due to be going back to Japan imminently. Deep down it would never have worked out anyway. Her family fiercely loved fish and, also, Ayucka was a girl. Future me would understand. Future me wouldn't be concerned by this situation. Future me would have realised this wasn't love. But in that moment, something in me knew that I felt something so strong. There was an unseen pull towards this girl that I couldn't explain. And surely, I'd never feel this way again if she left. She was my chance.

So, I cried my eyes out in the playground when she finally went.

Ugly, Kim K emoji crying. That's it. The end of my love life. The week after she had gone, I told my mum that I now loved Lizzie Bolton.

Ayucka who?

I wish I could fall in love as quickly as that these days. Not over-think things constantly, playing games and wondering if they love me back. Quick, uncomplicated "love" that didn't cost you money or your feelings. But that wasn't love. Or at least not the love that I think I now know at the age of thirty-three.

I think.

True love. Whatever that was. Love is love, apparently. But if that's the case, I'm going to need a better explanation. Because frankly, I'm confused.

❧

"I like the way that the French describe being in love as a form of 'folie'. The kind of passionate, powerful love we experience in an intense relationship often feels nothing like the kind of gentle, warm love we feel for family, children, friends or pets." Judi James says that "being in love" is the strongest form of love we ever feel. "It can feel exquisitely painful and involve all sorts of anxieties, paranoia and irrational jealousies that defy any form of logical thought."

Love has always been my end goal. You'll probably understand by now that I have over-indulged in the odd romantic comedy.

Or twenty.

I've got caught up in love stories, celebrities who seem to have it all and books that depict the kind of love that I'm looking for. If there's romance to be had in something, I'll find it. Love was on a pedestal. A holy grail to reach and a bloody mountain for me to climb. But it was up there, sitting pretty, looking perfect.

Coincidentally, I had fallen in love with writing because of a review I had read in the *Guardian* of *Love Actually* in 2004. A romantic comedy. I'd stumbled across it after always reading reviews ahead of watching a movie. I hated (there's that easy word again) nothing more than picking a bad movie. Having to sit through it. Annoyed. I was all about saving wasted time. I had no time to waste. Wasting time was ageing without getting anywhere. I did not need more ageing.

Peter Bradshaw, a journalist, had beautifully captured (and torn apart) the movie, and his words touched me in a place that I didn't know existed. His words became power. In the review he quipped, *was love actually enough?*

The question ignited two things inside of me. First, I wanted to be a journalist. I wanted to touch people's own deep dark places inside with my words. Cause people to question, ask questions and demand answers. So, I went to uni, got a degree and became a journalist. Second, it, along with my parents' divorce, made me constantly recite that question.

Was love actually enough?

Would it ever be enough? Could it ever be enough? I've never stopped thinking about that question. Without knowing entirely what love was, what I did know was that there were a lot of other things in life going on. More important things. More substantial things. Things that I could define and explain a lot more easily. Other areas of life that required our focus. A concentration on our growth, who we were and what we did. Our careers, our character, our path. There were other things to prioritise than being in love. And let's be honest, easier points to tackle. Love could wait, right?

Despite civil partnerships being recognised in 2005, love before that and for a long time after felt like a different journey for us. We couldn't love the same. Campaigning for our rights to marriage licences and applications was happening as early as 1992 in England – perhaps even earlier. After marriage licence applications by same-sex couples were refused, it ignited a very long battle for equal marriage. A fight. We literally had to fight for the right to recognise our love. Despite the obvious homophobia, not being able to display love in public without getting insults or worse, that fight was felt throughout our community. Whether you bravely campaigned on streets, in protests or in debates, or if you read the news behind closed doors, suffering in silence. Everyone felt it. And it affected everyone differently.

But could love wait?

Because in reality, for our community and for a lot of people, it had to wait. So, it did. Of course, after coming out, I'd dabbled in relationships. But I wasn't sure where that love would go, would be able to go. After a failed relationship at twenty-one and it still not being legal to "love" for our community, I had dreams outside of love. Other focuses. Career aspirations. I started scoring small goals, putting ambition ahead of anything else. I'd over-work, spread myself thin and burn out on a daily basis. Of course, I'd dabble with "love" on the side, but that is where it remained. A side hustle. A bit part. The supporting act. Never the main attraction.

The concentration on anything but love was like the blinkers a horse would wear when focusing on the road ahead. My peripheral vision was cut off so that I could only look forward. Keep concentration. But, despite the legalities and question mark over how far love could go, love, outside of family, friends or pets, couldn't be controlled. Couldn't be ignored. Despite all my efforts, unapologetically, "love" crept in. Sometimes it was unexpected, sometimes sought out during moments of procrastination, and often unplanned. Always unplanned. Even with the relentless support of Taylor Swift, Beyoncé and Demi Lovato advising me that I was doing okay on my own, love would find me. It had its way. Regardless of laws, career goals or Tinder rejection. It comes.

And slowly I realised that if I continued to turn my back on it, kept running, kept my focus elsewhere, I might regret my choices. Make the wrong turn. Life has an expiry date, so why wouldn't love? It was a relationship completely out of control. There, regardless. Waiting or available. Whenever we were ready for it. Whenever the world would acknowledge it.

Pure.

Honest.

Inconvenient.

Love.

❥

Ayucka, sorry my dear, but you were not my first love. I know that might be hard to read. But it feels good to now share that truth.

Sashay away.

My first love came in my early twenties. Like I said, I wanted love; I wanted it to happen bad. Yet, it wasn't my priority. It was far down on the list. I turned away from potential loves more often than I'd care to admit. Even now, at thirty-three, I constantly think about boys from the past. Odd dates that I didn't continue.

Where were they now?

However, nothing stopped me wanting it. I wanted to be Cinderella.

Of course I bloody did.

I wanted that man to hunt me down, to knock on every door until the shoe fit. I mean, I'd be slightly insulted that he had to see my foot in a shoe before he knew. It's not like we'd have met in a dark room! But that is what I wanted. A prince.

Although being in love was presented as only really an option to be obtained in a heterosexual way growing up, I had anticipated that I might experience this "love" feeling at some point. Hoped I would. I wasn't sure how it would look or feel, partly due to the poor representation at the time, but I was almost certain that it would be different to other people. It would not be a Cinderella moment. Hell, it would not even be a public moment. Since coming out, nothing I had experienced had been the same as it was for "other" people. I knew this. We just didn't get those fairy tales. And mine was not magical.

When it came, it wasn't obvious or mind-blowing. It was actually really hard to see. In fact, I would have loved it to have been as clear as the number nine bus turning up with a sign saying "love, all aboard." To be frank, I nearly missed the damn bus.

There wasn't a movie moment, or a flash mob that made it clear. It nearly slipped away before I even got to see it. To feel it. Blink and I'd have missed it. It was a gradual, a steady incline that grew with pace. A moment that made me realise what love might be. A lesson. Something that showed me, once and for all, that love between a man and a man was the same love that is experienced between a man and a woman, or anyone else in life. Love was love, and I finally understood it. The one relationship that everyone shared no matter our differences. No matter laws.

We could all be Meg Ryan. Love really was love.

❧

Marc Chattem.

For ages those two words did things to me that I can barely even describe. Things that I shouldn't describe, especially if my dad is reading this. Sorry, Dad. That name was love. Embodied in one person. It made me weak, anxious, lose my appetite and find it hard to concentrate. Really hard to concentrate. I'd daydream about marriage, houses and holidays to hot countries where I'd be smiling. Grinning like the cat that had the cream. Where I'd laugh like Meg Ryan.

When it was good with Marc, it felt like the best thing in the world. Nothing could compare. Nothing would compare. It was a high. I've never taken ecstasy before, but I imagine it's a heightened version of that. A trip that you really didn't want to end and that felt like it could last forever. I wanted it to last forever. Love was a drug. So good, but definitely bad for you too. Awful in fact. The feeling of love produced smiles, conjured up a sunny day when it was raining and inner confidence. It made you feel warmer, happier and whole.

Are you sick yet?

But when it was bad, it would tear you down to your bones and leave you out in the cold. Freezing. Uncomfortable. Love. It could cause tightness in your chest where happiness once resided and turn you into a crazy person who you'd be sure not to recognise. You'd be Kathy Bates. Yes, that's who you'd be. A psycho. Because love makes you crazy.

Folie.

Whoever described love as a rollercoaster was absolutely right. I hope you enjoy rides.

I met Marc in a local nightclub in Southend. It was a straight nightclub, and he was straight. Or at least that was the line he was peddling to friends and his girlfriend at the time. We became "friends" after an initial chat at the bar, and after a few weeks spent turning up at the same places, we exchanged numbers. As mates. Just mates.

Of course, in my head I'd fantasised a whole host of scenarios with him. I'd given us a fake love life, which was happy and normal. It was the same sort of daydreaming that I now do over Jake Gyllenhaal. A fantasy coupling in which we've been happily married for around twelve years now. Congrats Jake!

Crazy.

A year after meeting him, Marc came out. Shortly afterwards, he pursued me. I played hard to get. I wasn't interested. Sure, he was lovely, handsome and would be a magazine-cover boyfriend. But I was young, having fun and only just becoming comfortable in my own skin. Love wasn't my focus because I didn't know if we could have it. He was available and I was occupied. So, he stopped trying. Stopped contacting. Stopped turning up to the same places. And left me to it.

Love could wait, right?

The feeling that came next was foreign. I missed him. I felt myself going to message him, then realising I shouldn't. Then wanting to. I stopped being attracted to other people and constantly compared them to him. I thought about what he was up to as I lay in bed, and I wondered if I had thrown away something that could have been incredible. It was torture. Indiscernible and foreign, torture.

And so, I messaged. I arranged to meet up. I swallowed my pride. I stopped playing. We had drinks, he wore a tight grey jumper that showed off his arms and chest, resembling Thor, and we sat down at a bar. He looked hot. We chatted and conversation flowed. Easily. So easily.

I was an idiot.

If ever there was a light-bulb moment, it happened then and there. A puzzle piece slotted into place and when it came time to part ways, I didn't really want to.

Marry me illegally, Marc!

Like the gentleman he was, he drove me back to my home. We sat in silence on the ride. I wanted to say so many things, but my pride didn't allow me to speak. As he pulled up to my house, I found courage. I told him that I wanted to go out on a date. Wore my heart on my sleeve. Gulped and waited for his response. He told me, "No."

If I wasn't interested before, then why now?

He had a point. I was an idiot. I watched him drive off and felt that tightening in my chest.

Goodbye, Thor.

Deep down I knew I couldn't explain why; I just took my time. This feeling was far stronger than my Ayucka episode, and, not to label it, but I'm pretty sure this anxious feeling bubbling inside was love. It certainly was not the feelings I felt for my sister, parents, friends and dead rabbit. Three days later he wrote me a letter. Back when letters were a thing. Rather than long text messages, emails or a WhatsApp video message. Four pages, FRONT AND BACK, explaining how he had felt when I showed no interest. How much it took for him to come out and how his heart felt heavy and he had felt a little lost. He wanted me and I shrugged him off.

I felt awful. Really awful.

He had just come out and wanted to be with me. Me, in a sea of men, he chose me. I read the letter multiple times and didn't know how to respond.

I still have that letter.

He had poured out so much of his heart, and I knew I didn't want to break it any further. And so, I sent him songs that reminded me of him. Cringe! Yes, I was that kid. I texted when I thought of him, breaking all the courting rules and playing no games. There was no "cool" response. An apology wasn't enough. I needed to show him. I went from colourful beating-around-the-bush messaging to black-and-white facts. Because this was it. This was love. And he felt it too.

Together, after breaking him down and realising he was stalking my Myspace page, what we built were foundations. Core footings that turned into something that resembled love. Blind-siding, all-consuming and devastating love. Nothing like what I'd experienced before. Because before Marc, I had been wrong about love. I had always thought that the agonising and lusting for him that I endured was love. I thought not being with him and how my heart ached was love. I thought love wouldn't be the same for me as it was in movies or as it was for straight people. I thought I couldn't be Meg. Marriage wasn't (originally) on the table. I couldn't have love.

Wrong.

All wrong.

Love was just instinct. A feeling towards a person. Indescribable. Brilliant. And for everyone.

I'm not going to write forty pages on how good that love was. Don't worry, I don't think my stomach could take it either. But for three years, Marc and I had this incredible bond, a relationship that at times felt like it was all that mattered in the world. A car with the brakes cut, passengers left waiting for the crash, waiting for it to end. To stop. Will it?

Judi James says: "Love will nearly always change our behaviour as we try to assimilate this important person into our lives and form a complementary match. Too strong a change can be risky, though. It can be natural to change your behaviour to be pleasing and loveable but too much flexing will either end in you morphing back into your true self once the relationship has been established or keeping up an act for the rest of your life together."

Change. That is love. Love makes us change. Being in love changed me. It made me realise that we deserve to experience this love. Openly. It made me fearless about the legalities.

At the beginning of Marc and I, we did change, altered our single ways and I certainly put on an act in certain situations. It was pretty exhausting. When he didn't want to introduce me to his parents as his boyfriend because he wasn't out to them, I acted okay. I went along with being the "mate" who had popped round, despite his mum sensing the truth. This was even more evident when she didn't offer me cake and only spoke to me through her son. Damn that cake looked good. It was made clearer when she threw herself through a glass window, needing his assistance and pulling him away from our "date night." I went home and ordered pizza. I acted okay with it. My act continued when I wasn't introduced to friends and smiled through my teeth when he took my sister to a work event because he couldn't take me. We weren't allowed that open love.

Okay.

I did it because I loved him. An act that I was willing to partake in. Exhausting. But it was also an "act" that neither of us could keep up. Because I realised you can't keep up an act. Jake couldn't for Liberty on *Love Island* 2021, and I couldn't back then.

Sadly, the curtain closed on our relationship together. And that was love. Everything that consumes us and a journey we go on that changes us. It has to.

Of course, after Marc came heart-wrenching pain – love part two. You can't experience love without the pain that comes after. Curling up on your best friend's sofa after not speaking to anyone for two weeks and crying uncontrollably. Too sick to eat (yes, even pizza). Convincing yourself that you'll never experience a love like that again.

How can you?

You'll never get that moment of connection between two people that feels like an electric spark shooting through you as you touch each other.

Of course not, gone!

Don't even think you'll ever again have that insanely orgasmic sex on that fun ski trip with your friends. The one where you couldn't take your hands off each other. Late down to dinner, messy hair and smiles across our faces – sex faces. Over! How would you be able to recreate that with others?

So long great sex!

No one else would talk of your future home together. Painting your perfect life with that white fence in the Kent countryside.

Perhaps a kid running around that he'd look after. Chickens, there would be chickens for fresh eggs. He cooks because you can't. Shattered. Dead. Gone. Convincing yourself that you'll never know love like that again while staring at his old Myspace page.

Myspace!

Waiting for his next status. The next you. The replacement. Then there'll be the new Facebook photo of him smiling as the relationship status goes back to single.

What a wanker, how can he do that?

Facebook has a lot to answer for those status updates. You'd have been so happy to put "in a relationship" and add his name. Smugly enjoying the likes and comments that come flooding along with it. Comfort in a confirmed union. Even though his Facebook was private due to his family. Deleted. Then of course comes the next boyfriend.

Er, boyfriend? You said we couldn't be together because of your family! Bastard!

You inevitably then go down the rabbit hole, looking at their profile and reciting all the reasons they are better than you.

Younger, nicer hair, better cheekbones, probably better in bed. Definitely a higher paid job and sexy. He looks sexy. Fucker.

You go through denial, acceptance and regret, over and over. If you happen to see them out, you want to look good. Even on a trip to the local shop you now wear your good clothes. You work out harder than ever and eat healthier. Because you have a new act. Separation is your improved performance to show that you were okay, regardless. You were not okay. But this extended part of love is healing. It's the stages and moments we have. Day by day, month by month, you get better. Or numb. You learn.

Because what that love teaches us is a lesson in life. Yes, I'm aware lots of people stay with their first loves, but we aren't all lucky enough to live in Disneyland.

Okay.

But that first love, regardless of length, taught me that love is important. No matter who you are or who you love. Love is love. I only realised this with Marc. He showed me this. Or maybe experiencing it showed me this.

But finally, after thinking that it was unattainable, avoiding it as a focus, I surrendered. Because everyone can ride this rollercoaster.

❧

It's often the most uncomfortable thing to do, sitting down with an ex and speaking about your love.

Can you imagine!

In theory, I had three main "ones" who I could choose from. None of whom I particularly wanted to talk about this subject with. Not because it wasn't good. But they were personal experiences that we had together in the past. That's where they should stay, right?

However, how could you understand our relationship with love without confronting it?

My relationship with my second love (who has chosen to remain anonymous) lasted just over a year. A complete journey. A complete whirlwind. A complete ride. One that I got off. Enter, the awkward conversation with a love.

"Could this be any more uncomfortable?" he started. "Love, in my head, was a very different version of what love is in reality. It was not going to be like Rose and Jack from *Titanic*. We couldn't have that love. Not as gay men.

"Growing up, there was no representation of what love was like for gay people. Now there is representation on TV in shows like *Love, Victor*, but back then there wasn't. You viewed other people's love and had to figure out your own."

He said that the lack of representation not only reflected in his feelings towards love but showed in how our community moved forward with their own versions of it.

"It's weird to talk to you about love. But okay. When you are young, I think you are conditioned to think you need love and a two point four family. And for a gay man, you couldn't have that, or not in the way others did. So, you kind of thought, well what happens to me? Therefore, I didn't know, at the time, if it was accessible to me. I wasn't sure I'd have what they had."

He said that when he had romantic relationships he never thought, this is the one; he instead thought, let's see how it goes.

"Gay people were not like straight people. When you are younger, growing up, our lifestyle as gay men – it didn't fully lend itself to finding a partner, it was more like finding your next thing, whatever that was. You weren't sure where it could go. Even now, so many friends of mine are in open relationships, on Grindr as couples and living a very different version of the 'love' we once thought we'd have.

"We've evolved with our own loving way because we couldn't love how others did at first. It's now rippled and changed. Each to their own, but I think it's actually clouded the term 'love' for me. It will always be different because of the fight we had. As I've got older, I've actually sought it out less. It's almost become less important to me."

He suggested that he could still be content and happy having a career, having hook-ups and keeping it loose.

"To be honest, I thought to myself, this love thing isn't working out for me. I'm just going to concentrate on work. Apart from our relationship, the others weren't great. Gay relationships are harder to obtain than straight ones. Yes, it might be more accepted, easier to hold hands down the street etc., but to get to that place is the hard part. Our community is awful and shallow on apps like Tinder and Grindr. We discriminate on our own. Femmes, mascs, camp, short, fat, ugly. We are brutal.

"We have rights in place, others have accepted us, but we are still living in a time where we aren't loving in a way that we are now allowed to. Granted, not everyone is in an open relationship – there are of course people who are monogamous – but gay relationships that I've encountered are different. Creating their own rules. Small and large."

As we chatted, we agreed there was a love for our community.

"I take it for granted that I can love freely right now. I can go on a date. In other countries and cultures you can't. I don't think many people think of this privilege. But it is, and one we've fought for."

He said that he is lucky to have always felt love, but suggested that is different for everyone.

"Most of my experience of love is negative – because it hasn't lasted. For me, that's love. Realistic. I mean, what is good love? Each person has a different perspective. I think as I have a 'love' replacement with a good job, family and life, I don't think about it nonstop. Love is too hard to define. It's different to me from what it is to you. Our experiences change how we see love. Influence changes how we see love.

"But I have never had a relationship 'being in love' that I've been completely happy in. Which is awkward to say to you. So, my goals are focused on different things at the moment. I'm not saying I am not open to love. I'm just not sure what that is or what it looks like. I think this stems back further than relationships and how society made us feel about loving. I guess love is contentment for me. But dangerous because you can lose yourself in it."

He and I got together when I was twenty-four. Our love grew from friendship and laughter.

"Obviously, our love was good. We laughed loads, didn't we? I'm not sure what it was, but I remember just nonstop laughing. It was a nice experience. We were close. We did some fun things. There are good memories there. Would I describe it as love? At the time, yes. But how do you quantify love? If it was real love, then why aren't we still together? It would be unfair to say that I didn't love you, because I did. But was it *Titanic* love? Obviously not, as we didn't fight until we were on a door in the freezing sea. *Titanic* is probably not the best film reference."

He, a writer and editor for TV, claimed that this was a really hard topic to discuss.

"Our love hurt me. I disliked how it ended. How flaky you were. This is like therapy. Honestly, our love was disappointing. At the time, I had hoped it would be forever despite how illegal it was. My friends still think you're the 'one' – whatever that is. I believed that too at one point. And that's sad to admit and to feel. Love hurts us, no matter the sexuality."

Is love different with every different person you are with?

"It's never the same. It can't be. You are different people. Love changes you and how we love is different because of past loves. You can't control love, but you can manage it. You can control your feelings."

He said that although love isn't his focus, who he chooses to love will always remain his choice.

"The whole love is love thing means that it's my choice. Mind your own business. We all love. No matter race, sexuality, gender, career – it's untouchable. There are positives and negatives to it.

"I'm cynical with it. I don't think I need to fall in love or settle down. Do I want to? Yes. I'm human. But love is complicated. I'm not hopeful, I'm realistic when it comes to this subject. Everyone wants to hear those three words. And everyone should be able to openly. But will we? Love is the biggest thing we do. The first thing we do. The last thing we do. Ultimately, we have the ability to love as gay people and now we have the right to if we want to do so."

Movies and novels always showed me what love was. But they weren't true. They were fiction.

Love is fact. Love is different and looks different to how it was portrayed when I grew up. And despite our community having to fight hard for it every step of the way, we have always felt and known love.

I grew up with poor representation in the subject. I thought it was unrealistic, unattainable in the way "others" had it. I sometimes wonder if it still is. If we are bruised by our struggle. If our past has created a present that some of us find harder to navigate. We've made our own rules, and some can't play by them. But without love, we are starving ourselves.

Everyone deserves to experience it openly. In whatever way works for them. It's the one relationship that we experience the same as everyone else. However, it's one we weren't allowed at first.

It's still a struggle. We still have a fight. Yes, we can love easier these days, thankfully. But two men or two women holding hands in the street or kissing will still get abuse or double takes. We'll still feel awkward at times in declaring it. Shouting it from the rooftops.

Nothing changes the fact that love is love. It feels the same for us all and is completely unique at the same time. It's universal.

When I was younger and before love existed to me, I assumed that the concept of love was perfect. I assumed it would make me rounded if and when it came. I assumed Meg had it. Her characters did and that laugh surely showcased it. But love is not perfect. It's not definable by a person. We'll never experience the love we might think we deserve.

We all deserve better.

Or the love you see in movies, read in books or that is portrayed in *Fifty Shades of Grey*. I repeat. This is not a Disney movie. You are not Snow White. No one will come and kiss you, waking you from a spell, and you will not have seven men who will basically serve you until you die.

Lucky Snow!

Love is toxic.

Love is beautiful.

Love is hate.

Hate is love.

Love is love.

I don't think I've ever had a healthy relationship with love. It started as a forbidden fruit and now it's something I think about too much. But then, no one really has a healthy relationship with it. We can't. Because we can't control it. There are elements in our control, granted. Thankfully, people, marches and pride have allowed us to love more openly. The way we should all be able to. But we can't control it.

It's meant to be indescribable, unpredictive and life-changing. The only thing we know is this. We should be able to love outside of closets, in clothes we want to wear, in the streets and in the bedrooms. All of our letters in the LGBTQIA+ community deserve it. It separates us all, but also brings us together. Love shows us that it's okay to love. Love is the same for everyone. The only difference is that we had to wait for a green light before we could do it openly.

Gay love is no different to straight love. Straight love is no better than gay love. Love is love and it unites us all.

It might not complete us; nor does it need to. But it will complement us. If we let it. And the beauty is, we are all allowed to do it.

We'll have what she's having.

couple

/ˈkʌp(ə)l/

---

noun

1. two people or things of the same sort considered together.
    "a couple of girls were playing marbles"

2. two people who are married or otherwise closely associated
    romantically or sexually.
    "in three weeks the couple fell in love and became engaged"

verb

3. link or combine (something) with something else.
    "a sense of hope is coupled with a palpable sense of loss"

4. mate or have sexual intercourse.
    "as middle-class youth grew more tolerant of sex, they started
    to couple more often"

conversations with a couple

Couples. The mere term makes me, as a single person, shudder.

It's powerful, isn't it? The word itself feels strong, together, united. That's what a couple is. People who got their shit together and made it work. Because it's a job. We know this. We know that the honeymoon period does not last forever, and we know that being in a couple means putting in effort.

Putting them first.

Communicating.

Choosing them.

Prioritising.

Ignoring your selfish traits. Thinking of another person. Making it work. Love, that was the easy part, that was the job application that you passed with flying colours. Well done. Love, especially now being able to do it freely and legally, was a breeze. But the couple bit. That's the hard part. Now comes the work.

That's what scares me about couples. That, along with any couples who seem to have successfully nailed it.

How the hell have they nailed it? How can they endure each other forever?

When did they reach the Holy Grail and become so bloody perfect? Powerful. United. Together.

Couples. They scare me and fascinate me. Because how, in a community of desire, open relationships, hook-up apps, people frowning at us holding hands in the street and thirst traps ready to blow up every second, have they dodged the bullets? Endured. Survived.

What was their secret?

❧

Five years ago, I stood next to someone at a hotel reception desk. We were both checking in, or at least I assume he was too. We were strangers.

I was in Mexico for a wedding. A location ceremony always felt just that extra bit special. An event, spanning across multiple days. Allowing you to enjoy a moment and live amongst love at its highest point in a foreign place. Then go home, back to reality and FaceTimes with your mum asking what you're having for dinner. It was single life escapism.

I'd never fancied Cancún, but it was warm, beautiful and all inclusive. A holiday. A break. A wedding. Seeing two friends, a happy couple, marry.

"We have a lovely room for you both," the receptionist said with a beaming smile. I frowned at her instantly. The stranger next to me, who she'd confused as my partner, shot a look my way, and I blushed with embarrassment. He smiled. I wanted the ground to swallow me up. This was a couples' resort, of course; why would a single guy be checking in alone to a couples' resort?

Ground swallow me up. Now.

"No, sorry. We aren't together. It's just me." I laughed and rolled my eyes. Completing my single comedy act. To be fair, it was lovely that she suggested we might be together. That two men could be here romantically. Normal. But this moment was not enjoyable.

My fake husband-stranger smiled again, staying mute. Making me feel even more awkward, alone, embarrassing me further.

Stop talking, Daniel.

"I'm here for a wedding. Not mine, obviously." I laughed and rolled my eyes again. Then a tall, model-like lady came over and joined the handsome man who wasn't talking and put her arm around him. They stepped away from me as I continued to check in and I'm sure they both started sniggering at the mess-up. I blushed red. As if this wasn't hard enough. Single, attending a wedding full of couples. *Powerful couples that had their shit together.* Here I was, solo, being forced into a coupling because that was the "norm." Even for me, a gay man. That's what happened in a couples' resort. Single people be aware.

However, this was not the only time this has happened, I'm embarrassed to say. Once, just over a year ago, I sat working from a trendy London eatery. I'd been tapping away on my laptop, agonising over an unmanageable workload while sipping on an iced latte. Yes, I realise I sound like one of *those* people. The latte also was made with oat milk...

Do you hate me?

Suddenly, a lady plunged into the seat opposite me and introduced herself. She was called Vicky, and she had been running late due to a meeting but was here now.

Hi, Vicky.

I stared, confused, while she apologised for being late, again, and started to take off two of her seven layers. She smiled. Then the realisation set in.

"Oh my god, are you not Max?"

I was not Max. Vicky was here for a blind date. The hostess, who clearly couldn't be bothered to look any harder, searched for a single man and decided that I was Max. I, amongst tables of couples, was her date. We laughed, awkwardly. I joked that she wasn't my type.

Shut up, Daniel.

Then she found her man. Later, her and Max sent me over an espresso martini. I'm not totally sure why, but I accepted it. They felt sorry for my single self. I raised my glass and acknowledged a thank you, then downed the drink.

To Max and Vicky.

I bet they are married now. *Bastards.*

I share this because, wherever you go, regardless of sexuality, people are so quick to couple you up. Dinner, cinema, holidays, working from a café. More acceptable when there are two. I might have been intimidated by couples, but it turns out people are even more unsettled by the singles. The universe wanted me in a pairing. Because that was the norm. That is what's comfortable. Duos. That's what we should be in. Even us gays. Couples. And when you aren't in one, you notice them more.

They are everywhere. Holding hands. Kissing in line for restaurants. On planes. On trains. On buses. The other week I even saw two loved-up colleagues in Pets at Home.

You have to be kidding me!

Flying solo makes you acutely aware of the fact you are ALONE. But this is my point of view, and we are the ones that people fear. The singles. Regardless of how we feel. We are conditioned into thinking that a partner will complete us, and when we don't have one, we either look incomplete, feel incomplete or are a threat. A couple is the one relationship that we need to have to fit in and make others feel comfortable. It's the relationship that we *should* be in through the eyes of society. And a couple makes "different" people a little more normal. Less threatening.

Yippee.

In the beginning, it's fun. Everything at the start of an intimate relationship is exciting. There is an adrenaline driving you through this fun period. Encouraging you, making you smile, laugh and get excited. The honeymoon. A new beginning without knowing where it will take you. A period you just enjoy, and as it gets better, you become even more surprised. Even more committed. Insatiable for more of them. Thrill.

The morning sex, the conversations, the late-night phone calls, the evening sex. Ecstasy. Getting ready and putting on the good outfits because you care. Making effort, worrying about your hair and making sure you look okay. *Worrying you look okay.* Then changing your outfit again. *The previous outfit looked better, but you want to be sure.* Butterflies. You are feeling stomach-tingling butterflies. You want this to go okay. You don't want the honeymoon to end.

No one does.

Frankly, getting into a relationship might just be worth it for those first few months of passion. Even writing about it is making me lust for it.

Re-downloads Tinder.

However, that's what it is. A lust. A moment. A honeymoon. And it's called that for a reason. Pretty soon, late-night phone calls for an hour make you frown rather than smile.

Frankly, who has that time?

Who also wants to hold a phone that long? Your arm will be aching. Especially if it's a FaceTime. You roll your eyes at the number flashing up, *it's him again*, and you actually relish in the nights that you have the bed all to yourself. That whole bed to starfish in and snore or not hear their annoying repetitive breathing. *Bliss.* Their snoring, which was once cute, piglet like, is now annoying and causing bags under your eyes. You resent them. They did this. They made you look like this. You come to hate the nights that they are in your bed. Then you feel bad. You'll miss them, briefly. See them, then need nights apart again. A relationship circle. Soon, you'll move past the honeymoon period. You'll wonder how you fitted in sex five times a week, preferring to snooze in the morning rather than get it up. Sex will become something on your to-do list, but not the most important thing. But it's worth it. You are in a partnership. You got what you wanted.

Right?

A relationship that's going somewhere, finally more than just a flash in the pan, something that comforts you. Something that feels right. Instead of the tired game-playing, it becomes like an old pair of well-worn slippers, snug and reassuring. You have become a couple. Goal achieved.

But the confusing thing about this word, or should I say, branding, is that you are therefore forever associated or linked to another person. You are not a single. You are a plus one. A pair. The mere definition of the word suggests that you are *two people or things of the same sort considered together.*

Considered together.

Is this the goal that we wanted? Is this the couple we want to become? We strive, we swipe, we yearn to be in this duo. Complete our lonely solo act. Be "normal." I can't help but fear: in our quest for a match, do we lose ourselves, and is it worth it?

What are we coupling up for?

❧

Perfect. What an ugly word.

We all know that this is a fake term. A word that we put on a pedestal and aspire to be. I've often pondered the *perfect* couple.

Does it exist? The recipe for them, the attributes, the appropriate age gap, the ease, the right amount of passion and jealousy. The sex. Oh god, the sex needs to be good.

I'm aware most people will argue that this doesn't exist. I know this deep down too. Most people in their current couples will tell me it doesn't exist. The friends in our community who are in a couple tell me it's hard. Harder for us than heterosexuals. *I believe this.* Some even tell me that perhaps we aren't meant to be in monogamous relationships. *It's not realistic for us.* I worry this is also true.

Perfect is an idealisation, right? For every sexuality. But if that's true, why can't I stop imagining people who look like they have achieved it? Especially in the heterosexual world, leading the jealousy we all feel towards their somewhat perfect lives. Their portrayal of it across social, news and one hundred and forty-character tweets.

They have it.

Kate and William, Chrissy Teigen and John Legend, Barack and Michelle. *Got it.* If they have their own issues, problems and struggles, we aren't seeing it. Or I'm ignoring it. Barack and Michelle. I mean, that's "it," right? *I bet they don't argue!* But then I think about the people who I once thought had "it." Brad and Jen had it all, until they didn't. Brad and Angelina had it all, until they didn't. My mum and dad...

I realise that I held so many straight relationships in high regard, even though loads of the ones I have rated have ended. But I ignore this. I turn my back on it. Replace it with beautiful new examples that I look up to. Hetero couples that "have it." Perfectly. And despite the LGBTQIA+ community clearly having some contenders too, I'm doubtful if we can achieve the same level of coupledom. Perfection.

Neil Patrick Harris seems to have an amazing marriage and family set up. Matt Bomer seems completely happy and content in his love life. Ellen DeGeneres and Portia have been going strong for twelve years of marriage. *Twelve years!!!!!* But perfect? These people seem just as happy as the heterosexual ones. Just as Instagram "perfect." But something won't let me fully believe it. I can't. I've convinced myself they are selling a lie.

Maybe they aren't monogamous. Maybe they have side bits. I'm sure they argue, have heated text debates, sometimes even sleep in separate rooms. I bet they snore too.

For some warped reason, I can only see perfect existing for heterosexual couples. It's not that I don't want it to happen for "us"; I crave it and daydream about it constantly. Two words: *Jake Gyllenhaal.* But when I wake up, drink my coffee and get back to work and reality, I have a sense of disappointment.

Relationships end. The honeymoon period ends. Especially in the LGBTQIA+ community. I've seen it. It's not my fault that I think this way. I'm conditioned to think this way. Due to the history of LGBTQIA+, the branding and the provocative nature we project, I have been tuned into thinking that we couldn't have it all. We could have a portion, yes, but not everything. I'd seen the non-sticking couples of our community. Witnessed wandering eyes first hand, not encountered "forever" relationships and assumed everything would expire eventually.

Open relationships. Distractions. Thirsty Thursday. Cheats. Lies. Aubergine emojis. I've also had the STIs to prove it.

Shout out to my ex.

Perfect was an ugly word. *A lie.* I knew this. A pill I swallowed and often believed. But a dangerous one, as I could only see it working for straight couples. My head told me that there were too many roadblocks for a couple in our community to survive.

It still does.

❧

Of course, I've sampled them. I know that being in a couple is work. I've been in one and I can attest. I clocked in and out, put in the hours, grafted, wondered if I was doing a good job. Worried about the review. Desperately tried to impress the boss, and still, the contract finally came to an end. But when we work, we earn money; we do it for a reason. So, what's our reason in a couple? Because frankly, I'm having doubts if it's worth the paycheck.

Our community deals with being in a couple differently. The other week I went on a date – a pre-couple screening – with a bisexual man. He told me that being in a couple with a guy is so much different to being in a couple with a girl. For us gay men, subjects are discussed much earlier; a more open conversation is on the table and it's more than likely the other person is talking to more people than just you. Their eggs are not solely in your basket. Then when you are in the couple, you have decisions to make that come up far more often than in a heterosexual couple. Sex, relationship rules, threesomes, open relationships, cheating: all more apparent in a homosexual coupling.

Why?

Because we are different. We believe we are different. We do things differently. We continue to evolve because we have, because we can, because that's what we know. So, our couplings follow the same suit. The date had a point. We *worked* on our couples, put in the effort for the hope it would work out. Not always believing it can.

A couple in our community is complicated. I already know this to be true. Currently, I know two couples that are in open relationships. One that is public knowledge and one that isn't. Behind closed doors. Three couples I know who have had threeways, but only together. Two couples that are married, one that also adopted a child. One couple that is engaged to be married. And the longest standing gay relationship that I know is currently at nine years. I also have a friend who is the guest star in another couple's relationship. A role he plays just three times a month. Then there are seven gay friends who do not want to ever be in a couple. You see? Complicated. Not simple. Not all it's cracked up to be. Even the couples that seem happy and secure often tell me they are aware it might not be forever. The work, the effort, the time – this job might end.

Why do we feel this is our reality?

●

"The 'perfect' couple is often described and perceived externally rather than by the couple themselves. We see 'perfect' lifestyles and idyllic displays of affection and we easily stick on labels in a bid to prove perfect love and romance exist," Judi James says.

And that's exactly what I'd done. Idealised these unattainable hetero beings, ignoring the flaws and watching their lives through filters. A fantastic view that we are only merely spectating and not getting a behind the scenes tour of. Because we all know: behind the scenes is often a reality that we want to hide. We don't want to show what happens when the cameras stop rolling. Our realities.

As a gay man, I've been in a "couple" – I've known that it's not perfect, understood my own flaws and endured arguments that at times felt like World War 2. And all of these couples ended.

My good friend Darren always says to me, "a couple is a fleeting time in your life, but everything has an expiry date. More so for gay men. We expire early." *We are fucked.* He says that with wit, but a glimmer of honesty; he believes it. And it's a feeling that I've had for a long time.

Can we beat this gay expiry date?

●

I'm cynical. I know this at thirty-three because I'm still single and pondering if a couple can survive. I want it to. But society, history, community and the fact that nothing has stuck makes me question. So, I wanted to chat to a couple that are gay and seem to have something that I coveted. Something that didn't look simple but seemed not to have an expiry either. As close to perfect as I might ever get in "our" world.

Chris and Dan. I loved their love. And despite them repeatedly telling me that their love wasn't perfect, I viewed their relationship through rose-tinted glasses. Because it looked fucking incredible. As merely a spectator of their life, here is what I saw.

They live on a farm. They have two pigs, Robert Redford and Barbara Windsor; three dogs, Stanley, Elsie and Dolly; ducks; chickens; bees; and a goat called Alf. Both of them are kind. Both caring, interested in what you have to say and full of heart. Both into each other. *Goals.* As an outsider looking in, I think they pretty much have it made. But I was outside, looking in. "Come live with us for a week and you'll know it's not," Dan joked. And so, much to his regret, I did, and we sat down to chat.

Chris: "I'm slightly nervous. I wonder how many arguments we'll have after this."

Couple is the end goal. It's something I aspire to but that I'm not confident I'll get.

Chris: "To me, a couple was a realistic goal. But through being in one, my perception of what a couple is has changed."

Dan: "I never thought about a life without being in a couple." Dan confessed that his first and last relationship is with Chris. He hasn't been with anyone else. "When I was younger, growing up, I was never exposed to gay people. Even representation wasn't available. But despite this, all I knew was couples. All of my family are still with their partners, no divorce. So, in my head when I came to terms with who I fancied, for me, it was the same goal. Find my couple. Be in it for the long run."

Chris: "Even though there was not one couple I can publicly think of that was gay at the time, I was the same. All I'd known was couples and that was what I wanted."

Chris and Dan both experienced their starts to gay life differently. Chris had relationships before Dan, with the hope to find "the one," and Dan fell in love with the first person he met.

Dan: "We grew up in a period of change. Gay men weren't seen as couples; they were seen as singles. But gradually as we moved forward this was challenged and different milestones allowed us to be seen."

Chris: "I jumped from boyfriend to boyfriend, since I was sixteen. I was always looking for someone who I could settle down with. That was my goal."

Dan: "I just wanted to get out of the deep closet I was in. I never thought it was possible to get married; I thought I'd be able to be a couple, but I didn't think, what's my end goal? We got engaged and it was still illegal to get married at the time. We were heading for a civil partnership, the best we could do as a couple."

Dan and Chris got together after meeting on Grindr, an app they both acknowledged has changed throughout the years.

Dan: "It wasn't a sex app at the time, or at least, not just that. I was in the closet and needed to find someone. Grindr allowed me to come out at my own pace. Chris was on it to get laid!"

Chris: "Hang on a minute! I was on there, yes, maybe to 'hook-up,' but that wasn't it! Ultimately, I wanted someone. It was just an accessible app at the time."

After meeting and going on dates, their relationship was a whirlwind. They both stated that they instantly knew this was "different" to other feelings and fell in love.

Chris: "Dan didn't come out until after he met me."

Dan: "He was my reason, but he never forced me."

Chris: "I was hesitant, though. I didn't want to be his reason to come out and change his life. That was a lot of pressure on one person. What if it went wrong?"

Dan: "But it went oh so right, Chrissy."

It wasn't plain sailing, though; after a wobble on Dan's side after worrying about being gay, the pair had a "break."

Chris: "I had just got over a heartbreak and wasn't going to date for a while. And then Dan came out of the blue, inconveniently, but because Dan wasn't out, he couldn't fully cope with coming out and falling in love. So, he pushed me away."

Dan: "It was never about Chris. I just went from zero to one hundred."

Chris: "Gay whiplash."

Dan: "Exactly, most people hope to hit one hundred, and I did it in a matter of weeks. So, I pushed him away. But Chris was patient, and deep down I knew what I wanted, even if it scared me."

Chris: "I didn't need another friend, and him having a wobble made me protect myself. Then all of a sudden, he pulled me back and faced his fear. Which is actually incredible when you think about it."

Three months into their relationship, they were happy and content. And it wasn't long until they moved in and made plans for their future. To them, this was it.

Dan: "I think we were on the same page at the same point. Chris falls in love quickly, but we both felt it."

Chris: "When Dan asked me to move in with him, I thought to myself, okay, I've moved in with exes before, but something feels different. It felt like he was serious; for me this felt like the home straight."

Dan: "But we've never compared ourselves. We don't follow

hetero norms, don't feel like we need to do things to fit in, which ended up working for us. There was a moment that I thought – right, I'm never going to do the 'gay thing' as I'd found the one already. I never had the freedom to be gay first. It isn't that I wanted that, or needed it, but I don't think you can be in a couple and not realise it. I'd never have that."

Chris: "That was a huge worry for me. But actually, there was something else that we had, an unspoken trust."

Dan: "I realised my own 'freedom' was just about being true to who I was. Just in being out and lucky to be in a relationship, that happened to be enough. We wrote our rules. That was enough."

Chris confessed he had an ideal in his mind of what a relationship should be.

Chris: "I feel like Dan was my first 'real' relationship. This was not a Disney storyline. I had held my breath through past relationships, not fully being myself because I wanted it to be perfect, to be who they wanted me to be. But with Dan I stopped the act of what I thought my partners needed. He allowed me to be me. I hadn't been my authentic self – I had been playing a character before. Which was unhealthy."

Dan: "I think I did change him, not because he needed to, but because he hadn't before felt like he could be himself."

Chris and Dan said that the base of their relationship is trust.

Dan: "Everyone goes into a relationship wanting it to work. Other than you, Dan! And that's what we did. Two feet in."

Chris: "I threw my heart into him."

Dan: "I think that's why we weren't scared for this interview. There is nothing you can't say to us together. If you aren't being your authentic self, the partner will find out."

Chris: "You can't hide from your partner. You can't be an act the whole time. To make it work, we have to be completely true and that's what I've learnt from this relationship."

Dan: "In our heads, everyone has an ideal of who we want to end up with. But the person we actually end up with is often different. You have sexual attraction and then you have the personality that you fall in love with. That doesn't always look or feel like what you might have imagined. That's why you have to be open to it. Luckily, we were each other's type, but it was more than that. Or I think so."

Chris: "Yeah, there's that – but also you have to have something invisible that can't be explained, something that works. An 'it' factor."

Dan: "Exactly, you could date someone who was your absolute type and be bored shitless in their company. Chris and I could live in a caravan park and be skint, but if we had each other, I know we'd be okay."

After getting engaged in 2012, the couple were due to get a civil partnership in 2014.

Chris: "I remember when Dan told me that we could actually get married, not just have the civil partnership. He shouted up the stairs and said, it's passed, we can actually get married."

Dan: "For us, it was never about getting married as a 'normal' person. It was about being equal. I didn't need to be normal; I needed equality. That's why we wanted marriage. Why should we be excluded from that for being gay? Our relationship was just as important. We didn't need to prove anything, we just wanted it."

Chris: "My reason was romance. I wanted marriage before it was even legal. I'm romantic. That is what I wanted."

Dan: "It also meant a lot to me that we had the same name. We are a team and that is proof. There are two of us. Well, five of us with the dogs."

In 2014, Chris and Dan became the first gay couple in Essex to get legally married.

Chris: "We are lucky. We feel lucky. I'm well aware people look at us via social and think we are one thing. But we have our struggles."

Dan: "We do have it all, I feel. But 'it all' means something different to us than what single people are perhaps looking for."

Chris: "Marriage and happiness are not the same word. Marriage can be going through bad times. But it's also a dedication to being together. We have it all – because we work for it. It doesn't mean that it's perfect. It's far from it. We have something brilliant."

Dan: "We have ups and downs, but actually as a couple we are incredibly lucky. I'm not one hundred per cent sure why, but we are."

The couple gave me a very honest look into their marriage, sharing the hard times that come with it.

Dan: "I don't find marriage difficult. I'm sure that's annoying to hear. If you pick the right person, it should make life easier. We have difficulties in our relationship, sure, but there isn't an itch happening."

Having always viewed their relationship through rose-tinted glasses, I asked if they thought that they, in being in a couple, are in the minority.

Chris: "I think location means everything. We were able to date without distractions, to focus on just us. And I think that helps your start."

Dan: "Yes, I think city gay men have more options. Maybe too many. I think if you came and lived in a small town, you'd fall in love and ease into a relationship, able to give it time."

They both agreed that we are still trying to shake the stigma of our past, the eighties and nineties, and find our pace.

Dan: "We are in the minority in the community. Well at least within the people we know. Most people aren't in couples or married. I believe we are still finding our way in a straight world. I think we still aren't widely sure about being in confident couples that last in our community. We want them, and a lot of people are in them, but still, there's so much doubt."

Dan and Chris say that it's a choice to be in a couple.

Chris: "Is being in a couple the best thing ever? No. Could I be without this? No."

Dan: "But it's a choice we make. If me and Chris split up, I don't think I'd marry again. Because I had that already."

Chris: "No, I wouldn't get married again either."

Dan: "We married the one we loved. We are realistic, and if we split, I'd feel like we failed. So, I wouldn't want to do it again."

The couple confessed that you have to keep on putting in effort, no matter how long you've been together.

Dan: "You have to keep the spark. Sounds basic, but it's true. I always tell Chris he looks amazing."

Chris: "Even on my worst day, he makes me laugh. If he can keep doing that, I think we'll be okay."

Is being in a couple the answer to happiness?

Chris: "I know this older gay man who is single and on Twitter. I don't know why, but there is a sadness in his tweets. I don't know him, but I think I'd worry when I'm older if I wasn't in a couple as a gay man. I'm not sure how happy I'd be outside of a couple when I'm older."

Dan: "I don't think you need to be in a couple to be happy. But perhaps it gives you something else. Comfort?"

Chris: "Most single gay people I know are always looking for something. So maybe there is an element of happiness that comes from reaching it. I don't think it's the ultimate answer, though. Everyone has a scary age, that one that we fear getting to."

Dan: "I guess I like to think that when you are older you have someone there. I think in later life, especially as a gay person, you need it, as you may choose not to have kids etc. But a partner complements you; it's not crucial, but it is sort of a blessing."

Both have said it's easier to be in a couple as a gay person, as any barriers you face you experience together.

Chris: "Being in a couple changed me, for the good. Helped me."

Dan: "Yeah, you are influenced by your partner."

Chris: "Everyone puts on a performance when you walk out the door, but with your partner is the one place you don't need to act. That's the way I feel."

Dan: "We help each other. A perfect couple doesn't exist. Don't be fooled. We are happy, but there is no such thing as perfect."

Chris: "Is being in a couple important to our community? I'm not sure. Yes, I wanted it and have it. But how much importance is there in it? I'm not sure."

Dan: "Being in a couple to me is nothing about being gay or straight, it's just having someone in life who helps ease it – or it should be. That is across the board."

Chris: "There's companionship in friendship too; perhaps a couple is whatever you need it to be. It's just nice having someone at the end of the day."

Dan: "Ultimately that's it. You have to put in effort constantly, it's hard, it's brilliant, it's work. But having that person you love to come home to – I couldn't think of a better reason to keep going. Keep working."

Chris: "As a community, we are different. But sometimes I don't think we realise the visibility that we give off."

Dan: "Yes, it's incredible to be a gay couple in a straight world. We are fortunate to be able to be that. The visibility we share, showing that a man and a man can have marriage, be in a couple and be together, is important."

Chris: "Perhaps that's what being in a couple in our community might do for others. Help to show that we can. And we can."

Dan: "The end goal should be happiness, regardless of being in a couple. For us, the couple made us happy. Maybe it is a rare thing, but I think anyone can have it."

After the interview we hugged, and Dan said one more thing.

Dan: "What we have, you can't have. No one can have what

others have; you have to find your own version of that. Not compare. That's the issue."

Chris: "Don't search for a person, search for happiness."

Dan: "Now get your trunks on; we are going in the hot tub. You're going home tomorrow, thank Christ."

❧

I realise that I get more cynical the longer that I'm single. That's okay. That's natural.

Judi James told me that "Perfect couples tend to only exist in sofa ads or in that over-filtered world of the social media influencer. 'Perfect' in real life usually means a relationship that is riddled with imperfections, compromises and lows as well as highs."

I think my fear and doubt has been born out of what I thought was a "realistic" view of a future as a gay man. A cushion for my heart.

The couples that I've idolised, both heterosexual and homosexual, clearly put in that work. Keep working. They have to. But Dan was right, it was time to stop comparing.

"We can't have what they have."

And perhaps we don't need to.

I know lots of LGBTQIA+ people who think we shouldn't conform to heteronormative traditions. Who declare this isn't for "us." That is one thing, and we are another. Why conform? Then there are people who find embracing those traditions empowering, a right, a privilege. We fought for this; we deserve it. Both have points. We are different and yet we are deserving.

For me, I still worry for my future couple – whatever it looks like. Will we have wandering eyes, desire a three-way with the farmer next door and eventually crave an open relationship – because we can? Because as a community we have written our own "love rules"? And that's okay – it's okay to worry. Every couple will face questions. Challenges. I've always known this. Maybe, as gay men, we just have slightly more openly obvious choices and problems to solve as couples. But until you are in one, you can't solve those problems, so why worry now? Because what I always forget is that when those obstacles come, you have someone else to do it with you. You aren't alone. That's what a couple is, regardless of how yours is or what rules you rightly follow.

Perhaps I've had a negative relationship with the thought of being in a couple.

Do they last in our community? Can we be monogamous? Can we survive?

Pushing my fears on how we do it differently. What I need to remember is this: no couple is the same. We have to ask ourselves what we want.

What do we really want?

What type of couple do we need for ourselves? We have to take risks and see for ourselves where that takes us.

Yes, couples scare me. Especially the happy, perfect-looking ones. They are intimidating and creating an unrealistic pressure mounting inside of me. But also, they don't exist. (Shout out to my friend Lou who always keeps it real with me and who has a fantastic coupling.) All of them are just working hard at what they have, unsure of their own expiry date. What Chris and Dan showed me is that maybe the work is worth it, even if the relationship expires eventually.

Judi James also suggests that "'Real' couples looking back on long-term relationships that have lasted decades often happily refer to them as though they have somehow survived a war." Perhaps the lucky ones are survivors.

Regardless of sexuality, no one knows their relationship's expiry date. So, what's the point in fearing it? I keep thinking of where

I might fail, or where it might go wrong, or how can it survive. But what if it does survive?

I'm still not sure if we can have the relationship that we desire without it having an end. But that's my own hang-up. *God, I'm a catch.* Perhaps I've not had a great relationship with couples because in reality, as a community we are still testing the water, finding our feet in a straight world.

Thankfully, some couples are making it visibly easier, showing people that we can ignore the expiry date. That being in one might just make our "different" lives a little easier. Even if it's just a companion for when we are older.

We write our own rules. One beautiful pairing (or thrupple) at a time.

a rant: gay-ging, our number is not up

We have parties to celebrate ageing.

Celebrate!

When I turned twenty-one, I cried. Not because of the lovely gifts, gestures and celebrations, but because of the fear bubbling inside me that I might no longer be a "twink" any more. I literally stood in Batchwood nightclub, St Albans, and cried. Actual tears. And I'm an ugly crier.

In a smelly bar, around so many first-year students who made me feel old (there was only a year and a half difference), I worried that I was "past it." Single and over. I also worried that I hadn't slept with enough men yet and that no one would fancy me. So, my bedpost notches would stay low. Fuck.

It didn't stay low.

It's laughable that this was my concern. My fear. Of course, my twink status lasted a few years longer. But that distress didn't go. Every year, every birthday, I assessed my age and worried that youth was slipping away. It was and is slipping away. That was factual. It still is factual, and I still obsess over it. But tears were not warranted. In fact, they are never warranted.

Heed this. Oh, how I wish I was twenty-one again. Obviously. I certainly wouldn't be crying, I'd be celebrating. Probably topless. Because that's what we do on birthdays. And we should. But it's only now that I realise why we celebrate. The privilege of it. The joy that you get from the fact that you get to keep going, move forward and live.

Age is just a number, but to me, to our community, it's a discriminative one. A swear word. Granted, we don't have biological clocks, but something is ticking. Counting down our diminishing relevance. So often I see people on Twitter referencing "younger gays" and how they have no idea what struggles were before them. They were lucky. But we are quick to forget. We were them; they will be us.

Struggles in our community have always been there and always will be in some capacity. The way we view age enforces this. It's so easy not to care when you have years ahead.

Twinks.

A good friend of mine, Rachel, always says that life can only be understood by looking back. But frankly, I don't have time to look back. I am ageing. As are we all.

We need to start celebrating. It's what birthdays are there for. I need to remember this. You need to remember this.

Note to self: I will stop lying about my age in certain situations. Okay, I will try to do this. I will stop comparing achievements by how old people are when they do it. We can and will achieve when we are ready to do so. I will stop asking Alexa how old certain celebrities are. Okay, I will try to do this too. I will enjoy the privilege of ageing.

I will enjoy living.

Community, our number isn't up even if sometimes we feel it is. Remind yourself of this daily.

The shelf does not exist. The shelf does not exist!

date

/deɪt/

---

verb

1. establish or ascertain the date of (an object or event).
    "they date the paintings to 1460–70"

2. reveal (someone) as being old-fashioned.
    "jazzy – does that word date me?"

conversations about dating

I have dated over one hundred men. Fact.

I know this because the year before last, I went on a quest. A journey. A new year's resolution to change my life. Determined to stop single life, fit in and find my normal.

Finally.

Because whether or not I think it will be "forever love," I've never stopped wanting to find out if it could be.

Did I win?

Clarify win.

That's a story for another book. But right now, I'm still dating. And, due to that fact, the number is now most certainly over two hundred. That makes me sweat.

Two hundred.

Two hundred possible husbands. Gone.

Two hundred expensive transactions.

Two hundred different people.

Two hundred people taking their time to go out with me.

Sweating.

It's a fact that actually makes me feel slightly sick inside. I realise there is a lot of pressure in the way that I'm describing it. That pressure is not just in the description, but also in myself too. I hate pressure. Despite this, I seem to put so much of it on this area of my life.

Pressure.

I am not a woman. I don't have a ticking time bomb, so my mum tells me. And men age better, *apparently.* But still, I worry. Sweat. Anxiety. Waking up in the middle of the night in the realisation that I'm *still* single. Often going over the two hundred men that could have been.

Could they have?

Okay, one hundred and ten that could have been. At least ninety probably didn't want me. Potentially a smart move on their part, to be honest. There. That's what I do. That's what I do when it comes to dating. Reason with myself about why I'm single. Why I'm still dating and why I haven't settled. Why others wouldn't want me. Settled is a disgusting word. Especially when you're dating. It's also completely offensive.

We shouldn't settle.

I know this. But dating had no longer become the fun thing I did during my twenties in between more serious relationships. And it *was* fun. The number of new bars, pubs or crazy golf venues I could go to now was limited. I'd been there. Drank that. Played that. Tried and failed.

Dating in your thirties as a gay man was a ticking time bomb. I'm sorry, Mum, you are wrong. I hear it ticking daily. Hourly. Every minute. I am *Hook* in my own ticking hell and I want to get out of it. The fun times have evaporated and I'm exhausted. Small talk, apps, witty conversation, banter, exercise, shaving, maintenance – all requirements when dating. And I'm knackered.

When you are a gay man in your thirties, losing twink status by the hour, this relationship is hard. No, it's terrifying.

Sweat. Anxiety. Waking up in the middle of the night with the realisation I'm still single.

You need dating rules. As dating could be our most pressured relationship of all. Because like my friend Chris said, "He feels sad for the old gay guy who's alone with no companion."

And in the gay community, if you are gay, old and single, you are apparently dead. Gulp.

❧

Dating can be ignited from just about any scenario. No. Dating *can* be ignited from *any* scenario. You name it, a spark can come.

It can come from drinks out with friends, eyes across the bar and a build-up of tension. Standing next to someone at a urinal or chatting to *that* colleague from work as they make tea the wrong way – *never milk first* – but you don't care because you're flirting your ass off and they're hot. It can come from shopping, ordering coffee or that annoying but sexy man from the call centre who keeps ringing you about the accident that you didn't have. The same man who makes you start to consider causing an accident just to speak with him again.

Breaks leg immediately in train station, blames wet floor. Hello, George, now I need you...

Clubs, supermarkets, Twitter, speed dating, holidays, commutes. All possible meeting places. It can even come from attending a funeral of an old teacher whom you admired. Yes, it happened. Anywhere. The possibilities are endless and available. All we have to do is one simple thing: look up. See who is around and engage. And yet, we look down; I look down. We ignore those potential people around us, who could be eye fucking you on the train, trying to make their move, and concentrate instead on our phones.

Single people now rely on tech. Both a blessing and a curse. Something that takes away a lot of the excitement from an event that could be life changing. The thing we've been looking for... But we have to. Don't we? If we don't, and everyone else is, we (I) worry that we won't be able to date at all. No one else is looking up.

Dating now starts with a profile. Welcome to single life. Tinder, Bumble, Hinge, Grindr, Scruff, Instagram DMs, Snapchat...your future matches all in the palm of your hand. Easy access. Often requiring three simple things.

ASL?

Three loaded letters that carry a lot of information: *age, stats, location*. The foundations of a great relationship, or a hook-up. I'm often not sure which. Because what I've come to realise is this: dating is a steady stream of interviews that you don't prepare for. But should.

What are you looking for?

The single most used question when it comes to dating life as a gay man. In two hundred matches, I have to have been asked that at least by eighty per cent of them. And, interestingly, it's actually an incredibly hard question to answer. What are we searching for? Let's face it, the LGBTQIA+ are "looking" for a multitude of things.

Casual, hook-ups, three-ways, husbands, wives, second husbands, right now, HNH, second wives, polyamorous, S&M, outdoors, dates...the one.

Our overly active community was constantly searching. Keeping minds and body parts open to potential. But to begin the quest, it helps to know what you want. And can you answer that honestly?

❧

Twelve months ago, I was looking for coffee. It was midway through the week, and it felt like it'd been a month since the weekend.

Yes, that sort of week. During a work from home day, I went in search and wanted to break my routine.

Pandemic, bedroom office, global crisis, desperate to see people, going crazy.

That was me. So, I walked out of my way to a destination unknown and stumbled across a little coffee shop. *The Brothers.* Unplanned, desperately needed and welcoming. Then I sipped the coffee. You know when you get a good cup and accidentally confess how good it is out loud and without meaning to through noise.

Mmhhmm.

Yes, that was me. It was good. I was hooked and so I started dating the coffee shop. Daily, I'd go back. Each time I got to know a little more about the brothers who owned it. Italians. Friendly. Smiled a lot. Not only did I enjoy the coffee, I enjoyed their faces. I enjoyed the fact that they'd learnt my name and that I'd learnt theirs. They asked me how I was. Made me feel valued and seemed to care about my answers. Pretty perfect if you ask me.

After just one month, the coffee shop owners knew my ASL, drinks order and shoe size. They knew that I came in at 10.20 a.m. daily. They knew that I sometimes came in again around 14.10 p.m. if the caffeine hit was required.

It was usually required.

If it was a Saturday, they knew that I'd be tempted to have one of their quinoa croissants that were fresh from the oven. *A food-gasm in pastry form.* These strangers had seen me when I was happy, sad, distracted, angry and lost. Frustrated with work, on calls or lost in a Twitter rabbit hole. *Chrissy Teigen, you have a lot to answer for.* They accepted me however I looked. Which was a task, considering they'd seen me sweaty, exhausted and horrendous multiple times in their presence. Not to mention the number of times that I'd been unshaven, tired and carrying an amount of luggage that could rival the Kardashian clan. They'd seen me. All of me. The me that

I'd hide in certain scenarios. The me that only my sister sees, and that's because we live together. All my flaws. All my traits. Seen. And still they asked me how I was, kept the relationship going.

It wasn't for the three pounds ten that I spent most days. Yes, I'm sure they appreciated that, but these were people that were genuinely interested. Much more than a warm cup of good coffee. Perhaps that was their intention, their act to lure me in. Make me come back. But I like to believe it was more.

This was a union without pressure. Without façade. No guard up, no wrong first impressions, no visual pretence or exposure to my flaws. I was an oat cappuccino with an occasional quinoa croissant. Simple. Effortless. The way it should be.

Why couldn't we date like this? Dating was not a simple coffee order. It was a venti, extra hot, half whole milk, one quarter one per cent, one quarter non-fat, extra hot, split quad shots (one and a half shots decaf, two and a half shots regular), no foam latte, with whip, two packets of Splenda, one sugar in the raw, a touch of vanilla syrup and three short sprinkles of cinnamon. *Keep them short!* The most over-complicated coffee order that you can get; I googled. And to be honest, with so much detail riding on it, probably not worth the order, and you'd most certainly get burnt. *Extra-hot, WTF.* Brutal, occasionally rewarding, but often a waste of effort. The oat cap was easy, felt good.

So why did we over-complicate our order? Why, when it comes to dating, do we need more? Give more? Want more? Why can't it be simple?

❧

Age. The ghost in my closet, the monster under my bed and the nightmare that keeps me up at night. It scared me. I've ranted about it, you know this. You read it.

At twenty-four, I had basically assumed that my thirties were a decade to fear and in gay years meant that I was nearing retirement. I'd probably have grey hair. Not the hot Phillip Schofield grey. The hideous type. Nigel from EastEnders. *Sorry Nigel.* I'd be cross-stitching, doing Pilates to keep my limbs supple and I'd have a laundry room within my house.

Surely by the age of thirty I'd have a house.

Not a flat share. Not living with my sister. At least that's what I thought, looking forward, at the ripe age of my early twenties. A decade quickly approaching, filled with quality time spent with close friends and us all wearing slippers.

My thirties did not look like that. I do not own slippers. Quality time, what was that? My hours are occupied juggling a work diary, grabbing dates where I can and deadlines. Lots of deadlines. A clown spinning plates, *badly.*

Dating was just another plate. But a time-consuming one. It became a laborious task. As a single gay man, it had become by far the most consuming thing in my life. And I defy any single person to tell me otherwise. I wish someone had told me to hurry up in my twenties. Instead, I was told, *you've got loads of time. Don't worry.* Unsurprisingly, the people who told me I had loads of time were not single. Not dating. Not in the boat I was sailing. If they had been, they'd have been sinking too.

Why in my thirties am I still dating? Age was and is creeping up upon me and I'm still in the same place. Still dancing on my own. Thank you, Robyn. To anyone in their twenties reading this: *hurry the fuck up.*

I'm reluctant to use the term, "back in my day," as I still feel like this is "my day." You do that when you get older – you push back old age and feel that you still have it. That you're still youthful. *Fools.* Back in my day, dating apps did not exist and a phone was deemed cool if it had the game Snake on it. That's the first phone I had.

Nokia. Apple were a few years off releasing their first iPhone and camera phones had just been discharged onto the world, allowing dick pics to become a thing. Lucky us. A pixelated penis that filled a tiny screen, making everyone look hung.

They wish.

The computer was a closeted gay man's best friend. If you weren't out, or if you were a little lost, you might have had a Gaydar profile. It was essentially the desktop version of Grindr minus exact locations. If you were out, you went out. Meeting people organically was both harder and easier "back then." And here's why.

When I finally came out, I used to love going to the local gay pub or a bar that was "friendly" or on the occasional trip to Soho, London. If you were lucky enough to have gone to G-A-Y at the Astoria before it closed, then you will know how good clubbing was back then.

Okay, I do sound old.

It was a moment. There were no phones to stare down at and search where the nearest hottie was. You weren't scrolling Instagram to see what everyone else was up to. You were in a moment. Your moment. Moments where you'd meet someone random on a night out and snog them on the stage or the dance floor. Moments where you didn't rely on technology to aid your horn. Times where you'd dance with your friends drunkenly and hug strangers. Who knows where those snogs would lead? Sex back at theirs or in a side alley. Or, like me, a polite number exchange and the hope that you might go on a date. Okay, and the occasional sex back at theirs. You'd get lost in "your" time. It was fun.

It was easier because you didn't have the distraction of everything else. Your options were in front of you and not limitless. Which was a good thing. And, on the other hand, it was harder because those moments weren't as accessible. Our current "right now" culture was years away, and these interactions took planning and time. They came about with the blue moons. Rare and few, easy but hard, and always special, regardless of how special they really were. Effort was required. More than you could ever imagine. It sometimes felt like you were living a secret life, all in the search of coming back out of the closet all over again. Dating till you didn't need to date.

Of course, by the time I went to uni, Facebook came along. Then came the iPhones.

Rejoice.

But dating wasn't as online and available as it is right now. You did the groundwork yourself. Imagination played its part. I remember if friends met boys, the first thing we'd say was "describe them." If you were lucky, they'd have a Myspace profile, or if you were at uni, they'd have Facebook. But the odds of meeting them in a club or a bar were higher than if they'd met online, and communication was everything.

It was exciting. We swam in a pond that was small and limited. Age wasn't an issue. We had time. Swimming in the hope that you'd meet a match that would stick.

Could it stick?

That pond, however, quickly became an ocean. *Thank you, technology.* Now the match options are endless, and we don't have time. Age is an issue. I'm not sure which was better for dating...

Now or then?

❧

PizzaExpress. The restaurant name that you never want to hear for your first date. Ever. Even if you are a pizza lover. Especially after you've had sex with a waiter who worked there. Surely there are also more interesting options?

Come on!

Nando's would be more exciting. Or maybe even a Harvester with that all-you-can-eat salad buffet in a bowl. I bloody loved that salad, with the bacon bits that you can sprinkle on top of it. *Do they still do that salad bar?*

The restaurant choice, despite my love of dough, should have been a red flag from the offset, but I was giddy in lust. I was eighteen years old. It was my first official date with a boy.

A boy.

Of course, I felt equal levels of nervousness and excitement. *IT WAS A DATE WITH A BOY.* Up until this point, it was the only date I'd ever truly cared about. Because this was not a drill; I had a date with a boy. I was gay now. It's what I did.

Pete. That was his name.

Pete, I know we are now friends, so if you are reading this, I'm sorry. You were shit.

I'd fancied him for ages, everyone knew this. Friends would call him "Lips." It was his nickname, but I didn't use it. "Pete" was more BF material than "Lips." The nickname was for the very obvious reason that he had a huge pair of them. Plump. Cushioned. Non-surgical. Lips. Lips to envy and admire.

Pete didn't really show any interest in me at first. In fact, he'd shown more interest in just about every other person before me.

Another red flag.

When I say interest, it was his interest inside of them. He was a shagger. A player. One who also happened to like PizzaExpress. I, on the other hand, was a hopeless dater. A romantic. Wistful, craving, hopeful. *Forever bloody hopeful.* Innocent. So, despite the location and the "type" he projected, the date was on.

On the night itself, I had been so consumed by emotions and nerves, I hadn't realised how much my hair was now swimming in wet-look gel. I'd been reapplying to ensure perfection. But grease was the word, and I needed it not to be. After de-gelling and changing again, I got the number nine bus. Looking back, I probably looked awful. I had worn a beige shirt, which on pale skin made me look ill, and bell-bottom jeans. *I'm surprised I never fell over.* To complete the hopeless look, I wore smart old black school shoes. *WHY?* See, tragic. Regardless, there I was, eighteen and ready to meet my future. The one. A pair of lips for our date on Southend high street...at PizzaExpress.

On the slow journey to the date, I tried hard not to fantasise about where this first date would lead. Not marriage, but maybe a happy life together? Because I did that. A lot. I imagined a life for each date before we had even got to kiss. Before sex. Before seeing the penis size. Before knowing if he was a top or bottom. Before asking if he even wanted marriage or kids. A love story played out before my eyes. Pure ecstasy and over-expectation ticking over in my mind. Tonight was the same. He was the one. Lucky Lips.

It was a Friday night and I think the only reason that he'd agreed to eating out was because he hated cooking and needed to line the stomach.

Red flag.

A stomach, which happened to look like a washboard, created without any effort at all, that belonged on a *Men's Health* front cover.

Bastard.

A pizza-eating, top shagger, plump-lipped Adonis. But here it was. My chance to start something real and stop swimming. A date with a boy. Otherwise, before I knew it, I'd be nineteen and worrying that I was getting too old. Time was ticking.

So, at eighteen years old, I was ready. This was it. Stop looking at other men and have sex with one person for the rest of my life, never to experience other people or dating anyone else. Slippers by thirty, for sure.

A perfect plan with only one problem. Pete was not thinking

like this. To be honest, I'm pretty sure the only thing he'd thought about was the pizza he'd be having. He definitely hadn't worried about his outfit, or his hair.

Still looked hot.

Our short dinner, where he ordered repeat Jack Daniel's and Coke to the table, was exactly what the restaurant had insinuated. Express. Fast, strained conversations and small talk. I'd nervously attempted questions around work, growing up and what his favourite movie was.

DJ, still spoke to parents, American Pie.

He didn't ask me...

Red flag.

He seemed to enjoy his spicy hot pizza with a side of garlic bread, though.

Garlic bread!

I had attempted to hide the shock when he ordered it.

This was a date. Who orders garlic bread on a date?

Not wanting him to think that I assumed we would be kissing, I went with it. Not touching it myself. However, I strongly believe that in the rules of dating, garlic bread – unless both consenting – should be banned. Unacceptable. Unless of course you are trying to purposely put the other one off. Then order it. Knock yourself out. Knock them out with the smell of your breath.

Was Pete trying to put me off?

As the date continued, painfully, a bit of bread fell from his lips and he smiled a garlicy grin. I offered him a sprig of parsley that sat limp on the side of my breaded-chicken salad, which he declined. Yes, I ordered a salad. Who knew where this date was going? Like I'd feel sexy after a ten-inch pizza sat in my belly!

My first date. First date with a guy. The one. Stop looking right now, you've found him. Was a disaster. And it didn't feel much like a date at all.

Turns out, I should have just had the pizza and garlic bread and not worried about the bloat. This was a meal of convenience. Not a date. Pete really was lining his stomach, but not for me, for the night out ahead. A plan that I wasn't in on. He ate garlic and I ate my words.

After the date, later that evening, he tried to kiss me. As tempting as the lips were, I refused. Later that year I surrendered, and we fumbled around for a few months. Turns out, I wasn't the only one on the roster, but it was worth the journey for his friendship.

Small-town dating was hard. At first, I blamed the location. Surely if I dated in a larger place, not everyone would know or have slept with your suitor. Surely. Somewhere bigger. Like London. Yes, if I lived in a big city that would be easier. More to talk about, more to do and more to see. Options that didn't end in the word "express" and didn't feel rushed either.

At eighteen years old, I convinced myself that it wasn't me. It was the town. Stupid naïve eighteen-year-old with wet-look gelled hair.

You fool.

❧

The more I dated, the more pressure I put on dating. I spread that word across this area of my life like it was Boursin on a cracker. It became a delicious anxious treat.

Determined not to waste my life, I wanted to sort out my ducks, get my shit together. I had wanted to do this even quicker once I'd come out. If I was to be gay, I still wanted my life to be like others'. That was my goal. Simple and hitting the *normal* milestones. Even if I couldn't marry (at the time), I needed a partner.

Dating was a gateway to many of those milestones. So, I needed to get it out of the way. Be rid of it. Be normal. Find one. Stick.

From first dates to more dates, to dates in bigger cities, to relationships and then back to dating once again, one thing had been consistent throughout: the bad ones. Awkward, uncomfortable and unavoidable. Bad dates. Pete was not the only one. Through searching, forming dating rules, playing the game and watching the years fly by as I dated from small towns to big cities, I clocked up numbers. Miles, men and memories. Most wouldn't be giving me wedding bells, but turns out, some gave me stories to tell.

❥

Okay, perfect dates don't exist. I know. It is a concept often dreamt up in fairy tales, Disney movies and teen rom coms. I'm realistic and cynical. But there are great dates to be had. I've had some. Dates that were epic for a multitude of reasons, perfectly imperfect anecdotes of love or potential romance. Moments. Unique moments that catch you by surprise.

The *best* one I ever went on did this. It was not thrilling, or expensive, or that imaginative. In fact, the guy, who I won't identify, threw up at the end of it. He also went home on a train in the opposite direction of my house. Alone. Plenty of factors that shouldn't have made it good but wowed me nonetheless. And it was the most enjoyable date I've had so far. Even after two hundred.

Westcliff station, Southend-on-Sea, 2007. After a steady stream of PG-rated conversation and late-night phone calls, we met. Our conversations had been on fire since first connecting. Everything felt easy, natural and exciting. This date had potential. I knew it. It was oozing with possibilities. I was high on the possibilities. My daydreaming was performing on next level. Marriage and horses and white suits were in our future. We hugged and he smelt good. It was a dark November evening, cold and crisp. We walked towards the beach – a stony bank of pebbles that look out on to the Thames Estuary.

His smile was incredible. He used it a lot. Constantly flashing it towards me as we chatted. Laughter filled our walk as we shared stories, exchanged conversations about travel, career expectations and long-term goals. These weren't particularly new conversations – some of them we'd covered before on our phone calls – but they were good. This was better than on the phone. Deeper and more meaningful.

He held my hand. I dropped it in embarrassment. I was awkward. Goofy. Heart thudding. Awkward. We got chips from a seafront takeaway and sat on the beach, listening to the waves. He kissed me. Knocking teeth. We tried again. Vinegar and salt to the taste, and just the right amount of tongue. Passion and desire in one hit. Good kissing. We sat closer, sitting for two hours. My bum was numb for the majority of it. There weren't many moments of silence, but when there were, it was fine. Natural. Easy.

Then he puked.

It didn't hit my leg, but it got a bit of his. I hated the smell of sick. He paced in front of me, embarrassed. His nerves were showing, they had bubbled over, and this was a sudden reaction as a result. He apologised. Over and over. He said that he really liked me.

I wish he had a chewing gum.

I believed him. This had felt good. I of course quipped that I made him sick, then worried instantly that it was true. He assured me it wasn't. There was that smile again. We walked back to the station, he refused to kiss and I think my taste buds were probably thankful for that. He smiled and I stood as his train left. My heart jumped. I could not wait to see him again. I liked him.

That was our date. Awkward. Amazing. Memorable.

Never have I ever started a date in Pret. Until September 2019. Nothing against it, but it's just not the romantic setting that I had in mind.

He asked me to meet him there after work. I assumed it was just a meeting point. Wrong. Never assume. Let's call him Michael for anonymity. And let's say that he was six foot two, like his profile said, and not actually five foot seven like...

Michael was eating a crayfish sandwich when I arrived. *I hate fish.* I took a seat in front of him, in the harsh lights of Pret, after a long working day. He had a good smile. Full of fish, but nice. He was the one who wanted to arrange the date. He had literally said, "Leave it to me, I'm going to arrange the date!" Nothing was arranged.

After he finished his fish sandwich, I offered him a chewing gum – I now always carried them. He refused it. *I hate fish.* After leaving Pret, we ended up outside a bar and had a drink. It started to rain, but having not booked anything in London, standing outside was our only option. The conversation did not flow. There was a lack of enthusiasm, questions or passion. Michael seemed to not want to know anything about me. I read this as disinterested. Not a Pete level, but just a couldn't-be-bothered-to-try level.

We finished the drinks, a little wetter than when we started, and I thought that was it. Date done. I was fully prepared to finish it there and then. Hopeful in fact. *Who had the time to waste; a pandemic was coming!* When he said, "Shall we go?" I assumed he was ready to leave too. Wrong. Never assume. We walked out to a rickshaw, in which he told the rider to take us on a tour, chucking cash his way. Considering he hadn't paid or offered up any money for the drinks, I was mildly impressed. This was spontaneous and had romantic potential. Or at least it could have with someone else. But this was Michael. A man who was hard to chat to and even harder to spend time with.

During the forty-five-minute ride, we went past Buckingham Palace, St Paul's, Soho (where I ducked in case someone I knew saw me) and the Shard. Michael looked down at his phone the whole time. I'd shouted "Stop" at the driver multiple times, but he hadn't heard me over his boom box. I was a prisoner. I'm not even sure Michael had heard me, to be honest.

"What next?" he said when we finally stopped. I stared at him. Were we on the same awkward date? Were cameras capturing us? Was this a prank?

I'm not exactly sure why, but we went for another drink. He bought us two negronis, despite me saying that I didn't like them. I sipped. He watched. I asked questions. He gave me one-word responses. I checked my watch fifty thousand times.

Ground swallow me up.

We clearly did not have that much in common, though I'm not sure what his actual interests were as he never told me. He offered up no conversation, liked his phone more than me and held me captive for nearly three hours. I was done. After checking my watch once more, I reached for my coat. The end signals were there.

Leave, Daniel.

I had told him earlier that I had an early start the next day and that I'd get an Uber home. He stopped looking at his phone. For once. Stared at me blankly. Paused. Then said, "Well, fuck you!"

Loudly. Shouted it. He spat out the words (literally – spit, or dislodged fish, landed on my cheek) and got up, bumping into the table next to us. Then he left. Everyone was looking at me. I was mortified.

Where did this go wrong? Why did I stay for this long? Why did he continue it? What was on his phone that was so interesting? I hate negronis.

The waiter came over with a sympathetic look. I thought he was going to give me a hug, but instead he handed me the bill. Michael hadn't paid. The drinks were pricey.

Bad date. Shouted at, not offered a sandwich, made to drink a drink I didn't want, uncomfortable silences, no questions, no interest, no apology, A BLOODY RICKSHAW.

He was a crayfish sandwich, and frankly, a little cray.

❧

Leg work. You get out what you put in. Dating is exhausting, confusing, brilliant and often endless. But when it's good, it's worth all the bad. It has to be. It's even worth the occasional crayfish.

Dating can be like the feeling you get when you put on a really good outfit, having your hair look perfect and feeling your own vibe as you stare in the mirror.

I look good.

It can make you smile without meaning to and catch you off guard. Dating is an investment. You have to invest time, money, conversation and a portion of yourself into it. If you don't, if you come half-hearted, disinterested or not giving it a chance, it isn't worth your time. You may as well eat the garlic bread. It is an act. A performance to woo. Effort. Make no mistake: it is effort. But the more you put in, the more you get out, the more you develop a process. The more you discover your rules.

My dating rules are simple:

- You have to be spontaneous and not boring. I once stated that *I go with the flow* on a dating profile, and as vomit-inducing as that sounds, it's required. Go with it.

- Be interesting. Have hobbies, even if you don't – white lies are acceptable and you can learn the hobbies later.

- Keep the chatter light. Don't darken their days with your work woes; lighten them.

- Meet. Don't just keep it as chat and an online pen pal. Be bold and arrange a date. Don't wait for them to ask you. If there's a connection and spark, go for it.

- Open up. There is nothing more honest and endearing than someone sharing themselves. It allows people to see you. Tell them your fails and triumphs, flaws and beauty. Be proud to be unique but smile as you talk.

- Dress up. Feel yourself. Really feel yourself, and dress however that looks for you.

- Move on. If it isn't working, and you've given it a try, don't dwell on it and keep making exhausting effort. Swipe forward. Move on.

There they are. The rules. You need these when you are single and getting through dates quicker than your pants. Especially swimming in a gay dating pool. This pool has sharks. Piranhas and stingrays. But we swim regardless. Because no one wants to be old, gay and single, right?

Wrong.

The only reason to date, the only good reason, is because you want to. And because as gay men, we can! Remind yourself of that. Not because of fear, or pressure, or thinking this was your way of fitting in. But because it's our right.

Yes, it's a series of interviews. An over-complicated coffee order. You might be looking for a partner, a husband, a three-way, the one. You might even just be bored. Or not looking for much at all. But it is a screening, and they're interviewing you too. We all need to take a moment. Stop and breathe. Especially as gay men.

As someone who has personally dated a lot of people, I've been every date "type" that you can imagine. I've been the embarrassing double messenger when they hadn't responded. I've been guilty of being "too busy" to meet and formed a library of unsaved-numbered pen pals. I've misread signals, pined for someone that didn't want me, been too keen, not been keen enough, ghosted and also looked at my phone too much during a date. I've been the bad date, the good date, the average date and the try-too-hard date. I haven't always gone with the flow. Haven't followed my own rules. And most commonly, I've been just sitting there wondering if this was it.

My ticket.

My person.

My one.

Wrong.

Now in my thirties, what I hadn't been for a long time was the fun date. Because that is what dating is. Fun.

I'd forgotten that I wasn't *yet* past any honeymoon period, or stuck with the same penis for life, or bored in a coupling. I was single. A label that I'd become wearied by. And for what reason?

We are so lucky to date. I might not know where it will lead, or if they are the one, but I'm privileged to find out. So many before us haven't been able to do that. Some still feel like they can't. For so long I've been looking for a husband, a partner, a plus one. My ticket to normal. And I regret this. We should make mistakes. Enjoy dating. Date wrong guys and right ones. We can ask ourselves what we are searching for, but we also don't always need the answer.

Heterosexual couples are often seen to fit into a coveted "society mould." They court, get engaged, get married, have babies, retire and then live out their lives on cruises. I assumed I needed a slice of that. Maybe I still do.

However, there is no cast for us in the LGBTQIA+ community. No yellow brick road to follow. No movie portraying what the average gay success story is. *There are multiple versions!* We are fortunate to make our own path. Legally and openly. We fight for that path.

A man once told me, in response to my classic question asking what he was looking for, "I'm looking for a reason to stop using Tinder." A reason. I now agree with him. But, at thirty-three, it needs to be a bloody good reason. And that's okay. I have time. We all do.

Dating has changed since I started and continues to as I go. It's updated, evolving and accelerating. We are a window-shopping generation. Hungry to see what other fish are in the sea, eager to soak up life's experiences and eat the apple that falls far from the tree. Frustrating and blissful at once.

We can date through apps, through meeting in bars, through friends, through work. And although, in an age where we are meant to "be kind" and the gay dating scene is far from kind, we can do it. We can grow from this relationship. Yes, when you are finally ready to take your Hinge date to a party, with other gay guys, the chances that one or five of the people at that party have already slept with your new boo might be high. But this is modern-life dating. Yes, it might lead to a relationship that isn't forever. Yes, your partner might want to be "together" differently. And the odds might feel like they are against us. It can be a brutal scene. I'm just as much to blame for this. But we get to decide. We get to date.

I need to take my own advice. *Go with the flow.* From the start of my dating life, I had rules.

Don't eat garlic bread, don't have the pizza, don't date a shagger, leave the small town, find a normal guy, go masc or go home, don't waste time on someone who isn't the one...

Well, I'm here to tell you, waste your time. Live. Be the fun date. It might not work out. You might marry, you might end in divorce. There is a running joke within my heterosexual school friends where we wonder which (if any) of us will divorce first. The odds are not in anyone's favour. They never can be.

We can't compare our dating lives to heterosexual ones or people in current couples. Friends that all met their partners a long while ago, back when dating felt fun and flirty and led to STIs, morning-after pills and dancing. Daters who are no longer dating. Because as we grow up, our dating life does too. Ever evolving.

For too long I have been dating while holding my breath. Waiting for the house of cards to fall on anyone I'm with. Expecting it to do so. Shattering that perfect dating union. Or wondering if I'll ever find it again. But we take those odds. Because that is dating. A chance to get to know ourselves better too. Growing. Learning.

In this game of roulette, in a casino full of people, we only have one number to play. Our own. The odds are stacked against us. Often, the house will win. Still, we gamble. Because the thrill of rolling that dice, being part of the race, is exciting.

WE ARE LUCKY TO BE ABLE TO RACE.

It's fun. And sometimes, fourteen comes in. Your number. You don't always believe it when you see it, but that feeling that sweeps over you is worth hoping for and repeating the process. Dating. Or whatever that looks like to you. Putting yourself out there, opening up to being hurt. Losing chips left right and centre. And gradually finding you. Or your companion. A chance in thirty-seven. A chance to call off the search and stop looking, if that's what you want.

You are the good date.

You are the bad date.

You are the average date.

Dating is the simplest relationship in our lives. You are in control. It's often not around forever. So, instead, enjoy it while it lasts. Ease off on the pressure. Sometimes it might be a brilliant ride or at the least, a good story. One day you'll look back on this relationship and strangely miss it. It's fun.

Don't fear being gay, old and single. As a community, we need to normalise this. Not fear it. Even if we do individually. We'll all be that at some point. And, if the coupe shouts out your number, after so many misses, you might just be a winner, baby.

Fourteen!

role model

/ˈrəʊl ˌmɒd.əl/

---

noun

1. a person looked to by others as an example to be imitated.

conversations with a role model

Imitation. That is what we do throughout our lives. It's part of who we are. Copying fragments of other people that we like, piecing ourselves together. Bit by bit. If someone is living their best life, fantastically, inspiringly and richly, we want it. We want a piece of it. Copycats of personalities, careers, style, lives. You name it, we strive for it. It's natural.

We gravitate towards people who we admire and like, so it's only normal that we imitate. Admire. Respect. I'm not talking *Single White Female*. That is not imitation through looking up to people in an inspiring way. That is just downright crazy. Do not *Single White Female* anyone. But all of us are part-created from what we've seen. Learnt. Followed. Sought. Unique in our own ways but often shaped by others.

So, when you can't relate, don't always like what you see or struggle to find "your people," it's harder to find yourself. To imitate.

Grow.

Live.

Survive.

You can't fully appreciate how valuable a role model is until you need one. Until you search for one, when you wonder if there are any out there. Feeling so alone. Feeling like there is no one else like you. Isolated. Because we need support. We need to see representation. We need trailblazers.

The right role models can be a light in the dark. A guide in a storm. A person who saves your life. To our community, they are brave, they are powerful, and they open doors. And they are also all of us too.

Without role models, we would not be where we are today. We need them far more than we realise. And still do.

❧

Setting an example. A concept that sounds easy, right? We follow good examples daily. They have one job to do. To help people. They come in many forms, mediums and guises.

Characters in our favourite movies. Actors representing different demographics, pushing boundaries. Athletes paving the way for others to feel included. Opening our eyes. Examples of different people, backgrounds and walks of life. Vital.

I'll never forget the moment that I went to the cinema to see *Brokeback Mountain*. It was 2006; I was a fresh-eyed uni student, still shy about my sexuality. Still struggling. I'd seen the trailers. I knew what this film was about. A cowboy movie with a huge difference.

I was an out gay man, there with my female friend Charlie, and this was the most nervous that I'd been to watch a movie in public. Far more nervous than any of the horror films I'd seen and screamed my way through publicly. That would have been less embarrassing to me compared to this. Give me a horror film any day. On a large screen, two men before my twinkling, innocent eyes had sex. They had gay sex openly, to a sold-out cinema audience. An audience that gasped and let out giggles. *Anal sex is hilarious.* It was the most uncomfortable and fantastic thing that I'd ever seen. My face was flushed red with embarrassment. I'd never felt so exposed and *uncomfortable* publicly.

It didn't make me want to stand up and shout, "They're my people!" Clapping and cheering, thanking Ang Lee for this incredible moment.

I wasn't proud. I was shitting myself.

It wasn't *fantastic* because it was horny. Instead, it was a moment. An incredible moment of visibility. There, in front of people who had paid money to watch this, a slice of our community was seen. A storyline had been put out there showing difference. Showing that people can love differently. It was overwhelming. Years of thinking that I'd never see two men be open, that open, in a mainstream setting, it happened before my eyes.

A moment.

In the Odeon in Hatfield Galleria, Hertfordshire, where I'd screamed to horrors, laughed at comedies and seen representation of all kinds, I finally got a glimpse of myself. I watched, awkwardly, but with a small smile. This was progress, acceptance and a track leading to a better time. Inspiring.

I walked out of that cinema a little taller, a little prouder and, of course, puffy faced from crying. *Brokeback Mountain* was an emotional rollercoaster; I defy anyone to get through it with a dry eye. What Ang Lee created was far more than a beautiful cinematic experience. It was a chance to show another point of view. Tell a different story. Of course, he wasn't the first. But it was my first encounter publicly of this.

That was sixteen years ago. Thankfully, examples are all around us. Showing themselves more regularly, more often. Speaking out and speaking up. They are our country leaders. Paving the way for new laws, better days and equality. Our parents. Our friends. Our loved ones. They are that teacher in school who understood us. Encouraged us, helped us. The one who didn't just join in with the bullies but the one who fought to help you. Giving you a knowing look when you were scared. They saw you. Before you saw you.

Thank you, Mrs Seal.

People in positions of power. Setting an example. Using that for good, and occasionally bad, but leading and showing that difference is okay, should be okay, will be okay. Notably, some examples being set are wrong. Very wrong. Look at conversion therapy being available to different countries. What message is that sending out? The wrong examples can take us in the wrong direction. Lead us astray, misleading us down a different path.

Judi James says that "Humans have flaws, and putting a role model on too high a pedestal can lead to disappointment." It can be dangerous to follow the wrong example. Detrimental to our health, well-being and own path ahead. Seeking out the right role models is crucial. "I'm not sure wholesale role models can't be dangerous to have if we take the entire person to role model rather than picking out specific behaviours we admire and would consciously choose to emulate."

We have to find the right ones. Let them help not hinder. A model that we want to emulate. A body, a goal, a weight, an outlook, a mindset, a job, a career, a moment, a marriage, a confidence, a drive, a voice. Hopefully a person to say or show us that *you are okay as you are*. A relatable person who leads by example, not astray.

We all have them, each one different. No two people's will be the same. They'll mean different things to different people. Role models who we put on a pedestal. Idolise. Important beacons of hope. Required for a moment in our lives. Serving a purpose.

People who are probably flawed too. Lost at times. Having their own issues, looking for their own models to look up to.

Think of that pressure. The pressure of being the person that people turn to. One foot wrong, one mis-tweet, they could shatter lives and hearts. They could drive us off course. Lose their own status. Ruin their following. It must be a pretty scary position to be in, leading by example. So, we can't expect someone to be perfect in doing it. Do no wrong.

Hopefully, they'll help us, drive us, save us. I don't believe that any role model puts themselves in that position without an element of fear. They have an important job. Examples are there, good and bad. Not an easy position to be in. All we can do is try to find our ones we relate to, and forgive missteps, if forgivable. Our role models are just as damaged as we are, but they are the ones trying.

Paving a way.

Setting an example.

Showing difference.

❧

Judi James says that "Often spoken advice from a role model is only sought when we are too scared to work things out for ourselves."

Anyone who comes out as gay in a small town will probably feel alone. Isolated. There was a moment where I really did think that I was *the only gay in the village.* I also assumed that no one knew. No one would know my secret if I didn't share it. Didn't tell people or trip up.

They bloody knew.

In that moment, before I came out at seventeen, I really did assume that no one else in the entire world was like me. At least, not exactly like me. There is not one example that I can think of that I related to twenty years ago. Alone. That's how it was. Surely, no one would be feeling the way I did, or anything remotely like how I felt.

How could they?

I knew no one gay; the TV my family watched was filled with heterosexual shows with two point four children. Nothing felt familiar. I felt disgusting, odd, dirty, different, wrong, ugly, secluded, confused, hopeless and weird. Hateful words to describe myself. Nothing admirable. Words. Loaded words that felt as nasty to read as when you said them out loud. And I told myself those words. Like affirmations.

That small, scrawny teenager, nervous about turning eighteen, who had recently lost his puppy fat, heard those self-destructive conversations played over in his head on a daily loop. The soundtrack to my youth. On repeat. Never tiring. Hateful words.

Where were my people?

Out of all the kids I knew, all the movies I'd seen, no one person felt even close to what I was like. I stagger to understand how kids at school even called me "gay" at the time. I'd love to know what they were comparing me to. Who they were comparing me to. I'd have liked to have someone to compare myself to, frankly. I'm sure my parents knew this too. They just didn't speak about it. At least not to me.

There were lots of people my mum related to. Compared herself to. She told me that Madonna was a lot like her. She'd even worn that pointy bra costume one Halloween. Her music spoke to her and inspired her. Then she told me that everyone used to say that she also reminded them of her mother. In both looks and personality. In fact, my mum actually rattled off a lot of people who she easily related to. Celebrities, actresses, show hosts, athletes, musicians.

Her people.

Her groove.

Her set.

I got compared to my dad. People said that I looked like him. I can see it now. But back then, that was where it ended. I looked like I should belong, but I didn't quite fit. Not one bit.

As a young gay boy, twenty years ago, I had no one to aspire to be. Not one person. Which, at the time, didn't feel particularly important, or like I was missing out. I just assumed it was my way. The way of the world. There weren't people like me. As all the people around me related in different ways, I just followed the crowd. Ignoring my internal battle. Because this was it, life. Smiling, pushing it down deep inside me.

I didn't know then, but I realise now that people assumed things about me. Things I wouldn't have even considered myself. Kids at school, parents worrying, teachers. Assuming I was something. Something at the time I hadn't dealt with or understood myself. Because how could I? How can you understand something unless you see it in others? All I really knew was a sense of "Why me?"

Why was I alone?

Where was my person?

❃

Easy. That is what I overheard on the train to Cardiff the other day.

"In this day and age, the year of 2022, it's easy to come out as gay," said a stranger on the train.

Okay.

I guess 2022 is in a decade of acceptance, experience and inclusion... There are a whole host of people from different backgrounds on our TV screens. We have some same-sex rights, marriage and adoption for the LGBTQIA+. *Yay.*

Okay.

It's not illegal or frowned upon to love who we love in the UK; we can relax and be ourselves.

Right.

People even wave flags in our honour, raise money and parade in our name. *Our name!* Banks get on board sometimes too. *How lucky are we? Thanks.* I mean, I'm sure it's for all the wrong reasons, but they do! Those financial powerhouses change their logo and support us. I guess.

Okay.

And although it's often only one month of the year, we, our community, are noticed. Pride. We are seen.

Fantastic.

Brilliant in fact. We must keep this up, do more and strive to push further boundaries. Despite what slurs people often say – "Why do you need a month?" – we do. We need that visibility. There are brutal homophobic attacks. Trans rights are still a huge and current issue, and recognising different genders seems to still be a problem for people.

Easy?

I'm sorry, no fifty-something white man talking to his fifty-something white colleague in first class on a train, wearing a suit, can state that it's easy to come out now. It's not.

No flag, or parade, or Netflix series will silence a host of internal feelings that we go through before we find that light. That hope. That ease. Our tribe. It can't.

Most of the time, we are embarrassed to even attempt to look at or engage with those things. We don't want to out ourselves in fear of rejection. Because that battle, the one that millions go through on a daily basis no matter how loving, accepting or diverse our families or upbringings are, is a fight that we suffer silently first. We often don't say a word. I didn't. Which, for a lot of people as it happens, will always be the case. Experiencing a moment of discomfort. A by-product in the process of coming out. Some will find it fleeting. For others it will linger longer than they realise, taking hold at different moments and consuming you. But I can say with honesty that there will be some variation of this feeling for everyone who is a part of the LGBTQIA+ community. A truth. One that is not *easy* in the slightest.

Having done it, struggled through it alone, I can say this with confidence. And when I was at my lowest, living in fear of a future and not wanting to accept myself, I never once realised how a role model could help me. How someone could help ease those feelings. Until I started to see. Our visibility.

Slowly, there were people who I could look up to. Brave individuals who were doing something about *their* uneasy moment, showing me a way, showing me that I was okay. I was enough. I was normal.

I am normal.

Because easing that journey is key. And seeing is believing. But *easy*, no. It isn't easy and it never will be.

After coming out, I was convinced that I didn't need a role model. I hadn't seen one, so I was stubborn. Something inside of me refused to need someone else to lead the gay. I'd come this far; I had myself.

It was Gale Anne Hurd who once said, "If you can't find a good role model, be one." That's what I intended to do. Of course, I'd respect my elders, but I wanted to find a path of my own. Then help others. That was my internal thinking. My stubborn thought process. Driving me forward.

As long as I had motivation, drive and a will spurring me on, that's all I needed. Not a role model. Not another gay. Friends, fine, but no role models required.

Stubborn.

Arrogant.

Wrong.

I might have thought that I didn't need them, survived. But the journey had only just begun. Doing it alone was never going to be the easiest option. We need them at every point. And others after me do too.

You see, it's incredible for people to become role models. People of influence who use that position to help, guide and make things easier. We should strive to be them ourselves. Because, fifty-year-old businessmen, nothing is *easy* about the coming-out process. Even if it looks like it. Seems like it. Feels like it. Nothing. And, even if you do want to become a role model, like my stubborn self, you're going to need your own one first. An inspiration.

People who won't make it easy but might make it easier.

❧

In 2022, they are everywhere. I'm sure all heterosexual people think this too.

If you turn on the TV or open up a magazine now, representation can be found.

Rejoice. I can literally hear my younger self releasing his breath and feeling a little easier about life ahead. We've come on leaps and bounds. We keep leaping and bounding towards a better life for everyone. For equality. For normality. But this wasn't always the case. Once upon a time, we were fucked. Limited, lost and lonely.

In 1999, I didn't know about *Queer as Folk*. Why would I? It was of no interest to my family and I was underage. Television was five channels – a few more if you were lucky. Sky was only just awakening.

Nathan Maloney.

After I came out, that was the first person I can remember seeing as a gay man who felt a little more like me. He was fictional.

A character in *Queer as Folk*. A blonde-haired, skinny twink who men wanted to be or wanted in their beds. Created for a storyline and a TV show. The character was also famous for *that* scene where Stuart took his virginity.

Stuart was so hot.

But fictional or not, something about Nathan I related to. This guy, living his life as a gay man in a TV show, was relatable. In real life, not so much. In real life, the actor was straight. Charlie Hunnam. Yep. The now ripped hunk who rides around on a motorbike in *Sons of Anarchy*. Amen.

That body is enough to make anyone forget their train of thought. The strong guns that bulge as he revs the bike, the sex appeal that he oozes. Him in sunglasses. Him out of sunglasses. His body. The effortless attitude he had. A dirty, un-showered look that you didn't mind. Leather. I don't even like leather, but on him, okay. The back, the front, the side. A god. To hold on to those broad shoulders and ride...

Okay, I'm back.

But before finding his muscles, he played a part in my life. A schoolboy finding his feet, penis and own way. Making mistakes and having fun. A character and gay man who was far more confident than me, but someone who seemed like he was paving the way for a lot of hopeful people. Me.

I wanted to be Nathan.

If this was on TV, then maybe it was a possible life for others like me. A pipe dream. Daydreaming was a thing that I'd do constantly before I came out. I'd daydream about men, what sex would be like, what sex with other men would be like, sex. So much dreaming. Not much living.

When I managed to watch an episode of *Queer as Folk*, in secret, after coming out, it was probably unsurprising that in my head I wanted to date Stuart. I wanted to be Nathan. I dreamt that I lived in Manchester, had a mum who was more like a friend and smoked.

I can't smoke. I'm that nerdy-looking guy who can't hold a cigarette and look hot doing it. Far from my reality. This was not my life. This was a TV show that I'd stumbled across a little too late. Fake. But seeing it on a screen, a life linked to mine, gave me a glimpse of a future. What could be. Hope.

Even though I was out, I started to think times were getting more accepting due to this. After *QAF*, I started to seek out more. Graham Norton was also on TV. He was adored. I didn't really understand it, but people loved him. Old ladies, mums, all tuning in to his show. The audience seemed to love his camp nature, and although he seemed to play up to it, he was in on the joke. He was at ease. Even if he sometimes allowed himself to be the joke. I watched him like I watch a horror movie. Peering through a gap in my fingers behind my hand. Holding my breath. Waiting. I'm not sure what for.

At first, I couldn't believe that he'd allow himself to be so *out* there. So available to be pulled down publicly. Any moment someone could call him a name, perhaps people were shouting at their TVs, shouting homophobic remarks. He was unapologetically queer. Himself. Whenever I heard someone speak of him, they'd often refer to him as *that camp gay character on TV*.

I hated the word "camp." It was everything I didn't want to be. Everything I feared I was. But, if you were a TV personality you had to have a category, right? That was the portrayal of gay men on TV in the nineties. Well, that was him. Unlike me, he didn't shy away from it. He owned it, embraced it, laughed and excelled with it. He laughed, consciously, on the screen that millions were watching. Some with him, some at him, but all because of him. All the time being himself. And I watched, behind my hand, starting slowly to piece together a picture. An identity.

Even though in the 2000s (yes, I feel old) representations were few and far between, when they came, each time it felt like another big ripple. Another piece to a puzzle. A wave closer to the shore. My shore. My people. Whenever you noticed or heard about someone else like you, living their life in the public eye, another cog started turning. Another step taken. Normality. If people were tuning in, talking about famous gay people or characters, perhaps there was a life for me. Perhaps acceptance was coming.

Led by example.

Led by role models.

❧

We are everywhere. Comparing ourselves constantly, judging and following. Unfollowing. Liking. Disliking. As more people portrayed their truth on TV or in a magazine, I started to do two things.

Checking their age, relationship status and audience likeability.

Judging how "gay" they were.

It was crucial. I wanted to compare them to me, my progress, where I was and how my future was shaping up. Strangely, the "queerer" they openly were, the more outrageous or "different" they acted, the more I fought against liking them. The more I judged. I didn't like them. Or at least I thought I didn't.

There I was, already trying to silence my own gay and dumb it down throughout my twenties. Not draw attention to it. Hold back campness, or my feminine traits. I didn't need any more influence in this area. I didn't want any more.

Slap.

That is the sound of me putting my younger self in place. I hate that I worried so much. Thought that way. Judged. That boy needed a slap. But at the time, I didn't want to be the joke. The typical gay guy who everyone expected me to be. I wanted a different role model.

In 2022, I would be so disappointed if I heard a younger guy thinking that way now. Comparing his campness, frowning and turning away from it. Fearing it. I'd be disappointed. But I'd also understand them. Fear.

These people stepped into the light and sacrificed themselves. Declared their witchlike status and waited for the hunt. I didn't see it then. I didn't understand the huge impact each wave would have and continue to have on me. I couldn't. You can't see it when you are trying not to look. Avoid contact. Avoid camp influences. Try to push away those examples out of fear that was you.

Luckily, I'm glad other people were able to look. Able to embrace. Able to change. Were stronger than I was. Fought for their light and shining it on our community. Because if they didn't, if they didn't normalise "difference," then they couldn't have actioned change. And they did. Each tsunami of gay that we encounter helps. Although younger me might not have been aware of it, my role models, queer, masc, hot, old, young and fantastic, were also my angels.

Guardians.

My tickets to freedom. Me.

❧

Rylan Clark, please accept this as a public apology. I'm sorry for the internal annoyance I projected your way. And I projected. You were frustrating, limelight stealing and proud of everything I thought I hated about being gay. People loved you. Enjoyed your comedy, your realness and yourself. You bravely put yourself up for ridicule, judgement and risk. And I was your judge. A harsh judge.

Drag queens, I'm sorry. It took me so long to allow myself to enjoy you. I hate that. Your humour, your wit and your spirit. Your shameless confidence and talent.

Epic.

Thank god you shine and stand tall on main stages and small ones around the world. I thought smiling with you would impact me negatively. I've been fortunate to meet so many of you and interview and work with and adore you. Keep slaying.

Russell Tovey, thank you. Thanks for showing people that gay comes in all forms. We need that. We continue to need that. Thank you for those big ears, kind heart and endearing smirk.

What a cheeky grin!

I thought that I could never be "like you," but I now realise that I don't need to be. You show a different side to a difference.

Russell T Davies, wow. I bet you had some tough times of fight. Times of pushing boundaries and facing "no"s. My goodness, you must have been told no. Thank god you persevered. You helped show, and continue to show, that we are just as important, bright and talented as the rest of them. We are enough. We are epic. We have stories too. What you have done more recently with *It's a Sin* is just flawless. Not only have you shown the world a time when gay men were the enemy, showcasing how hard it once was, you have also highlighted how normal it should be to love. Regardless. You shine a light on HIV and AIDS, you force people to learn. To grow. To see us. Thank you.

Tom Daley, Nicola Adams and **Gus Kenworthy** (to name a small few), thank you for coming out as athletes and sporting heroes. Thank you to all the people in this industry who bravely break down barriers and showcase that the LGBTQIA+ can be represented in sport. At least one hundred and eighty-five out LGBTQIA+ athletes took part in the Tokyo Olympics. Incredible.

Conor Coady, thank you for being a football ally to the LGBTQIA+

community. A hard and dangerous position to be in, but one that we desperately require. Thank you to all of the people coming out in sport. We need it.

It's 2022, and I'm so in awe of all the role models that we have. There are so many influencers, apps, podcasts, people, celebrities, politicians and allies to name. And I see them all. I thank them all. Because in the path to finding myself, I often didn't realise that each person that represented our community represented a part of me, an importance.

Sometimes I didn't want to see them. I didn't want to be them. I worried. But I needed them. I wish they were there sooner. We need more. Slowly, as you remove the hands from covering your eyes, shadowing your fear, you see that. You understand the importance. And what a glorious sight and encouragement we are.

Role models.

●

There are of course so many role models that I'd love to have a conversation with. Say thank you to. Many incredible influences in my life and in all of our communities. People who inspire and change.

So, when I got to have a chat to Daniel Newman, an American actor (*Walking Dead* and *EastSiders*) who risked his career for his sexuality (bisexual) and our community, I was eager to understand his thoughts on role models and on being one himself.

"That's so sweet of you to say, thank you. I never stop and think I am one."

Speaking from Georgia, USA, Daniel said that growing up he really struggled, like me, to find relevant role models.

"Growing up, my parents were my role models. We didn't have

any public figures that I was really aware of, therefore I turned to my own. I look back now and see the legacies of the likes of Elton John were available and trying to push awareness, but I was so isolated growing up and didn't have awareness of ground-breaking and incredible role models."

Having no immediate access to role models, Daniel said he struggled with his sexuality.

"It was nearly impossible for me to come out. On so many levels. For me, I didn't know anything about our community. I had been brainwashed by society to hate myself and gay people. I never knew any differently. I didn't know any gay people and it didn't have visibility at the time. All I knew was people in the church saying gay people were bad."

Daniel assumed that there was just "something wrong" with him.

"I tried to hide it. For so long. Then I started to do a lot of film and TV work. Where, even more so, it wasn't going to help me or anyone else if I brought up this thing I had that was different. It was my burden alone. Having also started acting from the age of eleven, I was no longer just me. I had all of these agents, managers and people whose livelihoods started relying on me. Keeping my mouth shut was a part of that."

As a kid in the eighties and nineties, he was brainwashed to believe that he had to keep this to himself. Not many were like him.

"It was just growing up with a feeling that you were alone and isolated, believing this was the only way. Don't talk about it or you'll be the weirdo. It was dangerous. No wonder people committed suicide."

As an actor with a platform, Daniel slowly saw a different path.

"I realised that the TV shows I was on created such a spotlight. As an actor, that's kind of like winning the lottery. It's so rare to get a job that becomes a huge show. I got to a point where I thought, I don't know if this will help anyone, but if my life is going to have some purpose or effect, then I need to do something. I thought, what would the little boy version of me want? And what I wanted back then was visibility. I had felt so alone, thinking that this was a defect and that I was different – I was unsure of myself. I didn't see the role models. So, I now had a platform and responsibility. It was do it or I might never do it."

Daniel posted a coming out video on YouTube – as a definitive choice that he had hoped would help others.

"We were doing promotions for the *Walking Dead* and hundreds of thousands of people were worshipping these characters and I was like, I hope there is a kid out there like me who sees this and helps identify. You can be someone and not be scared of your difference."

He became a role model.

"When someone says I'm a role model, it just makes me think of my flaws. But I see this as a job. I'm in the public eye and acting, and I have a responsibility to try to help people. We have that. Everyone should."

Daniel said that he just wanted to make life better for people, something he didn't have access to himself.

"Each one of us is part of this diverse rainbow. But it's not just the bright colours that we see so clearly; there are millions of different shades and versions of people. When we see the fantastic Elton John come out publicly, people might think they don't need to come out, someone else is doing it, but that is just one shade. One colour. The truth is, each one of us needs to come out. The businessman, the actor, the football player. Each one representing a niche, or a small group. Until we are visible, there is an unspoken void if you don't see yourself in that person. To be gay, is that just an Elton John type? Obviously no. To summarise a group of human beings by one person is never going to be a full representation. It's not enough to have one person come out. We all need to do it."

Daniel credits the media for showcasing so many different diversities and continuing to do that and give it a platform.

"Our community, and the visibility, is still such a baby culture. It's still so new to mainstream America and pop culture globally, despite it being seen more. So, we are still figuring it out. People hate when they don't understand. It's easy to be phobic about something we don't know much about. So, we must be visible. Honesty breaks down walls. That's important to me. If I'm honest, we can help to showcase *us* and break phobias."

I wondered if Daniel worried about being stereotyped and his career being affected by his sexuality.

"I realised quickly the true importance in life isn't about what people say or think about you. However, I'm a free man now and I have come out of the other side of it. Up until I came out and after it, I was petrified of how this would affect and change my life. I had built a career since I was eleven years old and now this one thing, something that was a part of me, could affect it. It's scary.

"Everyone in the industry said, do not come out. You will never be a star. You'll never get your dream job. You'll never have sustainable income as an actor if you come out. There is no one in history that had been a leading male actor (at the time). They said I would be labelled and stereotyped. They also said, threatened, that I'd significantly hurt the careers of other people too. There was a lot of weight on my shoulders."

Daniel said it was an ugly and brainwashing industry as a child actor, keeping him in the closet for a long time.

"There was also this narcissistic side to it. Like, how do you think you are that important that it's going to help people? Are you so vain and self-absorbed that you think you'll make a difference? There were so many layers to why a male actor shouldn't come out. And finally, I snapped. I didn't care if it would hurt my career or if it would change, all I could think about was the kids out there who needed representation. Kids like myself."

Daniel realised that he loved himself and was proud of who he was. Having worked with and met gay people on sets, and moving to New York, he fell in love with the community and finally felt like he belonged.

"If people stereotyped me as being 'like' these other people I'd met, I started to not see it as an issue, but more of a dream. When you grow up thinking it's just you, you appreciate the diversity. Gay people are my heroes. I stopped caring and realised the value of visibility."

Daniel acknowledged that he is a good-looking guy, but also said we need more diverse role models.

"I grew up as a ginger redheaded scrawny boy. Then I had a tyre belly and acne, then braces. In 2009, I got run over and had to learn how to walk again. I looked like a mess. Seeing just 'hot' men come out, whatever that is, isn't enough. The bigger picture is to drive awareness of global issues that matter to me and make our lives visible. We are more than a six pack; we are a human being."

As an actor, Daniel is thankful for the roles that he's had. Where possible he loves to do roles that are impactful, but says this platform doesn't come easily.

"Actors play the lottery. They hope they get parts and want to do well. I took years off it and invested in property. I was fortunate to work on incredible projects like *EastSiders*, but you have to work hard. My passion is educating; I try to be honest with people wanting to come into acting. It's not easy. But when incredible projects that make differences come along, I feel blessed in taking them. We need to keep making them. Even being a part of Marvel's *Loki* right now is brilliant. I'm honoured."

Daniel said if he could give his younger self any advice, he would tell him that there are millions of people like him out there.

"It's taken decades to get the visibility to where it is today and everyone that is a part of that should feel so proud. We have so much more to do. I wish I'd told myself, come out as soon as possible. You attract what you embody. If you hide a part of you, other people won't come to you or share their lives with you. That's a sad, sheltered life to live."

Daniel agreed that role models can be present at any stage of life.

"We always need role models. We are always striving to grow. I struggled for gay role models when I was a child, which is why it's so important that we strive to show ourselves today. Whether you are a gay teacher, businessman, sportsman, in coming out you give the gift of confidence and show people that they can do that too. There is no glass ceiling to achieving your dreams. Being a role model is a responsibility. I'm thankful to be in a position to project this. A role model isn't just an actor, but there are so many around us. People who have changed and continue to change how people see us. So much hard work and dedication from grassroots to charities to large finance organisations that have really helped change the world we know."

As we ended the chat, I thanked Daniel for using his platform in a positive way and to help people.

"Sometimes we have to search for the role model that we need. But hopefully, as more people become visible, the fewer people will need to search. You should be proud of doing a project like this. This in itself will help people, Daniel. I feel thankful to be considered as a role model, but all I am doing is trying to show that being LGBTQIA+ is incredible, beautiful and important. There's nothing to be afraid of. We need to be seen."

What a guy.

My mum has always said that it's *people* that set examples for other people. She said that this is the only way that we learn. I never really appreciated the value in that sentence before. But *people* are the key. Learning from them is vital.

We are taught to respect our elders; *they always know best.* Then our teachers, the wise and brilliant people educating us. Shaping us. And then on to bosses, presidents and politicians. This is true. We need to show respect. Look up. But what we often forget are the people representing us and striving to show differences regardless of age, background or job title.

Last year, I went to the 2021 LGBT Awards in London (thank you, Benji). I put on a black suit and sat in a crowded room of people, celebrities, companies and allies.

My black suit had a toothpaste mark on it that I coloured in with a Sharpie moments before I got there.

In an evening of celebrating our role models, I was honoured. Sharing struggles, stories, differences, people spoke about the need of representation. The need for our community to have a voice and continue to use it. I don't think my sixteen-year-old self would have ever imagined being in that room, let alone being comfortable in who he was. We have come so far because of people.

Writers, publications, athletes, actors, podcasts, radio DJs, drag queens, trans activists, bisexual activists, non-binary activists, allies.

We need them all.

As Daniel Newman told me in our interview, our rainbows come in many shades, and it's in being able to see a version of yours projected for the world to see that we feel a little less alone. This continues to be an important relationship for our community. Finding our relatable examples. Then discovering yourself.

A role model is a person we judge, see ourselves in and who influences us. They scare us and inspire us, and so they should. They take a risk and set out to help others.

Perhaps they become role models because they needed one themselves. At times we might need them more than others, but we do need them. We might not always notice the ones we have; I certainly didn't. We might fear different versions, or hide behind our hands. It's complex and a journey that often starts with hate, resentment and fear. Turning our backs. Not facing our truths. Often because that role model is doing things that we can't, yet. Thank goodness they are.

I didn't feel like I had a gay role model before I came out. But right now, I have millions. They provide a valued role that only you can understand once you go on a journey yourself.

Everyone should be setting an example. Becoming a role model. And forgive those missteps, slip-ups, slurs. They wanted role models too.

Let people try.

Find your people. Become one. Be one.

To the businessmen on the train, it's never going to be easy, but role models help it get easier.

❧

I spoke to a number of amazing role models who had advice to give.

Coming out in sport wasn't easy. But I felt like it was important to stand up and speak out about my experiences because during my playing career, no one else had. I have played across the world in different countries, cultures and continents, but during that time had never played with an openly gay teammate. At the highest levels of the sport, there was no one else I could confide in who had similar experiences to me. When I signed my first profession-al contract with the New England Free Jacks, I realised I had no excuses not to come out any more. I had already accomplished more than I had ever imagined would even be possible as a player and felt like I had nothing to lose.

I think for a long time I viewed myself as a failure because I hadn't felt confident enough to come out. I really wanted to come out and be visible in a way that I felt was really lacking in men's rugby. But being able to speak directly to students and athletes all over the world and share my story has been an amazing experience. To know that my rugby career and journey has been able to have that type of impact on others is incredible and I am so grateful for it.

I think that having visible representation makes you feel less alone. I really struggled with depression growing up and often felt like I had to keep my sexuality separate from my greatest passion of rugby. Knowing that it was possible to be openly gay and not lose opportunities in my sport or the respect of my teammates would have made my journey much easier.

Devin Ibanez, professional rugby player

❧

When I was younger, I don't think I had role models, but I had curiosities. People who intrigued me and made me feel a little less alone. The likes of Julian Clary and Paul O'Grady were there and surviving. Seeing them allowed me to feel a little more comfortable in myself.

You know, the further you get from that time of struggle [coming out] the easier it is to forget how hard it actually is. It's a real fight.

Although I don't think of myself as a role model, I'm aware I have a platform that could and does help people. And I'll always use it in that way. We absolutely need to continue having role models – so many people still don't see theirs represented yet, so the fight continues.

Darren Kennedy, Irish television presenter

●

I have always looked up to Ian McKellen. There were actually very few LGBTQIA+ role models around the turn of the millennium, so it was great that Ian McKellen became so vocal on LGBTQIA+ rights. He was a household name, familiar from stage and screen and it meant a huge amount to me as a teenager that he was visible and outspoken.

I see myself as a hard-working person, who is simply trying to do their best to change the world for the better. It was my HIV diagnosis, which took place in January 2010, that was the catalyst for my activism. It took me several years to come to terms with my HIV diagnosis and it was not until 2012 that I felt confident enough to tell my parents. I started campaigning a few years later, initially because I wanted to change the narrative around HIV. It was not long before I started speaking out about LGBTQIA+ rights, homelessness, asylum, faith inclusion and international human rights.

A role model doesn't have to be someone in the media; they come in many forms, and in the year following my HIV diagnosis I was able to turn to a range of people living with HIV, from long-term survivors to other newly diagnosed people. They inspired me and helped empower me to be the person I am today.

I am a gay, HIV positive Christian. I am proud of who I am. We need to celebrate diverse identities and continue to challenge stereotypes.

Philip Baldwin, gay human rights activist

❧

As someone who never saw myself as a role model, the love that I felt from finally being vocal about my own thoughts and feelings made me realise that role models are needed. You never know who you are going to inspire along the way. Be you; you never know who is watching, and nor should you care.

Nick Charles, radio DJ and queer positivity activist

❧

It's only in the last couple of years that I have realised the responsibility of the work that I do and how it can affect others. When I was a kid, my role models were the outcasts of society, famous faces like Pete Burns, Boy George, Lily Savage and some non-famous ones – there was a cross dresser that rode around my hometown on a pink bike – I lived for those sightings! These people had a profound impact on me, living authentically and unapologetically. It's lovely to be referred to as a role model to others now because of the things that I am trying to achieve; I certainly don't feel like I have all the answers, but I am fully aware that the output that I have can influence others. It feels good, the outcast getting a little win. I had a really hard time trying to work out who I was and why I felt different – that was until I saw myself reflected in the life of another.

Danielle St James, founder of Not A Phase

confessions of a bad gay

Forgive me LGBTQIA+ community, for I have sinned. Multiple times over.

I'm guilty of not watching RuPaul until it reached its season nine premiere. I also skipped episodes. Okay, a lot of episodes.

I'm sorry.

In all honesty, you can imagine how long it has taken me to catch up. *Hundreds of seasons!* Not to mention Canada, UK and Australia. Ru's been churning them out. And being behind as a gay man, especially when Twitter erupts with spoilers over season thirteen exits, is tough. For too long I've wondered who Gottmik, Kandy Muse and Tina Burner were. When friends started gushing about how much they love Rosé, I'm there thinking they're talking about wine. I still also don't know who is stuck in the VIP.

Sorry.

Ru, forgive me for also getting your name wrong. I assumed it was called Are You Paul...a search for the next Paul...

An easy mistake. Apologies.

I'm guilty for not having seen Studio 54...yet.

Forgive me.

I know that I should. I want to. I keep meaning to, but then forget, or get bogged down by work, dates or catching up on *Drag Race. So many seasons!*

Confession. I've never gone to a sauna, a sex party or an orgy. Nor have I had a three-way.

Should I?

I've never taken E, cocaine or speed. I have tried poppers. Accidentally. But that's an embarrassing story for another day.

I don't wear pink on Wednesdays, and if I do, it's a mistake. Pink is not my colour. I'm too pale for it. I look ill. Terrible in fact. Pink does not make any boys wink at me.

I've only been to London Pride three times. I've also never walked in a Pride parade.

Terrible.

I should walk. I am proud. Prouder now.

Forgive me.

Never have I done drag, seen *Priscilla Queen of the Desert* or enjoyed karaoke. I hate it.

Also, I'm ashamed to admit that I'm one of those people who originally thought bisexuality was a phase. A stopover, an easier way of coming out. It's not. I apologise to my good friend Lewis and thank him for my education on this. A role model for the Bs in our letters.

Forgive me.

Once I called a camp guy a "fag" under my breath. At the time, I didn't realise how mean that could have been. I didn't realise that I was the fag. It was cruel. That word is nasty. A nasty word amongst so many horrid slurs.

Wrong.

I have body shamed myself. Even while supporting others. Even while encouraging others that they look good. *They do look good.* I don't allow myself that same treatment. I've failed the man in the mirror. Royally. EVERY-body is goals.

Forgive me, my community, I have sinned. Repeatedly. I used to hate the rainbow flag. Shudder at it.

Twat.

We are at an age where acceptance is key. And yet, we struggle to accept ourselves. I've hated myself for being gay. Hated my voice.

My walk.

My hips.

Ageing.

My bum.

Forgive me.

From the smallest thing that you feel you should do to the larger things that we wished we hadn't done. We mess up. It's part of our make-up, our journey. I am making mistakes. Multiple times over. I'll continue to do so.

Forgive me.

I'm not perfect. And I'm not sure I want to be.

But.

I'm learning.

We learn.

We teach.

We grow.

We forgive.

We've all been a bad gay. But we can be better.

gay

/geɪ/

---

adjective

1. (of a person) homosexual (used especially of a man).
   "the city's gay and lesbian people"

2. DATED light-hearted and carefree.
   "Nan had a gay disposition and a very pretty face"

noun

3. a homosexual person (typically referring to a man).
   "the capital is a popular destination for gays and lesbians from all over the world"

conversations with myself

Who am I?

It's incredibly hard to define who you are. To really pinpoint exactly that definition. You. Because we change. We are forever changing and evolving.

When I came out at seventeen years old, I assumed that was it. Job done.

Move forward, do not pass go, do not collect two hundred pounds.

There was no medal to be received, no trophy to put on a shelf. It was what it was. Move on. Get on with it. And I didn't want a medal; I didn't want to even discuss it. After holding my breath, I wanted to breathe. I thought in saying the words, the actual confession, that would be the end of it. It had to be the end of it. For years I'd bottled up something that I didn't want to address. Denied. Pushed so far inward that I didn't even realise it was there at times. Others may have clocked it, but I was oblivious. It was literally a huge part of me that I suffocated out of fear of addressing. Facing the plain fact that there was a difference in me. I was different. Something that I didn't see, even while others shouted it out across the street at me.

Faggot.

I ignored it. And it was easy to. It wasn't a siren call or a glittery object that I needed to have. It was something that I couldn't deal with. Refused. Buried. It was something glaringly obvious that I just couldn't handle. The only way I can describe it to people that haven't lived through it is this: denial.

Something only you felt but that you never address yourself. You know it's there, nagging at you, but you ignore it. Which becomes easier. Because strangely, you stop remembering that there might be an issue or a resolution to this feeling, and you just accept the words slung your way.

Poof.

You start to embody them. Meaningless words. You are just the chosen one to receive them. And the more you keep denying, keep running, the less you question.

Who am I?

Because you don't care who you are. The boy with the target. You become a master of training your brain to believe the one truth you can accept.

You're just the unlucky one.

The more you don't address it, the more you feed the cover up. The more you ignore the real issue. You move and get nowhere.

Bum boy, faggot, uphill gardener, AIDS victim, paedo, fag, cocksucker, fudge packer, poof.

Soaking in the insults said with passion, hatred and intent. Words that become negative but normal to you. Because you aren't normal.

I was running. Until one night close to my eighteenth birthday, in a bar, a man reached through a crowd and grabbed my bum. A bum that was flat and far from the peach emoji that it now strives to be. *Still striving, damn you squats.* No light-bulb moment, no huge realisation.

Just a simple, inappropriate gesture that stopped me in my tracks. Stopped me running. Because the people shouting it in your face, pushing your head down toilets or tripping you up, aren't people you want to listen to. Aren't people who will get through to you.

Their words were just negative. But when someone *like* you sees you in a crowd, and shows you a glimpse of who you are in a different way, your life begins. Slowly.

Thanks, Del.

I was still ashamed and continued to be for many years. Still running, it was just perhaps more of a light jog after the pinch moment.

In coming out, I thought I'd squashed the issue. Silenced the noise. Addressed it. Move on. I didn't need a party, a card, sympathy. I didn't even want to discuss it. Let alone with my family. I was still the elephant in the room, in every room, and I did not want to be there. So, I came out and shut up.

It wasn't that I didn't embrace my reality. I did. Dating, sexual exploration, making new friends in my community and finding my way. Living. But living quietly. A secret life. Still on the side.

And, for a large part, that's what it's been. That's what I thought it had to be. Not once did I stop and ask myself, "What does this mean now?"

Who does this make me become? Has my life changed? Am I okay? Are the people around me okay?

Instead, I just shut up. I'd become good at it. Coming out was enough. But it wasn't. It can't be. Not after years of repression and fear. Not after months of holding your breath, not showing who you are to your nearest and dearest. It was a foot on the ladder, yes, but you'd only just begun. The tip of an iceberg that was melting. A ticking time bomb. Insecure, fragile, gentle and still denying yourself the conversations that you needed. The conversations others needed.

And as I jogged through my birthdays, my twenties and hopping into my early thirties, I didn't realise that I was on an unknown quest to find comfort and acceptance. Not from others, but in myself. The most important relationship of all.

Because never, since coming out, did I ever imagine that I'd talk so openly about being gay, let alone be proud of it. Until I listened to the conversations and the things we didn't say.

❧

On my thirtieth birthday, I had a lot of mixed emotions.

Would this be the year that I have Botox? Will my metabolism finally catch up with me? Am I past it? Can I arrange a shot-gun wedding in time for my thirty-first? Can I find a man willing to do the shot-gun wedding? Is divorce legal for gay men?

But I didn't cry. *Result!*

At my party, friends shared old pictures of me from school, from uni and first jobs, as they do on birthdays. Moonpig cards were also created with montages from my life. A picture gallery of awful fashion choices and puppy fat.

One picture stood out. A photo of me in a red polo top, a little bit chubby, in the school playground, around fourteen years old, with my curtains and something in my hand, pretending to sing into it like a microphone. Performing.

I instantly hated the picture. In fact, I was worried that people at the party (especially the gays) would see it. Would see that embarrassing image of who I didn't like. It screamed camp gay kid.

Shortly after the party, two of my best friends, Shane and Darren, took me to Bratislava as a birthday surprise. An odd destination, but an absolutely hilarious trip. After nights out drinking and a Segway tour that started with me on my arse (don't lean forwards on a Segway), on the final day they were taking me to a spa.

How lovely!

Although, this spa was not lovely. It was located in an old, haunted hospital-style building with flickering lights. We were there to have a mud massage, or be murdered – a Brat special.

I'm sure they did this deliberately. Spooky destination. Scaring me stupid. Ageing me more.

We were asked to put on disposable underwear by "surgeons" who didn't speak English. And then separated. For our deaths.

I shit myself.

There, in a hospital-like room with flickering lights, I laid on a bed realising far too late that I'd put the pants on backwards. Before I could do anything about it, a dumper truck of mud suddenly came hurtling down onto my now naked body. Filling the uncovered cracks and suffocating me.

Goodbye world.

Now, I already have a fear of being buried alive as it is, but for one uncomfortable hour I lay in what might as well have been concrete. I could not move. Mud was in places it shouldn't be. *Thanks, back-to-front underwear.* Very cold surgeons worked around me, and I thought, "This is it." I couldn't even speak. I just heard drills.

Okay, there weren't drills. But it was not relaxing, or youth defying, and it smelt disgusting. With nothing else to do, as I waited for my death, I thought about the fact that I was entering a new decade, and the photo came into my mind.

That photo. Red polo shirt. Don't let the gays see it. Cringe camp curtain boy.

Embarrassing. I cringed as I was restrained in mud. But then the more I thought about it, the more I remembered how I felt in the picture at the time. The more the memory of the moment came back to me.

I was smiling in the photo. I was happy. It was a happy picture, and all of a sudden under my blanket of mud, I felt the overwhelming emotion of happiness.

And I laughed. I'm sure the surgeons around me assumed it was the mud slowly suffocating me to death making me delirious, but it wasn't. I just remembered how much I laughed with the girls during those school lunchtimes. With Jo and I spitting laughter, or Harri linking my arm and making me wet myself, and then Rosa and I dancing nights away at uni. How stupid we were and the fun we had. The fact that we had friendships, enjoyed our down-time and enjoyed each other's company. The fact we were label-less.

Repeatedly, we brought light to dark days. Yes, often there were horrendous times at school, but I had been constantly looking back at them with a frown. Viewing those days as a cringe-worthy camp guy. Ashamed of a picture of me. A part of me. A huge part of my life and journey.

It didn't feel right at all. I felt disappointed that I was so bothered by my innocence, by the fact that in those rare moments with the girls who loved me, all of me, I was able to be a slice of myself. Moments where I didn't hide.

After surviving the mud slide, and Darren controlling his laughter at the fact that I'd lost my disposable pants somewhere in the ruins, we chatted about embarrassing photos.

With two gay friends who couldn't care less, we shared stories and pictures and laughed. Because they were funny, and we all have them. Embarrassing memories that make us up. That build us up. Unashamedly.

Moments. Not to be hidden or covered in mud.

❧

It's very easy to be negative. Especially when it comes to ourselves.

We hate before we love. In fact, we are pros at this. We are the first ones to spot our flaws. Often revealing them before others get the chance to. Much like a comedian will focus on their shortcomings so that they're already in on the joke. Comfortable. But maybe they're not. Maybe they just want to be in control of the narrative. Of their insecurities.

Many people will tell you that your flaws are what they love about you. Your quirks, anxieties or the way your face wrinkles when you are happy. Which is lovely. But it's also not enough, and probably not always true.

I do not like the way my face wrinkles when I am happy. In fact, it makes me instantly stop showcasing a happy face. Insert frown here. So, we quickly correct. We quickly consider. And we shield ourselves, protecting our feelings. Ignoring what others see.

When I look in the mirror and see a guy in the reflection, often tired, often frowning, the more I look, the less I'm sure of who I see. The more I find those flaws. I see lines around my eyes. I see scars across my chest. I see stubble even though I shaved that morning, something I've inherited from my dad. *Thanks Pa.* I see receding hair that I hope doesn't go back any further, a belly when I slouch, and I see a diamond earring that multiple people have told me I'm too old for. But I can't stop wearing it because it brings back memories. Then I stop. I stop looking. Because I know they keep coming. I know I'll find another flaw. They are endless.

I've come to realise that I'm also an over-compensator. Along with being negative on myself, I talk too much. *Another flaw!* Regularly I fill awkward silences, which frankly only makes things more awkward. Sometimes I don't even take a breath. Then there's the fact that I hate the thought of upsetting someone, even if I one hundred per cent couldn't have. If there's a chance that I offended, flowers are straight in the post to them.

I also project. I fill people up on the stuff that I want to chat about, distracting them with stories, anything to lead them away from questions I'd prefer not to answer about myself. Pushing, driving the conversation in a different direction. I hate answering questions. I'd prefer to ask them, to listen and to detract. It's actually my job to do so, classic journalist! I talk a lot. My cameraman (friend) Ash is a saint, or so he repeatedly tells me. I prefer to be the fun, easy-going and unburdened man. Not having to answer to any other buried pockets.

And sometimes, I am that. Quite often actually. I like that person. That fun, easy-going dude. I'm sure that's the person the relationships around me also like. But sometimes, I realise that I'm hiding someone else. I'm avoiding questions. Still jogging. When I should be answering and being more positive. Because... we are great.

❥

Life is a journey. At least, that's what I tell myself when shit things happen. I breathe in and say, "Regrets are stupid, Daniel. Life has a path. There is a reason you aren't dating Wentworth Miller, yet. He will find you. You can write that chapter."

Then I have a sleepless night anyway, worrying about the stupid things occupying my mind at that current moment.

Work. Money. Love. Body confidence. Illness. Pandemics. Family. Will I marry?

Often these nights come with sweats too. They're horrid. I once woke up and didn't know if I'd wet myself, someone had poured water over me or the ceiling had caved in from a flood.

Anxiety.

Because as much as we try, we can't control everything. We can't control our journey. We especially can't control our minds.

I thought I knew everything about my own relationships. Assumed so much and didn't ask questions. Perhaps I didn't want to ask questions that would lead somewhere towards me; perhaps I just wanted to sweep it under the carpet and move forward. Well, sweeping never helps. It just silences it for a short period. Life is a journey that's better spent being shared. Being open. Accepting things and being your full self.

I know that. I knew that. I've learnt that.

Relationships that we are born with and that we encounter through our lives are our guides, our downfalls and our saviours. They're also on a journey. But we can only get through things if we let them be a part of ours and become a part of theirs.

So, let them be a part of yours.

❧

Gossip is damaging. Sure, it feels great when you first share it. Fantastic in fact. You know something that others don't; it falls out of your mouth like a comedian feeding jokes to a hungry crowd. They're starving. Everyone wants your information. People crave it. Hell, I want to hear it too. Whatever you have for me. But it has implications. Repercussions. It's damaging. We should try to censor ourselves in this department. Be kinder. Control those urges to spill. Gossip has hurt me and our community. Gossip makes us fear diseases, and realities, and often misses out facts.

In my twenties I dated someone. The journey wasn't the best. However, there were plenty of great moments in that relationship. Tonnes in fact. Good and bad. The start of our relationship came on the 31st of October.

It was Halloween. I remember as I have a photograph imprinted in my memory of the outfit that I wore.

Not a photo I hated, but quite slutty to be honest.

A skeleton costume. I didn't work out back then because my metabolism was enviable, and the black all-in-one clung to me in all the right places.

Yes, all of them.

I was feeling myself. Confident, sexy and happy. I had also just started dating this new guy who I was into. It's so nice when you are "into" someone. You feel good. Outwardly and inwardly.

That night he would be there. At the local gay pub where people would be dressed sexy not scary and ready to have the night of their lives. In your mid-twenties, every night was the night of your life.

Again, you only appreciate this when looking back. I'm old.

It was cold, but I had a jacket laced in alcohol to keep me warm. My drink was topped up regularly due to the gay group doing rounds each time the next person finished. I was at an age where I loved that group so much. (Shout out to my Southend gays and gals!) We'd been through so much. I felt so included, so happy, so giddy on life. I had acceptance and it felt good.

Damn, I looked good too.

We danced, we drank and we laughed. Laughter spilt out of us and onto the floors of the pub. Sticky floors. We all laughed a lot. Then I saw him. Through the crowd with his mate. He saw me too. Our smiles found our faces and couldn't leave them. We kissed. Two faces with different make-up drawn across, neither caring.

That night was brilliant. I went home with the guy. Then he told me a secret. A secret that hadn't been ruined by gossip. Which was rare. It was one that he was incredibly scared to share. But he trusted me with it. A damaging confession, but an honest one.

At the time, I didn't think I'd keep it. Had you asked a younger me, he probably wouldn't have kept it. But this was precious. Important to keep.

As time went on, the guy in question would share it himself when he was ready; he also allowed me to tell who I felt needed to know. But this was not my truth to share. This was not gossip.

People would have eaten it up. Devoured it. They'd have taken it and it could have damaged that man's own journey. I knew it.

So, there and then I knew that I wouldn't want to change someone's life because of words that fell from my mouth. Words can be weaponised and hurt. Gossip was damaging.

That relationship made me grow up quickly. Made me need to learn. Made me ask questions. Made me face questions. It changed me and slowly, each relationship has continued to do so.

We do not need gossip; we need conversations before others get there first.

❧

"I would say it is undeniable that your relationship with yourself will impact on your relationships with other people," says Judi James. "If you *don't* think you're okay you will either see others as better than you and suffer low self-esteem or you will be unable to understand how they could like you and therefore find it hard to trust or to open up."

See me as gay.

See me as camp.

See me as anything but straight.

Because I no longer care.

I can't define who I am. I don't think anyone really can. But I do know that I am made up of the relationships and experiences that I've encountered on my way.

Blessed.

If anyone has become instantly comfortable with who they are, I applaud you. You are lucky to feel that way. It's truly remarkable to be comfortable with who you are. The majority of us don't. Not at first.

It can take time to find your comfort. To accept who you are. To find your fit. You might try being straight, dabble with a different sex or not realise things till a little bit later. You might not need to do anything. But there is no stopwatch timing you; you can go at your own pace. Take your time.

I'd put so much pressure on myself and my relationships to be a certain way. To be a certain gay type, or to like things that I felt I should as a gay man after coming out.

My body should be like this, I should wear those colours, be masc, be fem, like this, listen to new music, tweet this, try that, he'll like you, he'll hate you. Don't do drugs. Do drugs. Have a three-way. Get married. Don't be single. Do be single.

Pressure. An unrealistic amount of pressure. All trial and error. Unavoidable.

Even now, in 2022, we will still struggle. Around the world, young and old LGBTQIA+ people are coming out of the closet in their own way, daunted despite the level of acceptance we might see. It's far from easy. Still is, and will be.

But we don't have to do that alone. Not now and not ever again. We don't have to face the pressures by ourselves. Ever.

Each relationship helps form us, shape us, encourage us to feel good in our own skin. Accept who we are.

So, please, see me as gay, see me as camp, see me as talented, kind, caring and loyal. See me in whatever way I shine. Because I shine. Hell, even see me as that camp boy in the red top with curtains. As long as I'm seen. Regardless of labels, that's the important part. Being seen. Noticed. Not a side part or a supporting act.

I stopped having conversations about who I was because I thought I'd closed that discussion. Ended that chapter. Moved on and came out. But what I've learnt from forcing myself to have them through the chapters of this book is that we should never just shut ourselves up. Close the book.

After spending time talking to family, friends, loved ones, people from our community, sex workers, role models, and then looking back in the mirror at myself, I now know why I was running. Jogging through life. Avoiding those conversations. I didn't want to be defined by something that others saw in me as different.

Gay.

I wanted to be more than the GBF, the gay friend, the gay son, a shade on the rainbow. So, I ran away from being *just* that.

In doing so, I continued to hold onto my fears. My labels.

Without realising it, I was putting myself into my own box. Slapping tape over my own mouth. When I should have instead used my voice. Listened. Because I had things to say. Conversations still to have. All the things we didn't say.

You see, we need the many relationships in our lives, each one bringing something different to our table. Variety, influences and difference.

For too long I hated that word: different. I wanted to be normal. To fit in. So, I was never able to notice when I finally did. When I became comfortable. Fitted. Accepted. We might not ever notice when that happens, but we all experience it at some point.

What we don't realise along our coming out journey, finding ourselves, feeling our way, is that the people and relationships around us also have internal opinions they probably haven't expressed to us. Haven't shared with us. Important things that actually can help us too. Their own voices.

Through people we learn. The straight man is educated by us; we are educated by the straight man. Talking about sex stops insecurities and allows us to become smarter, enjoying it. Speaking to your role models helps you understand the fight before us, and the fight ahead of us. Our families teach us lessons, which we then teach them in return. Some of us won't get accepted by people in our lives, but as long as we respect ourselves, there will be others who do.

I wish I could tell my younger self not to be scared. Not to run. To talk to the people around me. But that's just a conversation with myself that I had a little late.

Now I live in a world where we are so much more accepting. I feel hopeful for my future, not afraid of it. We embrace differences in and out of the community. We applaud them. It's the modern way.

If you go through life thinking that you have to be the same as everyone else, you will fail. If you worry your relationships are different because you are different, you'll miss out on what they can bring to your life and what you can teach them in return.

The truth is no one has the same relationship as anyone else. *Thank god! How boring would that be?*

We are all different. Never take that for granted. We are all just finding our people in a world where they are looking for us too. Thankfully we have a flag to wave helping guide us.

Hiding parts of us, photos or pockets of our lives will only stunt our growth. Because guess what, we are the lucky ones after all. *Who am I?*

I'm odd, awkward, with a voice that is probably too high, and I slightly mince when tipsy. I'm a man, brother, friend, son, voice, ally, sexual being, role model. I'm not *just* gay, but I'm damn proud to be it.

I am different. The boy with the big imagination being the whale in the pool. I'm that boy in the photograph and I'm happy about it. Always will be. *Just minus the curtains.*

I urge you to have conversations, even if you think that they have already been had. Because today as I write this final piece, I realised that I hadn't. Don't wait to say the things you didn't say.

They *will* save your life. They *will* make your life. Chances are, there is still so much more to say. It's a new world out there.

Find your comfort. You can't accept that *I'm okay* until you do. And shouldn't everyone be proud of who they are? I'm getting there myself, but ask yourself this:

Are you proud?

acknowledgements

Thanks to all the conversations that I had and to the ones that I'll continue to have in the future.

Thank you to the friends that feature in the pages and the ones who don't but are just as special to me.

Thank you to my family who love and accept me, they mean the world to me.

And thank you to Ashley, who puts up with my chatter on a daily basis.

In Their Shoes

Navigating Non-Binary Life

Jamie Windust

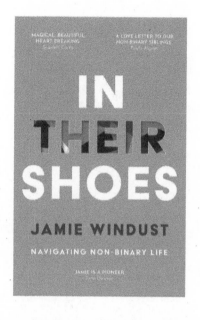

Combining light-hearted anecdotes with their own hard-won wisdom, Jamie Windust explores everything from fashion, dating, relationships and family, through to mental health, work and future key debates. From trying on clothes in secret to iconic looks, first dates to polyamorous liaisons, passports to pronouns, Jamie shows you how to navigate the world and your evolving identity in every type of situation.

£12.99 | $18.95 | PB | 208PP | ISBN 978 1 78775 242 9 | EISBN 978 1 78775 243 6

Bi the Way

The Bisexual Guide to Life

Lois Shearing

Whether you are openly bisexual, still figuring things out or just interested in learning more, this is your essential guide to understanding and embracing bisexuality. With first-hand accounts from bi advocates, it includes practical tips and guidance on topics including dating, sex, biphobia, bi-erasure, coming out, activism and gender identity, demystifying a community that is often erased or overlooked.

£12.99 | $18.95 | PB | 240PP | ISBN 978 1 78775 290 0 | EISBN 978 1 78775 291 7

Coming Out Stories

Personal Experiences of
Coming Out from Across
the LGBTQ+ Spectrum

*Edited by Emma Goswell
and Sam Walker*

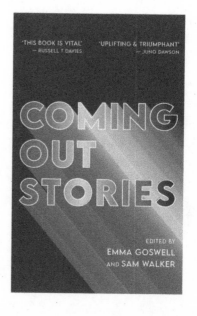

Based on the hugely popular Coming Out Stories podcast, this empowering, humorous and deeply honest book invites you to share one of the most important moments in many LGBTQ+ people's lives. Whether you're gay, pan, queer, bi, trans, non-binary, or an ally, this uplifting go-to resource is filled with helpful advice and tips on what to expect, and inspirational quotes from leading LGBTQ+ figures, to help you live your life as your most authentic self.

£12.99 | $18.95 | PB | 240PP | ISBN 978 1 78775 495 9 | EISBN 978 1 78775 496 6

How to Understand Your Sexuality

A Practical Guide for
Exploring Who You Are

*Meg-John Barker
and Alex Iantaffi*

Illustrated by Jules Scheele

This down-to-earth guide is the ultimate companion for under-standing, accepting and celebrating your sexuality. Written by two internationally renowned authors and therapists, the book explains how sexuality works in terms of our identities, attractions, desires and practices, and explores how it intersects with our personal experiences and the world around us.

£14.99 | $19.95 | PB | 352PP | ISBN 978 1 78775 618 2 | EISBN 978 1 78775 619 9